Subjective, Intersubjec...

Other volumes of collected essays by Donald Davidson

Essays on Actions and Events
Inquiries into Truth and Interpretation
Problems of Rationality (forthcoming)
Truth, Language, and History (forthcoming)

Subjective, Intersubjective, Objective

DONALD DAVIDSON

CLARENDON PRESS · OXFORD

2001

OXFORD

UNIVERSITY PRESS

Great Clarendon Street, Oxford OX2 6DP

Oxford University Press is a department of the University of Oxford.
It furthers the University's objective of excellence in research, scholarship,
and education by publishing worldwide in

Oxford New York

Athens Auckland Bangkok Bogotá Buenos Aires
Cape Town Chennai Dar es Salaam Delhi Florence Hong Kong Istanbul
Karachi Kolkata Kuala Lumpur Madrid Melbourne Mexico City Mumbai
Nairobi Paris São Paulo Shanghai Singapore Taipei Tokyo Toronto Warsaw

and associated companies in Berlin Ibadan

Oxford is a registered trade mark of Oxford University Press
in the UK and in certain other countries

Published in the United States
by Oxford University Press Inc., New York

British Library Cataloguing in Publication Data

Data available

Library of Congress Cataloging in Publication Data

Data available

ISBN 0–19–823752–9
ISBN 0–19–823753–7 (Pbk.)

1 3 5 7 9 10 8 6 4 2

Typeset in Times by Cambrian Typesetters, Frimley, Surrey
Printed in Great Britain on acid-free paper by
Biddles Ltd., Guildford & Kings Lynn

To Marcia Cavell

Contents

Provenance of the Essays and Acknowledgements

Essay 1, 'First Person Authority', was read at a conference on intentionality organized by Henri Lauener and held in Biel, Switzerland, in 1983. Earlier versions had been read at the University of Illinois at Chicago Circle, Stanford University, and the University of Colorado. It was first published in *Dialectica*, 38 (1984), 101–11.

'Knowing One's Own Mind', Essay 2, was delivered as the Presidential Address at the Sixtieth Annual Pacific Division Meeting of the American Philosophical Association in Los Angeles on March 28, 1986, and published in *Proceedings and Addresses of the American Philosophical Association* (1987), 441–58. It is reprinted here by permission of the American Philosophical Association. I am greatly indebted to Akeel Bilgrami and Ernie Lepore for criticism and advice, and to Tyler Burge, who generously tried to correct my understanding of his work.

Essay 3, 'The Myth of the Subjective', was read at a conference on Consciousness, Language, and Art in Vienna in 1986, and was published in the proceedings *Bewusstsein, Sprache und die Kunst*, edited by Michael Benedikt and Rudolf Berger, by Edition S. Verlag der Österreichischen Staatsdruckerei, 1988.

Essay 4, 'What is Present to the Mind?', was delivered at the Second International France Veber Colloquium, held in Bad Radkersburg, Austria, and Gornja Radgona, in what was then Yugoslavia and is now Slovenia. It was published in a book of essays on my work, most of them delivered at that conference. The editors of the book were Johannes Brandl and Wolfgang Gombocz, and it appeared as a special volume of *Grazer Philosophische Studien* (vol. 36, 1989) titled *The Mind of Donald Davidson* (Amsterdam: Rodopi).

'Indeterminism and Antirealism', Essay 5, was read at a conference on realism and antirealism at Santa Clara University in early 1992. It was published in *Realism/Antirealism and Epistemology*, edited by C. B. Kulp (Lanham, Maryland: Rowman & Littlefield, 1997).

Essay 6, 'The Irreducibility of the Concept of the Self', was written with the help and advice of Marcia Cavell for a book designed to honor the work of Dieter Henrich. The book, *Philosophie in synthetischer Absicht*, was edited by Marcelo Stamm (Stuttgart: Klett-Cotta, 1998).

Essay 7, 'Rational Animals', was delivered at a conference organized by Henri Lauener which took place in Biel, Switzerland, in 1981. It was first published in *Dialectica*, 36 (1982), 317–27.

'The Second Person', which is Essay 8, was given as a talk at a conference on Wittgenstein in Paris in 1989. It was published under the title 'Jusqu'où va le caractère public d'une langue?' in *Wittgenstein et la philosophie aujourd'hui*, edited and translated into French by J. Sebestik and A. Soulez (Paris: Méridiens Klincksieck, 1992). In the same year a somewhat modified English version was published in *Midwest Studies in Philosophy*, 17, which was edited by P. French, T. E. Uehling, and H. Wettstein (Indianapolis: University of Notre Dame Press). About four pages near the end are taken from 'The Conditions of Thought', a paper written for, and delivered at, a plenary session at the World Congress of Philosophy in Brighton, 1988. It was published in *Le Cahier du Collège International de Philosophie* (Paris: Éditions Osiris, 1989).

Essay 9, 'The Emergence of Thought', was given as a talk at a seminar on emergence held at the University of Frankfurt in 1993. Translated into German by T. Marschner, it was published with the title 'Die Emergenz des Denkens' in *Die Erfindung des Universums? Neue Überlegungen zur philosophischen Kosmologie*, edited by W. G. Saltzer, P. Eisenhardt, D. Kurth, and R. E. Zimmermann (Frankfurt am Main: Insel Verlag, 1997). It was subsequently published in English with its present title in *Erkenntnis*, 51 (1999), 7–17.

Essay 10, 'A Coherence Theory of Truth and Knowledge', was my contribution to a colloquium organized by Richard Rorty as part of the 1981 Stuttgart Hegel Congress. W. V. Quine and Hilary Putnam were the other participants in the colloquium. Our papers were published two years later in the proceedings of that congress,

Kant oder Hegel? After Stuttgart the four of us had a more leisurely exchange on the same topics at the University of Heidelberg. When the Pacific Division of the American Philosophical Association met in March of 1983, Rorty read a paper titled 'Pragmatism, Davidson, and Truth'. In it he commented on some of the things I had written in 'A Coherence Theory of Truth and Knowledge'; his paper was subsequently published (with revisions) in *Truth and Interpretation: Perspectives on the Philosophy of Donald Davidson*. I replied with 'Afterthoughts, 1987', which was first published in conjunction with a reprinting of 'A Coherence Theory of Truth and Knowledge' in *Reading Rorty*, edited by Alan Malachowski (Cambridge: Blackwell, 1990). 'Afterthoughts' as printed here is, aside from some bibliographical details noted above, a reprint of 'Afterthoughts, 1987'.

'Empirical Content', Essay 11, was read at a conference in Vienna (in the house Wittgenstein helped design) to celebrate the hundredth anniversary of the births of Moritz Schlick and Otto Neurath. It was published in the year of the conference in *Grazer Philosophische Studien,* 16–17 (1982).

Essay 12, 'Epistemology and Truth', was read at the Fourth Panamerican Philosophy Conference, held in Cordoba, Argentina, in September of 1987. It was published in the proceedings of that conference by the National University of Cordoba in 1988.

Essay 13, 'Epistemology Externalized', was read in an early version at a SADAF meeting in Buenos Aires in 1989. The next year it was presented at a conference in Biel, Switzerland, and published in 1991 in *Dialectica*, 45 2–3: 191–202.

'Three Varieties of Knowledge', Essay 14, was written to be delivered in February of 1991 as an A. J. Ayer Memorial Lecture, sponsored by the Royal Institute of Philosophy. When the date for the lecture arrived, a snowstorm disabled the transportation system of southern England to such an extent that the lecture was cancelled. It was subsequently published with other memorial lectures in *A. J. Ayer Memorial Essays: Royal Institute of Philosophy Supplement,* 30, edited by A. Phillips Griffiths (Cambridge University Press, 1991). With some changes it was delivered as a Heisenberg Lecture in one of the upgraded stables of the Nymphenburg Palace in Munich and published in German in *Merkur* with the same title as the title of the present book.

Introduction

The essays in this book are concerned with three sorts of propositional knowledge and the relations among them. We all have knowledge of our own minds, knowledge of the contents of other minds, and knowledge of the shared environment. The subsections of the book are titled Subjective, Intersubjective, and Objective. The words track real differences. First person knowledge is distinguished by the fact that we can legitimately claim a unique sort of authority with respect to what we believe, want, intend, and some other attitudes. Second person knowledge and knowledge of the rest of the world of nature do not have this authority, but they differ from each other in that our knowledge of other minds is normative in a way the latter is not. All three varieties of knowledge are, however, objective in the sense that their truth is independent of their being believed to be true. This is obvious in the second two cases, but it holds even in the case of beliefs about our own beliefs and other attitudes: such beliefs can be wrong. All our knowledge is also objective in the sense that it could for the most part be expressed by concepts which have a place in a publically shared scheme of things.

Essay 1, 'First Person Authority', asks what explains the presumption that a speaker is right when he sincerely attributes a belief, desire, or intention to his present self, while no such presumption is appropriate when others make similar attributions to him. It is argued that 'solutions' to the problem of other minds which merely restate the asymmetry leave the field open to the sceptic. A new explanation of first person authority is offered which traces the source of the authority to a necessary feature of the interpretation of speech.

Essay 2, 'Knowing One's Own Mind', takes up an apparent difficulty about first person authority: how can we reconcile the fact that the contents of our minds are in part determined by external factors of which we are ignorant with the claim that we know the contents of our minds without (normally) needing or appealing to evidence? I argue that the answer depends, among other things, on giving up the idea of 'objects before the mind' none of whose attributes can be hidden from the agent.

In *Essay 3*, 'The Myth of the Subjective', I try to make clear what it means to deny that there are objects before the mind when we have sensations or think. The idea that there is a fundamental distinction to be drawn between uninterpreted experience and an organizing structure of concepts is closely related to the supposed dichotomy of the subjective and the objective. These dualisms have dominated and defined the problems of much of modern philosophy, the problems not only of epistemology, but also of philosophy of language and philosophy of mind. In this essay I inveigh against the picture of the mind that is presupposed by the dualisms, and so against the dualisms themselves, and the epistemological and metaphysical positions based on them. The view that the subjective is the foundation of objective empirical knowledge is attacked; it is claimed that empirical knowledge has no epistemological foundation, and needs none.

Essay 4, 'What is Present to the Mind?', continues the theme of the last two essays with fresh examples and arguments restated.

A number of philosophers have questioned whether there is any 'fact of the matter' concerning the propositional attitudes. *Essay 5*, 'Indeterminism and Antirealism', attempts to put these doubts to rest. In particular it disputes the claim that if one accepts Quine's indeterminacy thesis, as I do, then one has abandoned first person authority.

Essay 6, 'The Irreducibility of the Concept of the Self', emphasizes the features of our beliefs about our present attitudes which remain in place after we give up the myth of the subjective and its mental objects. These features include, of course, the special authority that attends such beliefs and the irreducible role of indexical sentences. It is the thoughts such sentences express which relate us and our speech to the world around us. I also discuss briefly the fact that there is no final court of appeal beyond our own standards of rationality, a point that is raised again in Essay 14.

Essay 7, 'Rational Animals', is one of a number of attempts I have made to specify some of the ingredients of rationality. By rationality I mean whatever involves propositional thought. In an earlier essay

('Thought and Talk', essay 11 in *Inquiries into Truth and Interpretation*) I argued for a mutual dependence of thought and language. Many readers were not persuaded. Here I try again, taking a different tack, one I have subsequently developed in the essays that follow. The considerations I adduce for the close connection between language and thought do not constitute anything like a demonstration or proof. They depend in part on what I think we know about creatures like us.

In *Essay 8*, 'The Second Person', I dwell on the idea that language is necessarily social. It is argued that to have thoughts, and so to mean anything in speaking, it is necessary to understand, and be understood by, a second person. If Wittgenstein held that language is necessarily social, then the central thesis of this essay is Wittgensteinian. But it is denied that communication requires that one person speak as others do. Rather, the objectivity which thought and language demand depends on the mutual and simultaneous responses of two or more creatures to common distal stimuli and to one another's responses. This three-way relation among two speakers and a common world I call 'triangulation'. In the end, the idea is as simple as that of ostensive learning, but with an insistence that triangulation is not a matter of one person grasping a meaning already there, but a performance that (when fully fleshed out) bestows a content on language. This thesis, and its ramifications for philosophy of mind, language, and epistemology, turn up again and again in my work after 1982 (Essay 7). Carol Rovane, Akeel Bilgrami, and Marcia Cavell were early critics of this idea. Their suggestions and candid doubts helped greatly in shaping my thinking.

Essay 9, 'The Emergence of Thought', asks how we are to describe the transition from the prelinguistic, preconceptual mind of an infant to a child with language, beliefs, and the other propositional attitudes. I argue that we do not have a vocabulary for describing the early stages of such development, and that it is unclear what would satisfy the felt need for such a vocabulary. It is suggested that a few major steps can be distinguished by considering the strengths of the semantic theories required for various languages.

Essay 10, 'A Coherence Theory of Truth and Knowledge', was written in 1981, before any of the first nine of these essays. There is no paper I have written I would like more to rewrite. It has understandably attracted much criticism, which is why I reprint it here without change. Anyway, I have in effect been rewriting it ever since it was written; the nine essays that precede it in this book are partial evidence of my subsequent misgivings, and Essay 14 is further testimony. I have also tried to make amends in replies to various critics in *The Philosophy of Donald Davidson* (in the Library of Living Philosophers, edited by Lewis E. Hahn, (Chicago: Open Court, 1999)) and in 'Replies' to Barry Stroud, John McDowell, and Richard Rorty in *Critica* 30 (1998). What I would most like to correct is the impression that I think experience and perception play no role in our beliefs about the world. 'Experience' and 'perception' are perfectly good words for whatever it is that goes on in our minds when we look around us, smell, touch, hear, and taste. I was so eager to get across the idea (for which I should have given credit to Wilfrid Sellars) that epistemic intermediaries between the world and our beliefs are a mistake that I made it sound to many readers as though I were repudiating all serious commerce between world and mind. In truth my thesis then as now is that the connection is causal and, in the case of perception, direct. To perceive that it is snowing is, under appropriate circumstances, to be caused (in the right way) by one's senses to believe that it is snowing by the actually falling snow. Sensations no doubt play their role, but that role is not that of providing evidence for the belief.

Essay 11, 'Empirical Content', provides a historical background for, and commentary on, the theme of Essay 10. Although Neurath and Schlick were more enmeshed in a very old debate than they seemed to realize, their sense that they were saving philosophy from its metaphysical past gave zest and a linguistic turn to a well-worn problem.

'Epistemology and Truth', *Essay 12*, discusses the relation of epistemology to truth. Two positions are often seen as opposed: that truth is 'radically non-epistemic' (in Putnam's words) or that it is to be understood in terms of what it is possible (in practice, in theory, or ideally) for us to know. Neither of these alternatives, it is argued, is acceptable. Truth cannot be limited to what we can or could determine to be true; nevertheless, there are firm reasons to connect truth with true belief in one way or another. A way of partially reconciling the two positions, based on the ideas explored in Essay 10, is outlined.

From the time of Descartes most epistemology has been based on first person knowledge. According to the usual story we must begin with what is most certain: knowledge of our own sensations and thoughts. In one way or another we progress, if we can, to knowledge of an objective external world. There is then the final, tenuous, step to knowledge of other minds. In *Essay 13*, 'Epistemology Externalized', I argue for a total revision of this picture. All propositional thought, whether positive or skeptical, whether of the inner or of the outer, requires possession of the concept of objective truth, and this concept is accessible only to those creatures in communication with others. Third person knowledge—knowledge of other minds— is thus essential to all other knowledge. But third person knowledge is impossible without knowledge of a shared world of objects in a shared time and space. Thus the acquisition of knowledge is not based on a progression from the subjective to the objective; it emerges holistically, and is interpersonal from the start. Several forms of externalism are examined and found wanting. It is argued that triangulation, which has featured in many other essays in this book, corrects and augments both a version of perceptual externalism and a version of social externalism.

'Three Varieties of Knowledge', *Essay 14*, comes closest to pulling together the main ideas in this book. If all the essays had been written after my thoughts had gelled, 'Three Varieties of Knowledge' would certainly have come first, and a reader who wants an overview might well begin here.

I have tinkered with the essays in this book to improve the grammar or style and occasionally to delete repetition or what I now see as a minor mistake. I am sure many more errors persist, and there is probably too much hammering away at certain theses. But when I contemplated major rewriting I realized that either I must reproduce my past work pretty much as it stood or simply start over again, and this would take years. I console myself with the thought that a fresh start would mean wiping out what amounts to a history of my attempts to come to grips with the triangle composed of a person, his society, and the shared environment. It would also deprive my critics of some of their favorite targets.

Among those critics I must especially thank Richard Rorty, who has been egging me on for years to collect and publish these essays. Ernest Lepore generously gave up a week of his time to sort through and help order not only the essays in this volume but also those to appear in two subsequent volumes. I am indebted to Ariela Lazar who earlier gave me her discriminating advice on arranging my work, and to Arpy Khatchirian, who corrected the spelling, grammar, and thinking in many of the essays. Peter Momtchiloff of the Oxford University Press has been an encouraging, kindly, and forgiving editor; his assistance has made a task I found distasteful in prospect more endurable than I imagined possible.

A number of people, lectureships, universities, and other institutions have provided opportunities to try out many of the ideas in these essays. There has been welcome feedback from my students at Berkeley, and from audiences who attended lecture series in Mexico (1992), Rome (1993), Munich (the Kant Lectures, 1993), Gerona (the Ferrater Mora Lectures, 1994), Leuven (the Francqui Lectures, 1994), and Buenos Aires (1995). Finally, there were my Jean Nicod Lectures (1995), delivered in Caen and Paris, from which I hope to develop a more unified and detailed account of the thoughts scattered through the present volume.

I am indebted to all those who added to, subtracted from, or modified my thoughts. I did not keep track of those who made especially trenchant suggestions, so any list I draw up will be shamefully incomplete. But it must certainly include Rosario Egidi, Pascal Engel, Dagfinn Føllesdal, Olbeth Hansberg, Dieter Henrich, Pierre Jacob, Carol Rovane, and those who came to the ten lectures and seminars in Gerona, particularly W. V. Quine, Burton Dreben, Akeel Bilgrami, Ernest Lepore, Barry Stroud, and Bruce Vermazen. Marcia Cavell not only attended many of the talks where I tried out versions of my ideas, but was an intellectual companion throughout these years, gently trying to temper my armchair speculations with a more empirically oriented, and psychoanalytically educated, outlook.

SUBJECTIVE

1 *First Person Authority*

When a speaker avers that he has a belief, hope, desire or intention, there is a presumption that he is not mistaken, a presumption that does not attach to his ascriptions of similar mental states to others. Why should there be this asymmetry between attributions of attitudes to our present selves and attributions of the same attitudes to other selves? What accounts for the authority accorded first person present tense claims of this sort, and denied second or third person claims?

The point may be made, and the question asked, in the modality either of language or of epistemology. For if one can speak with special authority, the status of one's knowledge must somehow accord; while if one's knowledge shows some systematic difference, claims to know must reflect the difference. I assume therefore that if first person authority in speech can be explained, we will have done much, if not all, of what needs to be done to characterize and account for the epistemological facts.

The connection between the problem of first person authority and the traditional problem of other minds is obvious, but as I pose the former problem, there are two important differences. First person authority is the narrower problem, since I shall consider it only as it applies to propositional attitudes like belief, desire, intention; being pleased, astonished, afraid, or proud that something is the case; or knowing, remembering, noticing, or perceiving that something is the case. But I shall not discuss what are often taken to be central to the problem of other minds: pains and other sensations, and knowledge, memory, attention, and perception as directed to objects like people, streets, cities, comets, and other non-propositional entities. What holds for the propositional attitudes ought, it seems, to be relevant to sensations and the rest, but I do not explore the connections here.

All propositional attitudes exhibit first person authority, but in various degrees and kinds. Belief and desire are relatively clear and simple examples, while intention, perception, memory, and knowledge are in one way or another more complex. Thus in evaluating someone's claim to have noticed that the house is on fire, there are at least three things to consider: whether the house is on fire, whether the speaker believes the house is on fire, and how the fire caused the belief. With respect to the first, the speaker has no special authority; with respect to the second, he does; and with respect to the third, responsibility is mixed and complex. The question whether someone intends to lock the door by turning the key depends in part on whether he wants to lock the door and believes that turning the key will lock the door; and whether this belief and desire have caused, in the right way, a desire to turn the key. Special authority attaches directly to claims about the desire and belief, less directly to claims about the necessary causal connection. These differences among the ways in which first person authority may apply to propositional attitudes are important and worth exploring. But in every case, first person authority is relevant, and it is the general case I wish to consider here. Since in almost every instance, if not in all, first person authority rests at least partially on a belief component, I shall concentrate on the case of belief.

Though there is first person authority with respect to beliefs and other propositional attitudes, error is possible; this follows from the fact that the attitudes are dispositions that manifest themselves in various ways, and over a span of time. Error is possible; so is doubt. So we do not always have indubitable or certain knowledge of our own attitudes. Nor are our claims about our own attitudes incorrigible. It is possible for the evidence available to others to overthrow self-judgements.

It comes closer to characterizing first person authority to note that the self-attributer does not normally base his claims on evidence or observation, nor does it normally make sense to ask the self-attributer why he believes he has the beliefs, desires, or intentions he claims to have. This feature of self-attributions was remarked by Wittgenstein: 'What is the criterion for the redness of an image? For me, when it is someone else's image: what he says or does. For myself, when it is my image: nothing.'[1] Most philosophers have

---

[1] Ludwig Wittgenstein, *Philosophical Investigations*, §377.

followed Wittgenstein in this, and have extended the criterion to the propositional attitudes, as we shall see.

This feature of first person authority, suggestive as it may be, does not help explain the authority. This is so partly because of the caveats—'normally' we do not make self-attributions on the basis of evidence, but sometimes we do; 'usually' it doesn't make sense to ask someone why he believes he has a certain belief or desire or intention, but sometimes it does. Even in the exceptional cases, however, first person authority persists; even when a self-attribution is in doubt, or a challenge is proper, the person with the attitude speaks about it with special weight.

But the existence of exceptions is not the chief reason first person authority isn't explained by the fact that self-attributions are not based on evidence; the chief reason is simply that claims that are not based on evidence do not in general carry more authority than claims that are based on evidence, nor are they more apt to be correct.

Contemporary philosophers who have discussed first person authority have made little attempt to answer the question why self-ascriptions are privileged. It is long out of fashion to explain self-knowledge on the basis of introspection. And it is easy to see why, since this explanation leads only to the question why we should see any better when we inspect our own minds than when we inspect the minds of others.

A few philosophers have denied that the asymmetry exists; Ryle is a sturdy example. In *The Concept of Mind* Ryle suggests that what we take for 'privileged access' is due to nothing more than the fact that we are generally better placed to observe ourselves than others are. Ryle writes, 'in principle, as distinct from practice, John Doe's ways of finding out about John Doe are the same as John Doe's ways of finding out about Richard Roe'. He continues,

the differences are differences of degree, not of kind. The superiority of the speaker's knowledge of what he's doing over that of the listener does not indicate that he has Privileged Access to facts of a type inevitably inaccessible to the listener, but only that he is in a very good position to know what the listener is often in a very poor position to know. The turns taken by a man's conversation do not startle or perplex his wife as much as they had surprised and puzzled his fiancée, nor do close colleagues have to explain themselves to each other as much as they have to explain themselves to their new pupils.[2]

---

[2]　Gilbert Ryle, *The Concept of Mind*, 156, 179.

I agree with Ryle that any attempt to explain the asymmetry between first person present tense claims about attitudes, and other person or other tense claims, by reference to a special way of knowing or a special kind of knowledge must lead to a skeptical result. Any such account must accept the asymmetry, but cannot explain it. But Ryle neither accepts nor explains the asymmetry; he simply denies that it exists. Since I think it is obvious that the asymmetry exists, I believe it is a mistake to argue from the absence of a special way of knowing or a special mode or kind of knowledge to the absence of special authority; instead, we should look for another source of the asymmetry.

Ayer at one time took a line similar to Ryle's. In *The Concept of a Person* he emphasizes that first person ascriptions can be in error; and he allows that such ascriptions are privileged.[3] But when he comes to describe the authority of self-ascriptions, he compares it to the authority we sometimes allow an eyewitness when compared with secondhand reports. This analogy seems to me unsatisfactory for two reasons. First, it fails to tell us why a person is like an eyewitness with respect to his own mental states and events while others are not. And second, it does not suggest an accurate description of what first person authority is like. For first person attributions are not based on better evidence but often on no evidence at all. The authority of the eyewitness is at best based on inductive probabilities easily overridden in particular cases: an eyewitness is discredited and his evidence discounted if he is a notoriously unreliable observer, prejudiced, or myopic. But a person never loses his special claim to be right about his own attitudes, even when his claim is challenged or overturned.

Joseph Agassi has actually maintained that we know the mental states and events in other minds better than those in our own mind. He distinguishes privileged access from the commonsense truth that 'every person has access to some information available to that person alone, and it involves one's self, at least as an eye-witness'. He goes on:

The doctrine of privileged access is that I am the authority on all my own experiences . . . The thesis was refuted by Freud (I know your dreams better than you), Duhem (I know your methods of scientific discovery better than you), Malinowski (I know your customs and habits better than you), and

---

[3] A. J. Ayer, 'Privacy'.

perception theorists (I can make you see things which are not there and describe your perceptions better than you can).[4]

Aside from Freud's case, there is little here to threaten first person authority. Freud's views, by extending the concepts of intention, belief, desire, and the rest to include the unconscious, do mean that with respect to some propositional attitudes a person loses direct authority. Indeed, loss of authority is the main distinguishing feature of unconscious mental states. Of course, the pre-Freudian attitudes remain as subject as ever to first person authority. But more interesting is the fact that in psychoanalytic practice, recovery of authority over an attitude is often considered the only solid evidence that the attitude was there before being noninferentially appreciated by its holder. Thus those cases of unconscious mental states that were unsystematically recognized to exist before Freud are indirectly included in the scope of first person authority by psychoanalysis. So I do not think the existence of unconscious attitudes threatens the importance of first person authority.

I turn now to philosophers who have assumed that there is such a thing as first person authority, and have accepted Wittgenstein's description of the difference between first and third person attributions.

Strawson discusses first person authority in the context of trying to answer skepticism about other minds. According to Strawson, if the skeptic understands his own question ('How does anyone know what is going on in someone else's mind?'), he knows the answer. For if the skeptic knows what a mind is, he knows it must be in a body, and that it has thoughts. He also knows that we attribute thoughts to others on the basis of observed behavior, but to ourselves without such a basis. Strawson writes:

> In order to *have* this type of concept [of a mental property], one must be both a self-ascriber and an other-ascriber of such predicates [which ascribe mental properties], and must see every other as a self-ascriber. In order to *understand* this type of concept, one must acknowledge that there is a kind of predicate which is unambiguously and adequately ascribable *both* on the basis of observation of the subject of the predicate *and* not on that basis, i.e. independently of observation of the subject.[5]

[4] Joseph Agassi, *Science in Flux*, 120.

[5] Peter Strawson, *Individuals*, 108. (Anita Avramides has pointed out that Strawson has contributed more to this issue than I allow. See her 'Davidson and the New Sceptical Problem'.)

This cannot be deemed a satisfactory answer to the skeptic. For the skeptic will reply that though Strawson may have correctly described the asymmetry between first and other person ascriptions of mental predicates, he has done nothing to explain it. In the absence of an explanation, the skeptic is surely justified in asking how we know that the description is correct. In particular, why should we think that a predicate that is sometimes applied on the basis of observation, and sometimes not, is unambiguous? This question, to which Strawson has not addressed himself, is a major source of skepticism about knowledge of other minds. (On the apparent ambiguity of mental predicates, see Essay 2.)

Richard Rorty has attempted an explanation. We are asked to imagine that originally self-ascriptions were made on the basis of the same sort of observation or behavioral evidence as other-ascriptions. It was then noticed that people could ascribe mental properties to themselves without making observations or using behavioral evidence, and that self-ascriptions turned out in the long run to provide better explanations of behavior than third person ascriptions. So it became a linguistic convention to treat self-ascriptions as privileged: 'it became a constraint on explanations of behavior that they should fit all reported thoughts or sensations into the overall account being offered'.[6]

This account is not meant to be taken seriously as a piece of folk anthropology, but it is meant to make it seem reasonable that we should treat self-ascriptions as having special authority. But the question remains: what reason has Rorty given to show that self-ascriptions not based on evidence concern the same states and events as ascriptions of the same mental predicates based on observation or evidence? There is a difference in kind in the ways the two sorts of ascription are made, and how they explain behavior is different. What Rorty describes as the discovery that self-ascriptions not based on evidence explain behavior better will be described by the skeptic as the fact that what is being ascribed is on every count apparently different.

It may come as a surprise to realize that the philosophers I am discussing have not really dealt with the ancient problem of skepticism concerning knowledge of other minds. But I think it is easy to

---

[6] Richard Rorty, 'Incorrigibility as the Mark of the Mental', 416. Rorty's account is derived from Wilfred Sellars, 'Empiricism and the Philosophy of Mind'. With respect to the point at issue, Sellars's account does not differ from Rorty's.

explain. Historically the problem has been seen from either a Cartesian or an empiricist point of view, and both venues assume that each person knows what is in his own mind. The problem has therefore seemed to be that of supplying a basis for knowledge of other minds (and, of course, the external world). Philosophers now realize that part of understanding mental concepts (or predicates) consists in knowing what kind of observable behavior justifies the ascription of these concepts to others. But this answer to the skeptic does nothing to explain first person authority, or the asymmetry between self-ascriptions and other-ascriptions. We can still ask why we believe these two sorts of ascription pertain to the same subject matter. And this question is a good one, whether or not we recognize its traditional skeptical ancestry.

Perhaps it should be pointed out that no concepts aside from those applying to sensations, propositional attitudes, and the positions of our limbs show the sort of asymmetry we are discussing. Many concepts can be applied on the basis of multiple criteria, but no others are such that ascribers *must*, on particular occasions, use different criteria. If we are to explain this anomaly and avoid an invitation to skepticism, the explanation should point to a natural asymmetry between other observers and ourselves, an asymmetry not simply invented to solve the problem.

The first step towards a solution depends on becoming clear about the entities to which first person authority applies. William Alston proposes this principle to characterize the special status of self-attributions: 'Each person is so related to propositions ascribing current mental states to himself that it is logically impossible both for him to believe that such a proposition is true and not to be justified in holding this belief while no one else is so related to such propositions.'[7]

For this suggestion to be plausible, we must suppose that the proposition Jones expresses by the sentence 'I believe Wagner died happy' is the same proposition as the proposition Smith expresses by the sentence 'Jones believes Wagner died happy.' This is, of course, a highly questionable supposition. Once more, the epistemic contrast goes unexplained; and in the absence of an explanation, the question arises what *reason* one has in any particular case to believe that the proposition entertained by Jones and Smith *is* the same. Given only

---

[7] William Alston, 'Varieties of Privileged Access', 235.

a description of an epistemic difference, the natural conclusion is that the propositions differ.

I turn, then, to a formulation of Sidney Shoemaker's, which makes explicit mention of language: 'Among the incorrigible statements are statements about . . . mental events, e.g. . . . reports of thoughts . . . These are incorrigible in the sense that if a person sincerely asserts such a statement it does not make sense to suppose, and nothing could be accepted as showing, that he is mistaken; i.e. that what he says is false.'[8]

I shall ignore the incorrigibility condition and substitute something less strong—something that amounts to first person authority. (This is perhaps reasonable, since Shoemaker is mainly concerned with sensations such as pain, while I am exclusively concerned with propositional attitudes.) What is important here is that Shoemaker assigns the presumption of correctness not to a kind of knowledge, but to a class of utterances. This idea might lead to an explanation of first person authority if the class of utterances could be specified in syntactic terms. Unfortunately it cannot. If Shoemaker is right, a speaker who sincerely uses a certain sort of sentence must be presumed to be right in what he says. But of course this holds only if the speaker knows he is using the privileged sort of sentence; if he is not, he is misusing language. What would constitute a misuse here? Above all, one wants to say, sincerely asserting a sentence one has no special authority to assert. Perhaps so; but this is just to reiterate the uninformative and unexplained claim that it is a convention of language to treat self-ascriptions with special respect. Seen from the point of view of the interpreter, this implies that he should interpret self-ascriptions in such a way as to make them true—or to assign a special priority to their truth. The point of view of the interpreter is the only one we can take, given Shoemaker's principle, and this deprives the principle of independent application: our only reason for saying the speaker has special authority on occasion is that we are prepared to treat his utterance as a self-ascription. In other words, self-ascriptions have special authority: true; and that is where we began.

No satisfactory explanation of the asymmetry between first and other person attributions of attitudes has yet emerged. Still, focusing on sentences and utterances rather than propositions or meanings is

---

[8] Sidney Shoemaker, *Self-Knowledge and Self-Identity*, 215–16.

a step in a promising direction. The reason for this is relatively simple. As long as we pose the problem in terms of the kind of warrant or authority someone has with respect to claims about an agent's attitude to a proposition (or a sentence with a given interpretation), we seem constrained to account for differences by simply postulating different kinds or sources of information. Alternatively, we may postulate different criteria of application for the key concepts or words ('believes that', 'intends to', 'wishes that', etc.). But these moves do no more than restate the problem, as we have seen, and thereby invite skepticism about knowledge of the minds of others (or of our own mind). But if we pose the problem in terms of relations between agents and utterances, we can avoid the impasse.

We now need to distinguish two related but different asymmetries. On the one hand, there is the familiar difference between self- and other-attributions of the same attitude to the same person: my claim that I believe Wagner died happy and your claim that I believe Wagner died happy. If these claims are put into words, we have the difficulty of deciding what pairs of utterances are suitably related in order to guarantee that the claims have the 'same content'. On the other hand, we may consider my utterance of the sentence 'I believe Wagner died happy', and then contrast my warrant for thinking I have said something true, and your warrant for thinking I have said something true. These two asymmetries are of course connected since we are inclined to say your warrant for thinking I speak the truth when I say 'I believe Wagner died happy' must be closely related to your warrant for thinking you would be speaking the truth if you said 'Davidson believes Wagner died happy'. But for reasons that will soon be evident, I shall deal with the second version of the asymmetry.

The question then comes to this: what explains the difference in the sort of assurance you have that I am right when I say 'I believe Wagner died happy' and the sort of assurance I have? We know by now that it is no help to say I have access to a way of knowing about my own beliefs that you do not have; nor that we use different criteria in applying the concept of belief (or the word 'believes'). So let us simply consider a shorter utterance of mine: I utter the sentence 'Wagner died happy'. Clearly, if you or I or anyone knows that I hold this sentence true on this occasion of utterance, and she knows what I meant by this sentence on this occasion of utterance, then she knows what I believe—what belief I expressed.

It would once more make the account circular to explain the basic asymmetry by assuming an asymmetry in the assurance you and I have that I hold the sentence I have just uttered to be a true sentence. There must *be* such an asymmetry, of course, but it cannot be allowed to contribute to the desired explanation. But we can assume without prejudice that we both know, whatever the source or nature of our knowledge, that on this occasion I do hold the sentence I uttered to be true. Similarly, it would beg the question to explain the basic asymmetry by appeal to some asymmetry in our knowledge of the fact that I know what my sentence, as uttered on this occasion, meant. So again, let us simply assume we both know this, whatever the source or character of our knowledge.

So far, then, we have not postulated or assumed any asymmetry at all. The assumptions are just these: you and I both know that I held the sentence 'Wagner died happy' to be a true sentence when I uttered it; and that I knew what that sentence meant on the occasion of its utterance. And now there is this difference between us, which is what was to be explained: on these assumptions, I know what I believe, while you may not.

The difference follows, of course, from the fact that the assumption that I know what I mean necessarily gives me, but not you, knowledge of what belief I expressed by my utterance. It remains to show why there must be a presumption that speakers, but not their interpreters, are not wrong about what their words mean. The presumption is essential to the nature of interpretation—the process by which we understand the utterances of a speaker. This process cannot be the same for the utterer and for his hearers.

To put the matter in its simplest form: there can be no general guarantee that a hearer is correctly interpreting a speaker; however easily, automatically, unreflectively, and successfully a hearer understands a speaker, he is liable to serious error. In this special sense, he may always be regarded as interpreting a speaker. The speaker cannot, in the same way, interpret his own words. A hearer interprets (normally without thought or pause) on the basis of many clues: the actions and other words of the speaker, what he assumes about the education, birthplace, wit, and profession of the speaker, the relation of the speaker to objects near and far, and so forth. The speaker, though he must bear many of these things in mind when he speaks, since it is up to him to try to be understood, cannot wonder whether he generally means what he says.

The contrast between the grounds a self-ascriber has for his self-ascription, and the grounds an interpreter has for accepting that same ascription, would be stark if we were to assume that no question can arise concerning a speaker's interpretation of his own words. But of course it can, since what his words mean depends in part on the clues to interpretation he has given the interpreter, or other evidence that he justifiably believes the interpreter has. The speaker can be wrong about what his own words mean. This is one of the reasons first person authority is not infallible. But the possibility of error does not eliminate the asymmetry. The asymmetry rests on the fact that the interpreter must, while the speaker doesn't, rely on what, if it were made explicit, would be a difficult inference in interpreting the speaker.

Neither speaker nor hearer knows in a special or mysterious way what the speaker's words mean; and both can be wrong. But there is a difference. The speaker, after bending whatever knowledge and craft he can to the task of saying what his words mean, cannot improve on the following sort of statement: 'My utterance of "Wagner died happy" is true if and only if Wagner died happy'. An interpreter has no reason to assume this will be *his* best way of stating the truth conditions of the speaker's utterance.

The best way to appreciate this difference is by imagining a situation in which two people who speak unrelated languages, and are ignorant of each other's languages, are left alone to learn to communicate. Deciphering a new language is not like learning a first language, for a true beginner has neither the reasoning power nor the stock of concepts the participants in the imagined situation have to draw on. This does not, however, affect the point I wish to stress, since what my imagined interpreter can treat consciously as evidence is exactly what conditions the first learner to be a language user. Let one of the imagined pair speak and the other try to understand. It will not matter whether the speaker speaks his 'native' tongue, since his past social situation is irrelevant. (I assume the speaker has no interest in training the hearer to cope with the speaker's original speech community.) The best the speaker can do is to be *interpretable*, that is, to use a finite supply of distinguishable sounds applied consistently to objects and situations he believes are apparent to his hearer. Obviously the speaker may fail in this project from time to time; in that case we can say if we please that he does not know what his words mean. But it is equally obvious that the interpreter has nothing to go on but the pattern of sounds the speaker exhibits in conjunction with further events (including, of course, further actions on the part of both speaker and interpreter). It makes no sense in this situation to wonder whether the speaker is generally getting things wrong. His behavior may simply not be interpretable. But if it is, then what his words mean is (generally) what he intends them to mean. Since the 'language' he is speaking has no other hearers, the idea of the speaker misusing his language has no application. There is a presumption—an unavoidable presumption built into the nature of interpretation—that the speaker usually knows what he means. So there is a presumption that if he knows that he holds a sentence true, he knows what he believes.

2 *Knowing One's Own Mind*

There is no secret about the nature of the evidence we use to decide what other people think: we observe their acts, read their letters, study their expressions, listen to their words, learn their histories, and note their relations to society. How we are able to assemble such material into a convincing picture of a mind is another matter; we know how to do it without necessarily knowing how we do it. Sometimes I learn what I believe in much the same way someone else does, by noticing what I say and do. There may be times when this is my only access to my own thoughts. According to Graham Wallas, 'The little girl had the making of a poet in her who, being told to be sure of her meaning before she spoke, said 'How can I know what I think till I see what I say?'[1] A similar thought was expressed by Robert Motherwell: 'I would say that most good painters don't know what they think until they paint it.'

Gilbert Ryle was with the poet and the painter all the way in this matter; he stoutly maintained that we know our own minds in exactly the same way we know the minds of others, by observing what we say, do, and paint. Ryle was wrong. It is seldom the case that I need or appeal to evidence or observation in order to find out what I believe; normally I know what I think before I speak or act. Even when I have evidence, I seldom make use of it. I can be wrong about my own thoughts, and so the appeal to what can be publicly determined is not irrelevant. But the possibility that one may be mistaken about one's own thoughts cannot defeat the overriding presumption that a person knows what he or she believes; in general, the belief that one has a thought is enough to justify that belief. But though this

---

[1] Graham Wallas, *The Art of Thought.*

is true, and even obvious to most of us, the fact has, so far as I can see, no easy explanation. While it is clear enough, at least in outline, what we have to go on in trying to fathom the thoughts of others, it is obscure why, in our own case, we can so often know what we think without appeal to evidence or recourse to observation.

Because we usually know what we believe (and desire and doubt and intend) without needing or using evidence (even when it is available), our sincere avowals concerning our present states of mind are not subject to the failings of conclusions based on evidence. Thus sincere first person present-tense claims about thoughts, while neither infallible nor incorrigible, have an authority no second or third person claim, or first person other-tense claim, can have. To recognize this fact is not, however, to explain it.

Since Wittgenstein it has become routine to try to relieve worries about 'our knowledge of other minds' by remarking that it is an essential aspect of our use of certain mental predicates that we apply them to others on the basis of behavioral evidence but to ourselves without benefit of such aid. The remark is true, and when properly elaborated, it ought to answer someone who wonders how we can know the minds of others. But as a response to the skeptic, Wittgenstein's insight (if it is Wittgenstein's) should give little satisfaction. For first, it is a strange idea that claims made without evidential or observational support should be favored over claims with such support. Of course, if evidence is not cited in support of a claim, the claim cannot be impugned by questioning the truth or relevance of the evidence. But these points hardly suffice to suggest that in general claims without evidential support are more trustworthy than those with. The second, and chief, difficulty is this. One would normally say that what counts as evidence for the application of a concept helps define the concept, or at least places constraints on its identification. If two concepts regularly depend for their application on different criteria or ranges of evidential support, they must be different concepts. So if what is apparently the same expression is sometimes correctly employed on the basis of a certain range of evidential support and sometimes on the basis of another range of evidential support (or none), the obvious conclusion would seem to be that the expression is ambiguous. Why then should we suppose that a predicate like 'x believes that Ras Dashan is the highest mountain in Ethiopia', which is applied sometimes on the basis of behavioral evidence and sometimes not, is unambiguous? If it is ambiguous, then there is no reason to suppose it has the same meaning when applied to oneself that it has when applied to another. If we grant (as we should) that the necessarily public and interpersonal character of language guarantees that we often correctly apply these predicates to others, and that therefore we often do know what *others* think, then the question must be raised what grounds each of us has for thinking he knows what (in the same sense) *he* thinks. The Wittgensteinian style of answer may solve the problem of other minds, but it creates a corresponding problem about knowledge of one's own mind. The correspondence is not quite complete, however. The original problem of other minds invited the question how one knows others have minds at all. The problem we now face must be put this way: I know what to look for in attributing thoughts to others. Using quite different criteria (or none), I apply the same predicates to myself; so the skeptical question arises why I should think it is *thoughts* I am attributing to myself. But since the evidence I use in the case of others is open to the public, there is no reason why I shouldn't attribute thoughts to myself in the same way I do to others, in the mode of Graham Wallas, Robert Motherwell, and Gilbert Ryle. In other words, I don't, but I could, treat my own mental states in the same way I do those of others. No such strategy is available to someone who seeks the same sort of authority with respect to the thoughts of others as he apparently has in dealing with his own thoughts. So the asymmetry between the cases remains a problem, and it is first person authority that creates the problem.

I have suggested an answer to this problem in the first essay in this book. There I argued that attention to how we attribute thoughts and meanings to others would explain first person authority without inviting skeptical doubts. In recent years, however, some of the very facts about the attribution of attitudes on which I relied to defend first person authority have been employed to attack that authority: it has been argued, on what are thought to be new grounds, that while the methods of the third person interpreter determine what we usually deem to be the contents of an agent's mind, the contents so determined may be unknown to the agent. In the present essay I consider some of these arguments, and urge that they do not constitute a genuine threat to first person authority. The explanation I offered in my earlier essay of the asymmetry between first and other person attributions of attitudes seems to me if anything to be strengthened by the new considerations, or those of them that seem valid.

It should be stressed again that the problem I am concerned with does not require that our beliefs about our own contemporary states of mind be infallible or incorrigible. We can and do make mistakes about what we believe, desire, approve, and intend; there is also the possibility of self-deceit. But such cases, though not infrequent, are not and could not be standard; I do not argue for this now, but take it as one of the facts to be explained.

Setting aside, then, self-deception and other anomalous or border-line phenomena, the question is whether we can, without irrational-ity, inconsistency, or confusion, simply and straightforwardly think we have a belief we do not have, or think we do not have a belief we do have. A number of philosophers and philosophically minded psychologists have recently entertained views that entail or suggest that this could easily happen—indeed, that it must happen all the time.

The threat was there in Russell's idea of propositions that could be known to be true even though they contained 'ingredients' with which the mind of the knower was not acquainted; and as the study of the *de re* attitudes evolved, the peril grew more acute.

But it was Hilary Putnam who pulled the plug. Consider Putnam's 1975 argument to show that meanings, as he put it, 'just ain't in the head'.[2] Putnam argues persuasively that what words mean depends on more than 'what is in the head'. He tells a number of stories the moral of which is that aspects of the natural history of how someone learned the use of a word necessarily make a difference to what the word means. It seems to follow that two people might be in physi-cally identical states, and yet mean different things by the same words.

The consequences are far-reaching. For if people can (usually) express their thoughts correctly in words, then their thoughts—their beliefs, desires, intentions, hopes, expectations—also must in part be identified by events and objects outside the person. If meanings ain't in the head, then neither, it would seem, are beliefs and desires and the rest.

Since some may be a little weary of Putnam's doppelgänger on Twin Earth, let me tell my own science fiction story—if that is what

---

[2] Hilary Putnam, 'The Meaning of "Meaning" ', 227.

it is. My story avoids some irrelevant difficulties in Putnam's story, though it introduces some new problems of its own.[3] (I'll come back to Earth, and Twin Earth, a little later.) Suppose lightning strikes a dead tree in a swamp; I am standing nearby. My body is reduced to its elements, while entirely by coincidence (and out of different molecules) the tree is turned into my physical replica. My replica, Swampman, moves exactly as I did; according to its nature it departs the swamp, encounters and seems to recognize my friends, and appears to return their greetings in English. It moves into my house and seems to write articles on radical interpretation. No one can tell the difference.

But there *is* a difference. My replica can't recognize my friends; it can't *re*cognize anything, since it never cognized anything in the first place. It can't know my friends' names (though of course it seems to); it can't remember my house. It can't mean what I do by the word 'house', for example, since the sound 'house' Swampman makes was not learned in a context that would give it the right meaning—or any meaning at all. Indeed, I don't see how my replica can be said to mean anything by the sounds it makes, nor to have any thoughts.

Putnam might not go along with this last claim, for he says that if two people (or objects) are in relevantly similar physical states, it is 'absurd' to think their psychological states are 'one bit different'.[4] It would be a mistake to be sure that Putnam and I disagree on this point, however, since it is not yet clear how the phrase 'psychological state' is being used.

Putnam holds that many philosophers have wrongly assumed that psychological states like belief and knowing the meaning of a word both are (I) 'inner' in the sense that they do not presuppose the existence of any individual other than the subject to whom the state is ascribed, and are (II) the very states which we normally identify and individuate as we do beliefs and the other propositional attitudes. Since we normally identify and individuate mental states and meanings in

---

[3] I make no claim for originality here; Stephen Stich has used a very similar example in 'Autonomous Psychology and the Belief–Desire Thesis', 573 ff. I should emphasize that I am not suggesting that an object accidentally or artificially created could not think; the Swampman simply needs time in which to acquire a causal history that would make sense of the claim that he is speaking of, remembering, identifying, or thinking of items in the world. (I return to this point later.)

[4] Hilary Putnam, 'The Meaning of "Meaning" ', 144.

terms partly of relations to objects and events other than the subject, Putnam believes that (I) and (II) come apart: in his opinion, no states can satisfy both conditions.

Putnam calls psychological states satisfying condition (I) 'narrow'. He thinks of such states as solipsistic, and associates them with Descartes's view of the mental. Putnam may consider these states to be the only 'true' psychological states; in much of his paper he omits the qualifier 'narrow', despite the fact that narrow psychological states (so called) do not correspond to the propositional attitudes as normally identified. Not everyone has been persuaded that there is an intelligible distinction to be drawn between narrow (or inner, or Cartesian, or individualistic—all these terms are current) psychological states and psychological states identified (if any are) in terms of external facts (social or otherwise). Thus John Searle has claimed that our ordinary propositional attitudes satisfy condition (I), and so there is no need of states satisfying condition (II), while Tyler Burge has denied that there are, in any interesting sense, propositional attitudes that satisfy condition (I).[5] But there seems to be universal agreement that no states satisfy both conditions.

The thesis of this essay is that there is no reason to suppose that ordinary mental states do not satisfy both conditions (I) and (II): I think such states are 'inner', in the sense of being identical with states of the body, and so identifiable without reference to objects or events outside the body; they are at the same time 'non-individualistic' in the sense that they can be, and usually are, identified in part by their causal relations to events and objects outside the subject whose states they are. A corollary of this thesis will turn out to be that, contrary to what is often assumed, first person authority can without contradiction apply to states that are regularly identified by their relations to events and objects outside the person.

I begin with the corollary. Why is it natural to assume that states that satisfy condition (II) may not be known to the person who is in those states?

Now I must talk about Putnam's Twin Earth. He asks us to imagine two people exactly alike physically and (therefore) alike with respect to all 'narrow' psychological states. One of the two people, an inhabitant of Earth, has learned to use the word 'water' by being shown water, reading and hearing about it, etc. The other, an inhabitant of

    [5] John Searle, *Intentionality*; and Tyler Burge, 'Individualism and Psychology'.

Twin Earth, has learned to use the word 'water' under conditions not observably different, but the substance to which she has been exposed is not water but a lookalike substance we may call 'twater'. Under the circumstances, Putnam claims, the first speaker refers to water when she uses the word 'water'; her twin refers to twater when *she* uses the word 'water'. So we seem to have a case where 'narrow' psychological states are identical, and yet the speakers mean different things by the same word.

How about the thoughts of these two speakers? The first says to herself, when facing a glass of water, 'Here's a glass of water'; the second mutters exactly the same sounds to herself when facing a glass of twater. Each speaks the truth, since their words mean different things. And since each is sincere, it is natural to suppose they believe different things, the first believing there is a glass of water in front of her, the second believing there is a glass of twater in front of *her*. But do they know what they believe? If the meanings of their words, and thus the beliefs expressed by using those words, are partly determined by external factors about which the agents are ignorant, their beliefs and meanings are not narrow in Putnam's sense. There is therefore nothing on the basis of which either speaker can tell which state she is in, for there is no internal or external clue to the difference available. We ought, it seems, to conclude that neither speaker knows what she means or thinks. The conclusion has been drawn explicitly by a number of philosophers, among them Putnam. Putnam declares that he 'totally abandons the idea that if there is a difference in meaning . . . then there *must* be some difference in our concepts (or in our psychological state)'. What determines meaning and extension 'is not, in general, fully known to the speaker'.[6] Here 'psychological state' means *narrow* psychological state, and it is assumed that only such states are 'fully known'. Jerry Fodor believes that ordinary propositional attitudes are (pretty nearly) 'in the head', but he agrees with Putnam that *if* propositional attitudes were partly identified by factors outside the agent, they would not be in the head, and would not necessarily be known to the agent.[7] John Searle also, though his reasons are not Fodor's, holds that meanings are in the head ('there is nowhere else for them to be'),

[6] Hilary Putnam, 'The Meaning of "Meaning" ' pp. 164–5.
[7] Jerry Fodor, 'Cognitive Science and the Twin Earth Problem', 103. Also see his 'Methodological Solipsism Considered as a Research Strategy in Cognitive Psychology', p. viii.

but seems to accept the inference that if this were not the case, first person authority would be lost.[8] Perhaps the plainest statement of the position appears in Andrew Woodfield's introduction to a book of essays on the objects of thought. Referring to the claim that the contents of the mind are often determined by facts external to and perhaps unknown to the person whose mind it is, he says: 'Because the external relation is not determined subjectively, the subject is not authoritative about that. A third person might well be in a better position than the subject to know which object the subject is thinking about, hence be better placed to know which thought it was.'[9] Those who accept the thesis that the contents of propositional attitudes are partly identified in terms of external factors seem to have a problem similar to the problem of the skeptic who finds that we may be altogether mistaken about the 'outside' world. In the present case, ordinary skepticism of the senses is avoided by supposing that the world itself more or less correctly determines the contents of thoughts about the world. (The speaker who thinks it is water is probably right, for he learned the use of the word 'water' in a watery environment; the speaker who thinks it is twater is probably right, for he learned the word 'water' in a twatery environment.) But skepticism is not defeated; it is only displaced onto knowledge of our own minds. Our ordinary beliefs about the external world are (on this view) directed onto the world, but we don't know what we believe.

There is, of course, a difference between water and twater, and it can be discovered by normal means, whether it is discovered or not. So a person might find out what he believes by discovering the difference between water and twater, and finding out enough about his own relations to both to determine which one his talk and beliefs are about. The skeptical conclusion we seem to have reached concerns the extent of first person authority: it is far more limited than we supposed. Our beliefs about the world are mostly true, but we may easily be wrong about what we think. It is a transposed image of Cartesian skepticism.

Those who hold that the contents of our thoughts and the meanings of our words are often fixed by factors of which we are ignorant have not been much concerned with the apparent consequence of their views which I have been emphasizing. They have, of course,

---

[8] John Searle, *Intentionality*, ch. 8.
[9] Andrew Woodfield 'Introduction', in Woodfield (ed.), *Thought and Object*, p. viii.

realized that if they were right, the Cartesian idea that the one thing we can be certain of is the contents of our own minds, and the Fregean notion of meanings fully 'grasped', must be wrong. But they have not made much of an attempt, so far as I know, to resolve the seeming conflict between their views and the strong intuition that first person authority exists.

One reason for the lack of concern may be that some seem to see the problem as confined to a fairly limited range of cases, cases where concepts or words latch on to objects that are picked out or referred to using proper names, indexicals, and words for natural kinds. Others, though, argue that the ties between language and thought, on the one hand, and external affairs, on the other, are so pervasive that no aspect of thought as usually conceived is untouched. In this vein Daniel Dennett remarks that 'one must be richly informed about, intimately connected with, the world at large, its occupants and properties, in order to be said with any propriety to have beliefs'.[10] He goes on to claim that the identification of *all* beliefs is infected by the outside, non-subjective factors that are recognized to operate in the sort of case we have been discussing. Burge also emphasizes the extent to which our beliefs are affected by external factors, though for reasons he does not explain, he apparently does not view this as a threat to first person authority.[11]

The subject has taken a disquieting turn. At one time behaviorism was invoked to show how it was possible for one person to know what was in another's mind; behaviorism was then rejected, in part because it could not explain one of the most obvious aspects of mental states: the fact that they are in general known to the person who has them without appeal to behavioristic evidence. The recent fashion, though not strictly behavioristic, once more identifies mental states partly in terms of social and other external factors, thus making them to that extent publicly discoverable. But at the same time it reinstates the problem of accounting for first person authority.

Those who are convinced of the external dimension of the contents of thoughts as ordinarily identified and individuated have reacted in different ways. One response has been to make a distinction between the contents of the mind as subjectively and internally determined, on

---

[10] Daniel Dennett, 'Beyond Belief', 76.
[11] Tyler Burge, 'Other Bodies', 'Individualism and the Mental', 'Two Thought Experiments Reviewed', 284–93.

the one hand, and ordinary beliefs, desires, and intentions, as we normally attribute them on the basis of social and other outward connections, on the other. This is clearly the trend of Putnam's argument (although the word 'water' has different meanings, and is used to express different beliefs when it is used to refer to water and to twater, people using the word for these different purposes may be in 'the same psychological state'). Jerry Fodor accepts the distinction for certain purposes, but argues that psychology should adopt the stance of 'methodological solipsism'—that is, it should deal exclusively with inner states, the truly subjective psychological states that owe nothing to their relations to the outside world.[12]

Stephen Stich makes essentially the same distinction, but draws a sterner moral: where Fodor thinks we merely need to tinker a bit with propositional attitudes as usually conceived to separate out the purely subjective element, Stich holds that psychological states as we now think of them belong to a crude and confused 'folk psychology' which must be replaced by a yet to be invented 'cognitive science'. The subtitle of his recent book is 'The Case against Belief'.[13]

Clearly those who draw such a distinction have insured that the problem of first person authority, at least as I have posed it, cannot be solved. For the problem I have set is how to explain the asymmetry between the way in which a person knows about his contemporary mental states and the way in which others know about them. The mental states in question are beliefs, desires, intentions, and so on, as ordinarily conceived. Those who accept something like Putnam's distinction do not even try to explain first person authority with respect to these states; if there is first person authority at all, it attaches to quite different states. (In Stich's case, it is not obvious that it can attach to anything.)

I think Putnam, Burge, Dennett, Fodor, Stich, and others are right in calling attention to the fact that ordinary mental states, at least the propositional attitudes, are partly identified by relations to society and the rest of the environment, relations which may in some respects not be known to the person in those states. They are also right, in my opinion, in holding that for this reason (if for no other), the concepts of 'folk psychology' cannot be incorporated into a

---

[12] Jerry Fodor, 'Methodological Solipsism Considered as a Research Strategy in Cognitive Psychology'.

[13] Stephen Stich, *From Folk Psychology to Cognitive Science*.

coherent and comprehensive system of laws of the sort for which physics strives. These concepts are part of a commonsense theory for describing, interpreting, and explaining human behavior which is a bit freestyle, but (so I think) indispensable. I can imagine a science concerned with how people think and act purged of 'folk psychology', but I cannot think in what its interest would consist. This is not, however, the topic of this essay.

I am here concerned with the puzzling discovery that we apparently do not know what we think—at least in the way we think we do. This is a real puzzle if, like me, you believe it is true that external factors partly determine the contents of thoughts, and also believe that in general we do know, and in a manner others do not, what we think. The problem arises because admitting the identifying and individuating role of external factors seems to lead to the conclusion that our thoughts may not be known to us.

But does this conclusion follow? The answer depends on the way in which one thinks the identification of mental contents depends on external factors.

The conclusion does follow, for example, for any theory that holds that propositional attitudes are identified by objects (such as propositions, tokens of propositions, or representations) that are in or 'before' the mind, and that contain or incorporate (as 'ingredients') objects or events outside the agent; for it is obvious that everyone is ignorant of endless features of every external object. That the conclusion follows from these assumptions is generally conceded.[14] However, for reasons I shall mention below, I reject the assumptions on which the conclusion is in this case based.

Tyler Burge has suggested that there is another way in which external factors enter into the determination of the contents of speech and thought. One of his 'thought experiments' happens pretty well to fit me. Until recently I believed arthritis was an inflammation of the joints caused by calcium deposits; I did not know that any inflammation of the joints, for example gout, also counted as arthritis. So when a doctor told me (falsely as it turned out) that I had gout, I believed I had gout but I did not believe I had arthritis. At this point Burge asks us to imagine a world in which I was physically the same but in which the word 'arthritis' happened actually to apply only to inflammation of the joints caused by calcium deposits. Then the

---

[14] See e.g. Gareth Evans, *The Varieties of Reference*, 45, 199, 201.

sentence 'Gout is not a form of arthritis' would have been true, not false, and the belief that I expressed by this sentence would not have been the false belief that gout is not a form of arthritis but a true belief about some disease other than arthritis. Yet in the imagined world all my physical states, my 'internal qualitative experiences', my behavior and dispositions to behave, would have been the same as they are in this world. My *belief* would have changed, but I would have no reason to suppose that it had, and so could not be said to know what I believed.

Burge stresses the fact that his argument depends on 'the possibility of someone's having a propositional attitude despite an incomplete mastery of some notion in its content ... *if* the thought experiment is to work, one must at some stage find the subject believing (or having some attitude characterized by) a content, despite an incomplete understanding or misapplication'.[15]

It seems to follow that if Burge is right, then whenever a person is wrong, confused, or partially misinformed, about the public meaning of a word, he is wrong, confused, or partially misinformed about any of his beliefs that are (or would be?) expressed by using that word. Since such 'partial understanding' is 'common or even normal in the case of a large number of expressions in our vocabularies' according to Burge, it must be equally common or normal for us to be wrong about what we believe (and, of course, fear, hope for, wish were the case, doubt, and so on).

Burge apparently accepts this conclusion; at least so I interpret his denial that 'full understanding of a content is in general a necessary condition for believing the content'. He explicitly rejects 'the old model according to which a person must be directly acquainted with, or must immediately apprehend, the contents of his thoughts ... a person's thought *content* is not fixed by what goes on in him, or by what is accessible to him simply by careful reflection'.[16]

I am uncertain how to understand these claims, since I am uncertain how seriously to take the talk of 'direct acquaintance' with, and of 'immediately apprehending', a content. But in any case I am convinced that if what we mean and think is determined by the linguistic habits of those around us in the way Burge believes they are, then first person authority is very seriously compromised. Since the degree and character of the compromise seem to me incompati-

---

[15] Tyler Burge, 'Individualism and the Mental', 83.   [16] Ibid. 90, 102, 104.

ble with what we know about the kind of knowledge we have of our own minds, I must reject some premise of Burge's. I agree that what I mean and think is not 'fixed' (exclusively) by what goes on in me, so what I must reject is Burge's account of how social and other external factors control the contents of a person's mind.

For a number of reasons, I am inclined to discount the importance of the features of our attributions of attitudes to which Burge points. Suppose that I, who think the word 'arthritis' applies to inflammation of the joints only if caused by calcium deposits, and my friend Arthur, who knows better, both sincerely utter to Smith the words 'Carl has arthritis'. According to Burge, if other things are more or less equal (Arthur and I are both generally competent speakers of English, both have often applied the word 'arthritis' to genuine cases of arthritis, etc.), then our words on this occasion mean the same thing, Arthur and I mean the same thing by our words, and we express the same belief. My error about the dictionary meaning of the word (or about what arthritis is) makes no difference to what I meant or thought on this occasion. Burge's evidence for this claim seems to rest on his conviction that this is what anyone (unspoiled by philosophy) would report about Arthur and me. I doubt that Burge is right about this, but even if he is, I don't think it proves his claim. Ordinary attributions of meanings and attitudes rest on vast and vague assumptions about what is and is not shared (linguistically and otherwise) by the attributer, the person to whom the attribution is made, and the attributer's intended audience. When some of these assumptions prove false, we may alter the words we use to make the report, often in substantial ways. When nothing much hinges on it, we tend to choose the lazy way: we take someone at his word, even if this does not quite reflect some aspect of the speaker's thought or meaning. But this is not because we are bound (outside of a law court, anyway) to be legalistic about it. And often we aren't. If Smith (unspoiled by philosophy) reports to still another party (perhaps a distant doctor attempting a diagnosis on the basis of a telephone report) that Arthur and I both have said, and believe, that Carl has arthritis, he may actively mislead *his* hearer. If this danger were to arise, Smith, alert to the facts, would not simply say 'Arthur and Davidson both believe Carl has arthritis'; he would add something like 'But Davidson thinks arthritis must be caused by calcium deposits'. The need to make this addition I take to show that the simple attribution was not quite right; there was a relevant difference in the thoughts Arthur and I expressed when we said 'Carl has arthritis'. Burge does not have to be budged by this argument, of course, since he can insist that the report is literally correct, but could, like any report, be misleading. I think, on the other hand, that this reply would overlook the extent to which the contents of one belief necessarily depend on the contents of others. Thoughts are not independent atoms, and so there can be no simple, rigid, rule for the correct attribution of a single thought.[17]

Though I reject Burge's insistence that we are bound to give a person's words the meaning they have in his linguistic community, and to interpret his propositional attitudes on the same basis, I think there is a somewhat different, but very important, sense in which social factors do control what a speaker can mean by his words. If a speaker wishes to be understood, he must intend his words to be interpreted in a certain way, and so must intend to provide his audience with the clues they need to arrive at the intended interpretation. This holds whether the hearer is sophisticated in the use of a language the speaker knows or is the learner of a first language. It is the requirement of learnability, interpretability, that provides the irreducible social factor, and that shows why someone can't mean something by his words that can't be correctly deciphered by another. (Burge seems to make this point himself in a later paper.[18])

Now I would like to return to Putnam's Twin Earth example, which does not depend on the idea that social linguistic usage dictates (under

[17] Burge suggests that the reason we normally take a person to mean by his words what others in his linguistic community mean, whether or not the speaker knows what others mean, is that 'People are frequently held, and hold themselves, to the standards of the community when misuse or misunderstanding are at issue.' He also says such cases 'depend on a certain responsibility to communal practice' (ibid. 90). I don't doubt the phenomenon, but doubt its bearing on what it is supposed to show. (*a*) It is often reasonable to hold people responsible for knowing what their words mean; in such cases we may treat them as committed to positions they did not know or believe they were committed to. This has nothing (directly) to do with what they meant by their words, nor what they believed. (*b*) As good citizens and parents we want to encourage practices that enhance the chances for communication; using words as we think others do may enhance communication. This thought (whether or not justified) may help explain why some people tend to attribute meanings and beliefs in a legalistic way; they hope to encourage conformity. (*c*) A speaker who wishes to be understood must intend his words to be interpreted (and hence interpretable) along certain lines; this intention may be served by using words as others do (though often this is not the case). Similarly, a hearer who wishes to understand a speaker must intend to interpret the speaker's words as the speaker intended (whether or not the interpretation is 'standard'). These reciprocal intentions become morally important in endless situations which have no necessary connection with the determination of what someone had in mind.

[18] Tyler Burge, 'Two Thought Experiments Reviewed', 289.

more or less standard conditions) what speakers mean by their words, nor, of course, what their (narrow) psychological states are. I am, as I said, persuaded that Putnam is right; what our words mean is fixed in part by the circumstances in which we learned, and used, the words. Putnam's single example (water) is not enough, perhaps, to nail down this point, since it is possible to insist that 'water' doesn't apply just to stuff with the same molecular structure as water but also to stuff enough like water in structure to be odorless, potable, to support swimming and sailing, etc. (I realize that this remark, like many others in this piece, may show that I don't know a rigid designator when I see one. I don't.) The issue does not depend on such special cases, nor on how we do or should resolve them. The issue depends simply on how the basic connection between words and things, or thoughts and things, is established. I hold, along with Burge and Putnam if I understand them, that it is established by causal interactions between people and parts and aspects of the world. The dispositions to react differentially to objects and events thus set up are central to the correct interpretation of a person's thoughts and speech. If this were not the case, we would have no way of discovering what others think, or what they mean by their words. The principle is as simple and obvious as this: a sentence someone is inspired (caused) to hold true by and only by sightings of the moon is apt to mean something like 'There's the moon'; the thought expressed is apt to be that the moon is there; the thought inspired by and only by sightings of the moon is apt to be the thought that the moon is there. Apt to be, allowing for intelligible error, secondhand reports, and so on. Not that all words and sentences are this directly conditioned to what they are about; we can perfectly well learn to use the word 'moon' without ever seeing it. The claim is that all thought and language must have a foundation in such direct historical connections, and these connections constrain the interpretation of thoughts and speech. Perhaps I should stress that the arguments for this claim do not rest on intuitions concerning what we would say if certain counterfactuals were true. No science fiction or thought experiments are required.[19]

[19] Burge has described thought experiments which do not involve language at all; one of these experiments prompts him to claim that someone brought up in an environment without aluminum could not have 'aluminum thoughts' ('Individualism and Psychology', 5.) Burge does not say why he thinks this, but it is by no means obvious that counterfactual assumptions are needed to make the point. In any case, the new thought experiments seem to rest on intuitions quite different from the intuitions invoked in 'Individualism and the Mental'; it is not clear how social norms feature in the new experiments, and the linguistic habits of the community are apparently irrelevant. At this point it may be that Burge's position is close to mine.

I agree with Putnam and Burge, then, that (as Burge puts it): 'the intentional content of ordinary propositional attitudes . . . cannot be accounted for in terms of physical, phenomenal, causal-functional, computational, or syntactical states or processes that are specified nonintentionally and are defined purely on the individual in isolation from his physical and social environment'.[20] The question remains whether this fact is a threat to first person authority, as Burge seems to think, and Putnam and others certainly think. I have rejected one of Burge's arguments which, if it were right, would pose such a threat. But there is the position described in the previous paragraph, which I hold whether or not others do, since I think this much 'externalism' is required to explain how language can be learned, and how words and attitudes can be identified by an interpreter.

Why does Putnam think that if the reference of a word is (sometimes) fixed by the natural history of how the word was acquired, a user of the word may lose first person authority? Putnam claims (correctly, in my view) that two people can be in all relevant physical (chemical, physiological, etc.) respects the same and yet mean different things by their words and have different propositional attitudes (as these are normally identified). The differences are due to environmental differences about which the two agents may, in some respects, be ignorant. Why, under these circumstances, should we suppose these agents may not know what they mean and think? Talking with them will not easily show this. As we have noted, each, when faced with a glass of water or twater, says honestly, 'Here's a glass of water'. If they are in their home environments, each is right; if they have switched earths, each is wrong. If we ask each one what he means by the word 'water', he gives the right answer, using the same words, of course. If we ask each one what he believes, he gives the right answer. These answers are right because, though verbally identical, they must be interpreted differently. And what is it that they do not know (in the usual authoritative way) about their own states? As we have seen, Putnam distinguishes the states we have just been discussing from 'narrow' psychological states which do not presuppose the existence of any individual other than the subject in that state. We may now start to wonder why Putnam is interested in narrow psychological states. Part of the answer is, of course, that it is these states that he thinks have the 'Cartesian' property of being

---

[20] 'Two Thought Experiments Reviewed', 288.

known in a special way by the person who is in them. (The other part of the answer has to do with constructing a 'scientific psychology'; this does not concern us here.)

The reasoning depends, I think, on two largely unquestioned assumptions. These are:

(1) If a thought is identified by a relation to something outside the head, it isn't wholly in the head. (It ain't in the head.)

(2) If a thought isn't wholly in the head, it can't be 'grasped' by the mind in the way required by first person authority.

That this is Putnam's reasoning is suggested by his claim that if two heads are the same, narrow psychological states must be the same. Thus if we suppose two people are 'molecule for molecule' the same ('in the sense in which two neckties can be "identical" '; you may add, if you wish, that each of the two people 'thinks the same verbalized thoughts ... has the same sense data, the same dispositions, etc.'), then 'it is absurd to think [one] psychological state is one bit different from' the other. These are, of course, narrow psychological states, not the ones we normally attribute, which ain't in the head.[21]

It is not easy to say in exactly what way the verbalized thoughts, sense data, and dispositions can be identical without reverting to the neckties, so let us revert. Then the idea is this: the narrow psychological states of two people are identical when their physical states cannot be distinguished. There would be no point in disputing this, since narrow psychological states are Putnam's to define; what I wish to question is assumption (1) above, which led to the conclusion that ordinary propositional attitudes aren't in the head, and that therefore first person authority doesn't apply to them.

It should be clear that it doesn't follow, simply from the fact that meanings are identified in part by relations to objects outside the head, that meanings aren't in the head. To suppose this would be as bad as to argue that because my being sunburned presupposes the existence of the sun, my sunburn isn't a condition of my skin. My sunburned skin may be indistinguishable from someone else's skin that achieved its burn by other means (our skins may be identical in the 'necktie sense'); yet one of us is really sunburned and the other not. This is enough to show that an appreciation of the external

---

[21] 'The Meaning of "Meaning" ', 227.

factors that enter into our common ways of identifying mental states does not discredit an identity theory of the mental and the physical. Andrew Woodfield seems to think it does. He writes: 'No *de re* state about an object that is external to the person's brain can possibly be identical with a state of that brain, since no brain state presupposes the existence of an external object.'[22] Individual states and events don't *conceptually* presuppose anything in themselves; some of their *descriptions* may, however. My paternal grandfather didn't presuppose me, but if someone can be described as my paternal grandfather, several people besides my grandfather, including me, must exist.

Burge may make a similar mistake in the following passage:

no occurrence of a thought . . . could have a different content and be the very same token event . . . then . . . a person's thought event is not *identical* with any event in him that is described by physiology, biology, chemistry, or physics. For let *b* be any given event described in terms of one of the physical sciences that occurs in the subject while he thinks the relevant thought. Let '*b*' be such that it denotes the same physical event occurring in the subject in our counterfactual situation . . . *b* need not be affected by counterfactual differences [that do not change the contents of the thought event]. Thus . . . *b* [the physical event] is not identical with the subject's occurrent thought.[23]

Burge does not claim to have established the premise of this argument, and so not its conclusion. But he holds that the denial of the premise is 'intuitively very implausible'. He goes on, 'materialist identity theories have schooled the imagination to picture the content of a mental event as varying while the event remains fixed. But whether such imaginings are possible fact or just philosophical fancy is a separate question'. It is because he thinks the denial of the premise to be very improbable that he holds that 'materialist identity theories' are themselves 'rendered implausible by the non-individualistic thought experiments'.[24]

I accept Burge's premise; I think its denial not merely implausible but absurd. If two mental events have different contents, they are surely different events. What I take Burge's and Putnam's imagined cases to show (and what I think the Swampman example shows more directly) is that people who are in all relevant physical respects similar (or 'identical' in the necktie sense) can differ in what they mean

[22] Andrew Woodfield, in *Thought and Object*, p. viii.
[23] 'Individualism and the Mental', 111.
[24] 'Individualism and Psychology', 15 n. 7. Cf. 'Individualism and the Mental', 111.

or think, just as they can differ in being grandfathers or being sunburned. But of course there is *something* different about them, even in the physical world; their causal histories are different, and they are discrete physical objects.

I conclude that the mere fact that ordinary mental states and events are individuated in terms of relations to the outside world has no tendency to discredit mental–physical identity theories as such. In conjunction with a number of further (plausible) assumptions, the 'externalism' of certain mental states and events can be used, I think, to discredit type–type identity theories; but if anything it supports token–token identity theories. (I see no good reason for calling all identity theories 'materialist'; if some mental events are physical events, this makes them no more physical than mental. Identity is a symmetrical relation.)

Putnam and Woodfield are wrong, then, in claiming that it is 'absurd' to think two people could be physically identical (in the 'necktie sense') and yet differ in their ordinary psychological states. Burge, unless he is willing to make far stronger play than he has with essentialist assumptions, is wrong in thinking he has shown all identity theories implausible. We are therefore free to hold that people can be in all relevant physical respects identical (identical in the 'necktie sense') while differing psychologically: this is in fact the position of 'anomalous monism', for which I have argued elsewhere.[25]

One obstacle to nonevidential knowledge of our own ordinary propositional attitudes has now been removed. For if ordinary beliefs and the other attitudes can be 'in the head' even though they are identified as the attitudes they are partly in terms of what is not in the head, then the threat to first person authority cannot come simply from the fact that external factors are relevant to the identification of the attitudes.

But an apparent difficulty remains. True, my sunburn, though describable as such only in relation to the sun, is identical with a condition of my skin which can (I assume) be described without reference to such external factors. Still, if, as a scientist skilled in all the physical sciences, I have access only to my skin, and am denied knowledge of the history of its condition, then by hypothesis there is no way for me to tell that I am sunburned. Perhaps, then, someone

---

[25] 'Mental Events', in Donald Davidson, *Essays on Actions and Events*.

has first person authority with respect to the contents of his mind only as those contents can be described or discovered without reference to external factors. In so far as the contents are identified in terms of external factors, first person authority necessarily lapses. I can tell by examining my skin what my private or 'narrow' condition is, but nothing I can learn in this restricted realm will tell me that I am sunburned. The difference between referring to and thinking of water and referring to and thinking of twater is like the difference between being sunburned and one's skin being in exactly the same condition through another cause. The semantic difference lies in the outside world, beyond the reach of subjective or sublunar knowledge. So the argument might run.

This analogy, between the limited view of the skin doctor and the tunnel vision of the mind's eye, is fundamentally flawed. It depends for its appeal on a faulty picture of the mind, a picture which those who have been attacking the subjective character of ordinary psychological states share with those they attack. If we can bring ourselves to give up this picture, first person authority will no longer been seen as a problem; indeed, it will turn out that first person authority is dependent on, and explained by, the social and public factors that were supposed to undermine that authority.

There is a picture of the mind which has become so ingrained in our philosophical tradition that it is almost impossible to escape its influence even when its faults are recognized and repudiated. In one crude, but familiar, version it goes like this: the mind is a theater in which the conscious self watches a passing show (the shadows on the wall). The show consists of 'appearances', sense data, qualia, what is 'given' in experience. What appear on the stage are not the ordinary objects in the world that the outer eye registers and the heart loves, but their purported representatives. Whatever we know about the world outside depends on what we can glean from the inner clues.

The difficulty that has been apparent from the start with this description of the mental is to see how it is possible to beat a reliable track from the inside to the outside. Another conspicuous, though perhaps less appreciated, difficulty is to locate the self in the picture. For the self seems on the one hand to include theater, stage, actors, and audience; on the other hand, what is known and registered pertains to the audience alone. This second problem could be as well stated as the problem of the location of the objects of the mind: are they *in* the mind, or simply viewed *by* it?

I am not now concerned with such (now largely disavowed) objects of the mind as sense data, but with their judgemental cousins, the supposed objects of the propositional attitudes, whether thought of as propositions, tokens of propositions, representations, or fragments of 'mentalese'. The central idea I wish to attack is that these are entities that the mind can 'entertain', 'grasp', 'have before it', or be 'acquainted' with. (These metaphors are probably instructive: voyeurs merely want to have representations before the mind's eye, while the more aggressive grasp them; the English may be merely acquainted with the contents of the mind, while more friendly types will actually entertain them.)

It is easy to see how the discovery that external facts enter into the individuation of states of mind disturbs the picture of the mind I have been describing. For if to be in a state of mind is for the mind to be in some relation to an object, then whatever helps determine what object it is must equally be grasped if the mind is to know what state it is in. This is particularly evident if an external object is an 'ingredient' in the object before the mind. But in either case, the person who is in the state of mind may not know what state of mind he is in.

It is at this point that the concept of the subjective—of a state of mind—seems to come apart. On the one hand, there are the true inner states, with respect to which the mind retains its authority; on the other hand, there are the ordinary states of belief, desire, intention, and meaning, which are polluted by their necessary connections with the social and public world.

In analogy, there is the problem of the sunburn expert who cannot tell by inspecting the skin whether it is a case of sunburn or merely an 'identical' condition with another cause. We can solve the sunburn problem by distinguishing between sunburn and sunnishburn; sunnishburn is just like sunburn except that the sun may or may not be involved. The expert can spot a case of sunnishburn just by looking, but not a case of sunburn. This solution works because skin conditions, unlike objects of the mind, are not required to be such that there be a special someone who can tell, just by looking, whether or not the condition obtains.

The solution in the case of mental states is different, and simpler; it is to get rid of the metaphor of objects before the mind. Most of us long ago gave up the idea of perceptions, sense data, the flow of experience, as things 'given' to the mind; we should treat propositional objects in the same way. Of course people have beliefs, wishes, doubts, and so forth; but to allow this is not to suggest that beliefs, wishes, and doubts are *entities* in or before the mind, or that being in such states requires there to be corresponding mental objects.

This has been said before, in various tones of voice, but for different reasons. Ontological scruples, for example, are no part of my interest. We will always need an infinite supply of objects to help describe and identify attitudes like belief; I am not suggesting for a moment that belief sentences, and sentences that attribute the other attitudes, are not relational in nature. What I am suggesting is that the objects to which we relate people in order to describe their attitudes need not in any sense be *psychological* objects, objects to be grasped, known, or entertained by the person whose attitudes are described.

This point, too, is familiar; Quine makes it when he suggests that we may use our own sentences to keep track of the thoughts of people who do not know our language. Quine's interest is semantical, and he says nothing in this context about the epistemological and psychological aspects of the attitudes. We need to bring these various concerns together. Sentences about the attitudes are relational; for *semantic* reasons there must therefore be objects to which to relate those who have attitudes. But having an attitude is not having an entity before the mind; for compelling *psychological* and *epistemological* reasons we should deny that there are objects of the mind.

The source of the trouble is the dogma that to have a thought is to have an object before the mind. Putnam and Fodor (and many others) have distinguished two sorts of objects: those that are truly inner and thus 'before the mind' or 'grasped' by it, and those that identify the thought in the usual way. I agree that no objects can serve these two purposes. Putnam (and some of the other philosophers I have mentioned) think the difficulty springs from the fact that an object partly identified in terms of external relations cannot be counted on to coincide with an object before the mind because the mind may be ignorant of the external relation. Perhaps this is so. But it does not follow that we can find *other* objects which will insure the desired coincidence. For if the object *isn't* connected with the world, we can never learn about the world by having that object before the mind; and for reciprocal reasons, it would be impossible to detect such a thought in another. So it seems that what is before the mind cannot include its outside connections—its semantics. On the other hand, if the object *is* connected with the world, then it cannot be fully before the mind in the relevant sense. Yet unless a *semantic* object can be before the mind *in its semantic aspect*, thought, conceived in terms of such objects, cannot escape the fate of sense data.

The basic difficulty is simple: if to have a thought is to have an object before the mind, and the identity of the object determines what the thought is, then it must always be possible to be mistaken about what one is thinking. For unless one knows *everything* about the object, there will always be senses in which one does not know what object it is. Many attempts have been made to find a relation between a person and an object which will in all contexts hold if and only if the person can intuitively be said to know what object it is. But none of these attempts has succeeded, and I think the reason is clear. The only object that would satisfy the twin requirements of being before the mind and also such that it determines the content of a thought must, like Hume's ideas and impressions, 'be what it seems and seem what it is'. There are no such objects, public or private, abstract or concrete.

The arguments of Burge, Putnam, Dennett, Fodor, Stich, Kaplan, Evans, and many others to show that propositions can't *both* determine the contents of our thoughts *and* be subjectively assured are, in my opinion, so many variants on the simple and general argument I have just sketched. It is not just propositions that can't do the job. No objects could.

When we have freed ourselves from the assumption that thoughts must have mysterious objects, we can see how the fact that mental states as we commonly conceive them are identified in part by their natural history not only fails to touch the internal character of such states or to threaten first person authority; it also opens the way to an explanation of first person authority. The explanation comes with the realization that what a person's words mean depends in the most basic cases on the kinds of objects and events that have caused the person to hold the words to be applicable; similarly for what the person's thoughts are about. An interpreter of another's words and thoughts must depend on scattered information, fortunate training, and imaginative surmise, in coming to understand the other. The agent herself, however, is not in a position to wonder whether she is generally using her own words to apply to the right objects and events, since whatever she regularly does apply them to gives her words the meaning they have and her thoughts the contents they have. Of course, in any particular case, she may be wrong in what she believes about the world; what is impossible is that she should be wrong most of the time. The reason is apparent: unless there is a presumption that the speaker knows what she means, i.e. is getting her own language right, there would be nothing for an interpreter to interpret. To put the matter another way, nothing could count as someone regularly misapplying her own words. First person authority, the social character of language, and the external determinants of thought and meaning go naturally together, once we give up the myth of the subjective, the idea that thoughts require mental objects.

3 *The Myth of the Subjective*

This is an essay on an old topic, the relation between the human mind and the rest of nature, the subjective and the objective as we have come to think of them. This dualism, though in its way too obvious to question, carries with it in our tradition a large and not necessarily appropriate burden of associated ideas. Some of these ideas are now coming under critical scrutiny, and the result promises to mark a sea change in contemporary philosophical thought. The present essay, while clearly tendentious, is not designed primarily to convert the skeptic; its chief aim is to describe, from one point of view, a fairly widely recognized development in recent thinking about the contents of the mind, and to suggest some of the consequences that I think follow from this development.

Minds are many, nature is one. Each of us has his own position in the world, and hence his own perspective on it. It is easy to slide from this truism to some confused notion of conceptual relativism. The former, harmless, relativism is just the familiar relativism of position in space and time. Because each of us preempts a volume of space-time, two of us cannot be in exactly the same place at the same time. The relations among our positions are intelligible because we can locate each person in a single, common world, and a shared time frame.

Conceptual relativism may seem similar, but the analogy is hard to carry out. For what is the common reference point, or system of coordinates, to which each scheme is relative? Without a good answer to this question, the claim that each of us in some sense inhabits his own world loses its intelligibility.

For this reason and others, I have long held that there are limits to how much individual or social systems of thought can differ. If by conceptual relativism we mean the idea that conceptual schemes and moral systems, or the languages associated with them, can differ massively—to the extent of being mutually unintelligible or incommensurable, or forever beyond rational resolve—then I reject conceptual relativism.[1] Of course there are contrasts from epoch to epoch, from culture to culture, and person to person, of kinds we all recognize and struggle with; but these are contrasts which with sympathy and effort we can explain and understand. Trouble comes when we try to embrace the idea that there might be more comprehensive differences, for this seems (absurdly) to ask us to take up a stance outside our own ways of thought.

We do not understand the idea of such a really foreign scheme. We know what states of mind are like, and how they are correctly identified; they are just those states whose contents can be discovered in well-known ways. If other people or creatures are in states not discoverable by these methods, it cannot be because our methods fail us, but because those states are not correctly called states of mind—they are not beliefs, desires, wishes, or intentions. The meaninglessness of the idea of a conceptual scheme forever beyond our grasp is due not to our inability to understand such a scheme, nor to our other human limitations; it is due simply to what we mean by a system of concepts.

Many philosophers are not satisfied with arguments like these because they think there is another way in which conceptual relativism can be made intelligible. For it seems that we could make sense of such relativism provided we could find an element in the mind untouched by conceptual interpretation. Then various schemes might be seen as relative to, and assigned the role of organizing, this common element. The common element is, of course, some version of Kant's intuitions, Hume's impressions and ideas, sense data, uninterpreted sensations, the sensuous given. Kant thought only one scheme was possible; but once the dualism of scheme and content is made explicit, the possibility of alternative schemes is apparent. The idea that we have a choice of schemes is explicit in the work of C. I. Lewis: 'There are, in our cognitive experience, two elements; the immediate data, such as those of sense, which are presented or given to the mind, and a form, construction, or interpretation, which represents the activity of thought.'[2]

---

[1] I have argued for this in 'On the Very Idea of a Conceptual Scheme', Essay 13 in *Inquiries into Truth and Interpretation*.

[2] C. I. Lewis, *Mind and the World Order*, 38. Lewis declares that it is the task of philosophy 'to reveal those categorial criteria which the mind applies to what is given to it' (p. 36).

If we could conceive of the function of conceptual schemes in this way, relativism would appear to be an abstract possibility despite doubts about how an alien scheme might be deciphered: the idea would be that different schemes or languages constitute different ways in which what is given in experience may be organized. On this account, there would be no point of view from which we could survey such schemes, and perhaps no way we could in general compare or evaluate them; still, as long as we thought we understood the scheme–content dichotomy, we could imagine the unsullied stream of experience being variously reworked by various minds or cultures. In this way, it may be held, conceptual relativism can be provided with the element to which alternative schemes are related: that element is the uninterpreted given, the uncategorized contents of experience.

This picture of mind and its place in nature has defined many of the problems modern philosophy has thought it had to solve. Among these problems are issues concerning knowledge: how we know about the external world, how we know about other minds, even how we know the contents of our own mind. But we should also include the problem of the nature of moral knowledge, the analysis of perception, and many troubling issues in the philosophy of psychology and the theory of meaning.

Corresponding to this catalogue of problems is a long list of ways in which the supposed scheme–content contrast has been formulated. The scheme may be thought of as an ideology, a set of concepts suited to the task of organizing experience into objects, events, states, and complexes of such; or the scheme may be a language, perhaps with predicates and associated apparatus, interpreted to serve an ideology. The contents of the scheme may be objects of a special sort, such as sense data, percepts, impressions, sensations, or appearances; or the objects may dissolve into adverbial modifications of experience: we may be 'appeared to redly'. Philosophers have shown ingenuity in finding ways of putting into words the contents of the given; there are those strange, verbless sentences like 'Red here now', and the various formulations of protocol sentences over which the logical positivists quarreled.

Expressing the content in words is not necessary and, according to some views, not possible. The scheme-content division can survive even in an environment that shuns the analytic–synthetic distinction, sense data, or the assumption that there can be thoughts or experiences that are free of theory. If I am right, this is the environment provided by W. V. Quine. According to Quine's 'naturalized epistemology', we should ask no more from the philosophy of knowledge than an account of how, given the evidence we have to go on, we are able to form a satisfactory theory of the world. The account draws on the best theory we have: our present science. The evidence, on which the meanings of our sentences, and all our knowledge, ultimately depend, is provided by stimulations of our sense organs. It is these stimulations that provide a person with his only cues to 'what goes on around him'. Quine is not, of course, a reductionist: 'we cannot strip away the conceptual trappings sentence by sentence'. Nevertheless, there is according to Quine a definite distinction to be made between the invariant content and the variant conceptual trappings, between 'report and invention, substance and style, cues and conceptualization'. For,

we can investigate the world, and man as a part of it, and thus find out what cues he could have of what goes on around him. Subtracting his cues from his world view, we get man's net contribution as the difference. This difference marks the extent of man's conceptual sovereignty—the domain within which he can revise theory while saving the data.[3]

World view and cues, theory and data; these are the scheme and content of which I have been speaking.

What matters, then, is not whether we can describe the data in a neutral, theory-free idiom; what matters is that there should be an ultimate source of evidence the character of which can be wholly specified without reference to what it is evidence for. Thus patterns of stimulation, like sense data, can be identified and described without reference to 'what goes on around us'. If our knowledge of the world derives entirely from evidence of this kind, then not only may our senses sometimes deceive us; it is possible that we are systematically and generally deceived.

It is easy to remember what prompts this view: it is thought necessary to insulate the ultimate sources of evidence from the outside world in order to guarantee the authority of the evidence for the subject. Since we cannot be certain what the world outside the mind is like, the subjective can keep its virtue—its chastity, its certainty for us—only by being protected from contamination by the world.

---

[3] This passage, and the quotations that precede it, are from W. V. Quine, *Word and Object*, 5.

The familiar trouble is, of course, that the disconnection creates a gap no reasoning or construction can plausibly bridge. Once this starting point has been chosen, there is no saying what the evidence is evidence for, or so it seems. Idealism, reductionist forms of empiricism, and skepticism loom.

The story is familiar; but let me continue in my breathless way through one more chapter. If the ultimate evidence for our schemes and theories, the raw material on which they are based, is subjective in the way I have described, then so is whatever is directly based on it: our beliefs, desires, intentions, and what we mean by our words. Though these are the progeny of our 'view of the world'—indeed, taken together, they constitute our view of the world—nevertheless they too retain the Cartesian independence from what they purport to be about that the evidence on which they are based had: like sensations, they could be just as they are, and the world be very different. Our beliefs purport to represent something objective, but the character of their subjectivity prevents us from taking the first step in determining whether they correspond to what they pretend to represent.

Instead of saying it is the scheme–content dichotomy that has dominated and defined the problems of modern philosophy, then, one could as well say it is how the dualism of the objective and the subjective has been conceived. For these dualisms have a common origin: a concept of the mind with its private states and objects.

I have reached the point I have been leading up to, for it seems to me that the most promising and interesting change that is occurring in philosophy today is that these dualisms are being questioned in new ways, or are being radically reworked. There is a good chance they will be abandoned, at least in their present form. What we are seeing is the emergence of a revised view of the relation of mind and the world.

The action has centered on the concept of subjectivity, what is 'in the mind'. Let us start with what it is we know or grasp when we know the meaning of a word or sentence. It is a commonplace of the empirical tradition that we learn our first words (which at the start serve the function of sentences)—words like 'apple', 'man', 'dog', 'water'—through a conditioning of sounds or verbal behavior to appropriate bits of matter in the public domain. The conditioning works best with objects that interest the learner and are hard to miss by either teacher or pupil. But here is the point: this is not just a story about how we learn to use words: it must also be an essential part of an adequate account of what words refer to, and what they mean.

Needless to say the whole story cannot be this simple. On the other hand, it is hard to believe that this sort of direct interaction between language users and public events and objects is not a basic part of the whole story, the part that, directly or indirectly, largely determines how the learner's words are related to things. One consequence is that the details of the mechanisms that constitute the causal chains from speaker to speaker, and spoken-of object to speaker to language learner, cannot in themselves matter to meaning and reference. The grasp of meanings is determined by the terminal elements in the conditioning process, and is tested only by the end product: use of words geared to appropriate objects and situations. This is perhaps best seen by noticing that two speakers who 'mean the same thing' by an expression need have no more in common than their dispositions to appropriate verbal behavior; the neural networks may be very different. The matter may be put the other way around: two speakers may be alike in 'relevant' physical respects, and yet they may mean different things by the same words because of differences in the external situations in which the words were learned. Insofar, then, as the subjective or mental is thought of as supervenient on the physical characteristics of a person, and nothing more, meanings cannot be purely subjective or mental. As Hilary Putnam (misleadingly) put it, 'meanings ain't in the head'.[4] The point is that the correct interpretation of what a speaker means is not determined solely by what is in his head; it depends also on the natural history of what is in the head. Putnam's argument hinges on rather elaborate thought experiments which some philosophers have found unconvincing. But the case can best be made by appealing directly to obvious facts about language learning and to facts about how we interpret words and languages with which we are unfamiliar.[5] The relevant facts have already been mentioned above; in the simplest and most basic cases, words and sentences derive their meaning from the objects and circumstances in whose presence they were learned. A sentence which one has been conditioned by the learning process to be caused to hold true by the presence of fires will (usually) be true when there is a fire present; a word one has been conditioned to hold

---

[4] Hilary Putnam, 'The Meaning of "Meaning" ', 227.
[5] I argue for this in Essay 1.

applicable by the presence of snakes will refer to snakes. Of course very many words and sentences are not learned this way; but it is those that are that anchor language to the world.

If the meanings of sentences are propositions, and propositions are the objects of attitudes like belief, intention, and desire, then what has been said about meanings must hold true of all of the propositional attitudes. The point can be made without recourse to propositions or other supposed objects of the attitudes. For from the fact that speakers are in general capable of expressing their thoughts in language, it follows that to the extent that the subjectivity of meaning is in doubt, so is that of thought generally.

The fallout from these considerations for the theory of knowledge is revolutionary. If words and thoughts are, in the most basic cases, necessarily about the sorts of objects and events that commonly cause them, there is no room for Cartesian doubts about the independent existence of such objects and events. Doubts there can be, of course. But there need be nothing we are indubitably right about for it to be certain that we are mostly right about the nature of the world. Sometimes skepticism seems to rest on a simple fallacy, the fallacy of reasoning from the fact that there is nothing we might not be wrong about to the conclusion that we might be wrong about everything. The second possibility is ruled out if we accept that our simplest sentences are given their meanings by the situations that generally cause us to hold them true or false, since to hold a sentence we understand to be true or false is to have a belief. Continuing along this line, we see that general skepticism about the deliverances of the senses cannot even be formulated, since the senses and their deliverances play no central theoretical role in the account of belief, meaning, and knowledge if the contents of the mind depend on the causal relations, whatever they may be, between the attitudes and the world. This is not to deny the importance of the causal role of the senses in knowledge and the acquisition of language, of course.

It is an empirical accident that our ears, eyes, taste buds, and tactile and olfactory organs play an intermediate role in the formation of beliefs about the world. The causal connections between thought and objects and events in the world could have been established in entirely different ways without this making any philosophically significant difference to the contents or veridicality of perceptual belief. What is true is that certain beliefs caused by sensory experience are often veridical, and therefore often provide good reasons for further beliefs.

If this is right, epistemology (as apart, perhaps, from the study of perception, which is now seen to be only distantly related to epistemology) has no basic need for purely private, subjective 'objects of the mind', either as uninterpreted sense data or experience on the one hand, or as fully interpreted propositions on the other. Content and scheme, as remarked in the quotation from C. I. Lewis, come as a pair; we can let them go together. Once we take this step, no objects will be left with respect to which the problem of representation can be raised. Beliefs are true or false, but they represent nothing. It is good to be rid of representations, and with them the correspondence theory of truth, for it is thinking there are representations that engenders intimations of relativism. (It is, of course, harmless to say true beliefs and thoughts are true because of the way the world is: they correctly 'represent' the world.)

There is an abundance of puzzles about sensation and perception; but these puzzles are not, as I said, foundational for epistemology. The question of what is directly experienced in sensation, and how this is related to judgements of perception, while as hard to answer as it ever was, can no longer be assumed to be a central question for the theory of knowledge. The reason has already been given: although sensation plays a crucial role in the causal process that connects beliefs with the world, it is a mistake to think it plays an epistemological role in determining the contents of those beliefs. In accepting this conclusion, we abandon the key dogma of traditional empiricism, what I have called the third dogma of empiricism. But that is to be expected: empiricism is the view that the subjective ('experience') is the foundation of objective empirical knowledge. I am suggesting that empirical knowledge has no epistemological foundation, and needs none.[6]

There is another familiar problem that is transformed when we recognize that beliefs, desires, and the other so-called propositional attitudes, are not subjective in the way we thought they were. The problem is how one person knows the mind of another. Perhaps it is obvious that if the account I have sketched of our understanding of language, and its connection with the contents of thought, is correct, the accessibility of the minds of others is assured from the start. Skepticism about the possibility of knowing other minds is thus ruled out. But to recognize this is not to answer the question

---

[6] See Essay 10.

what conceptual conditions we place on the pattern of thought that make it possible for an interpreter to progress from observed behavior to knowledge of the intentional attitudes of another person. That this question has an answer, however, is guaranteed by the fact that the nature of language and thought is such as to make them interpretable.[7]

It should not be assumed that if we cease to be bullied or beguiled by the scheme–content and subjective–objective dichotomies, all the problems of epistemology will evaporate. But the problems that seem salient will change. Answering the global skeptic will no longer be a challenge, the search for epistemological foundations in preconceptual experience will be seen as pointless, and conceptual relativism will lose its appeal. But plenty of questions of equal or greater interest will remain, or be generated by the new stance. The demise of the subjective as previously conceived leaves us without foundations for knowledge, and relieves us of the need for them, but new problems then arise that cluster around the nature of error, for error is hard to identify and explain if the holism that goes with a nonfoundational approach is not somehow constrained. It is not problematic whether knowledge of the world and of other minds is possible, but it remains as a question how we attain such knowledge, and the conditions belief must satisfy to count as knowledge. These are not so much questions in traditional epistemology as they are questions about the nature of rationality. They are questions that, like the epistemological questions they replace, have no final answer; but unlike the questions they replace, they are worth trying to answer.

Familiarity with many of the points I have been making is fairly widespread these days. But we have not fully appreciated the scope of the entailed revolution in our ways of thinking about philosophy. Part of the reason for this failure may be traced to certain misunderstandings concerning the nature of the new antisubjectivism (as we may try calling it). Here are three of the misunderstandings.

1. People have been persuaded of the dependence of meanings on factors outside the head by examples rather than by general arguments. There is therefore a strong tendency to suppose that the dependence is limited to the sorts of expressions that recur in the examples: proper names, natural kind words like 'water' and 'gold',

---

[7] See Essay 1.

and indexicals.[8] But in fact the phenomenon is ubiquitous, since it is inseparable from the social character of language. It is not a local problem to be solved by some semantic trick; it is a perfectly general fact about the nature of thought and speech.

2. If mental states like belief, desire, intention, and meaning are not supervenient on the physical states of the agent alone, then, it has been argued, theories that identify mental states and events with physical states of and events in the body must be wrong. This is suggested by Putnam's claim that 'meanings ain't in the head', and it is explicitly claimed by Tyler Burge and Andrew Woodfield.[9] The argument assumes that if a state or event is identified (perhaps necessarily, if it is a mental state or event) by reference to things outside of the body, then the state or event itself must be partly outside the body, or at least not identical with any event in the body. This is simply a mistake: one might as well argue that a sunburned patch of skin is not located on the body of the person who is sunburned (since the state of the skin has been identified by reference to the sun). Similarly, mental states are characterized in part by their relations to events and objects outside of the person, but this does not show that mental states are states of anything more than the person, nor that they are not identical with physical states.

3. A third misunderstanding is closely related to the second. It is thought that if the correct determination of an agent's thoughts depends, at least to some degree, on the causal history of those thoughts, and the agent may be ignorant of that history, then the agent may not know what he thinks (and, *mutatis mutandis*, what he means, intends, etc.). The new antisubjectivism is thus seen as a threat to first person authority—to the fact that people generally know without recourse to inference from evidence, and so in a way that others do not, what they themselves think, want, and intend. The reaction has been to resort to maneuvers designed to insulate mental states once more from their external determiners.

The maneuvers are not needed, for first person authority is not threatened. I may not know the difference between an echidna and a porcupine; as a result, I may call all echidnas I come across

---

[8] Tyler Burge, 'Individualism and the Mental'; and Hilary Putnam, 'The Meaning of "Meaning" '.

[9] Tyler Burge, 'Individualism and the Mental', 111; and Andrew Woodfield, 'Introduction', in Woodfield (ed.), *Thought and Object*, p. viii.

porcupines. Yet because of the environment in which I learned the word 'porcupine', my word 'porcupine' refers to porcupines and not to echidnas; this is what I think it refers to, and what I believe I see before me when I honestly affirm, 'That's a porcupine'. My ignorance of the circumstances that determine what I mean and think has no tendency to show that I don't know what I mean and think. To suppose otherwise is to show how strongly we are wed to the idea of subjective mental states that might be just as they are independent of the rest of the world and its history.

Another reaction to the imagined threat to our real inner lives is to concede that beliefs and other mental states as we normally identify them are not truly subjective, but at the same time to hold that there are similar inner (or 'narrow') mental states that are. The idea might be, for example, that since nothing in my inner state or my behavior distinguishes between porcupines and echidnas, what I really believe when I see an echidna (or a porcupine) is that what is before me is an animal with certain general characteristics—characteristics that are in fact shared by porcupines and echidnas. The trouble is that since my word 'porcupine' refers only to porcupines, I apparently don't know what I mean when I say 'That's a porcupine'. This unattractive solution is unnecessary, for it is based on a confusion about what is 'inner'. Since there is no present physical difference between my actual state and the state I would be in if I meant 'echidna or porcupine' or 'animal with such and such properties' rather than 'porcupine' and believed what I would then mean, it does not follow that there is no psychological difference. (There may be no relevant physical difference between the skin of someone who is sunburned and the skin of someone burned by a sunlamp, but there is a difference, since one state was and the other wasn't caused by the sun. Psychological states are in this respect like sunburn.) So nothing stands in the way of saying I can know what I mean when I use the word 'porcupine' and what I believe when I have thoughts about porcupines, even though I can't tell an echidna from a porcupine. The psychological difference, which is just the difference between meaning and believing there is a porcupine before me, and meaning and believing there is a creature with certain common features of porcupines and echidnas, is exactly the difference needed to insure that I know what I mean and what I think. All that Putnam and others have shown is that this difference does not have to be reflected in the physical state of the brain.

Inventing a new set of truly 'inner', or 'narrow', psychological states is not, then, a way of restoring first person authority to the mental; quite the contrary. There remains the claim, however, that a systematic science of psychology requires states of the agent that can be identified without reference to their history or other connections with the outside world. Otherwise, it is said, there would be no accounting for the fact that I, who may refer only to porcupines by my word 'porcupine', can no more tell the difference between a porcupine and an echidna than if (physically unchanged) I meant instead 'porcupine or echidna'.

The prospects for a scientific psychology are not directly relevant to the topic of this essay, and so we may disregard the question whether there are inner states of agents which might explain their behavior better than ordinary beliefs and desires. But it is relevant to consider whether there are states of mind which have a better claim to be called subjective than the propositional attitudes as these are usually conceived and identified.

Two suggestions have been made. The more modest (to be found in the work of Jerry Fodor, for example) is that we might take as the true inner or solipsistic states selected states from among the usual attitudes, and modifications of these. Thoughts about porcupines and echidnas would be eliminated, since the contents of such thoughts are identified by relations to the outside world; but admissible would be thoughts about animals satisfying certain general criteria (the very ones we use in deciding whether something is a porcupine, for example).[10]

Such inner states, if they existed, would qualify as subjective by almost any standards: they could be identified and classified without reference to external objects and events; they could be called on to serve as the foundations of empirical knowledge; and the authority of the first person could plausibly apply to them. It seems clear, however, that there are no such states, at least if they can be expressed in words. The 'general features' or 'criteria' we use to identify porcupines are such as having four feet, a nose, eyes, and quills. But it is evident that the meanings of the words that refer to these features, and the contents of the concepts the words express, depend as much on the natural history of how the words and

---

[10] Jerry Fodor, 'Methodological Solipsism Considered as a Research Strategy in Cognitive Psychology'.

concepts were acquired as was the case for 'porcupine' and 'echidna'. There are no words, or concepts tied to words, that are not understood and interpreted, directly or indirectly, in terms of causal relations between people and the world (and, of course, the relations among words and other words, concepts and other concepts).

At this point one can imagine a proposal to the effect that there are inexpressible phenomenal criteria to which the publicly expressible criteria can be reduced; and here it is to be hoped that memories of past failures of such reductionistic fantasies will serve to suppress the thought that the proposal could be carried out. But even aside from nostalgic musings about phenomenalistic reduction, it is instructive to find the effort to make psychology scientific turning into a search for internal propositional states that can be detected and identified apart from relations to the rest of the world, much as earlier philosophers sought for something 'given in experience' which contained no necessary clue to what was going on outside. The motive is similar in the two cases: it is thought that a sound footing, whether for knowledge or for psychology, requires something inner in the sense of being nonrelational.

The second, and more revolutionary, suggestion was that the mental states needed for a scientific psychology, though roughly propositional in character, bear no direct relation to common beliefs, desires, and intentions.[11] These states are, in effect, stipulated to be those that explain behavior, and they are therefore inner or subjective only in the sense of being characterized exclusively by what is physically beneath the skin. But there is no reason to suppose that people can tell without observation when they are in such states and so no reason to call them subjective.

In summary, I have made five connected points about the 'contents of the mind'.

First, states of mind like doubts, wishes, beliefs, and desires are identified in part by the social and historical context in which they are acquired; in this respect they are like other states that are identified by their causes, such as suffering from snow blindness or favism (a disease caused by contact with the fava bean).

Second, this does not show that states of mind are not physical

---

[11] This idea has been promoted by Stephen Stich, *From Folk Psychology to Cognitive Science*.

states of a person; how we describe and identify events and states has nothing directly to do with where those states and events are.

Third, the fact that states of mind, including what is meant by a speaker, are identified by causal relations with external objects and events is essential to the possibility of communication, and it makes one mind accessible in principle to another; but this public and inter-active aspect of the mind has no tendency to diminish the importance of first person authority.

Fourth, the idea that there is a basic division between uninter-preted experience and an organizing conceptual scheme is a deep mistake, born of the essentially incoherent picture of the mind as a passive but critical spectator of an inner show. An adequate account of knowledge makes no appeal to such epistemological intermedi-aries as sense data, qualia, or raw feels. As a result, global skepticism of the senses is not a position we can coherently entertain.

Finally, I have argued against the postulation of 'objects of thought', whether these are conceived on the model of sense data, or as propositional in character. There are the many states of mind, but their description does not require that there be ghostly entities that the mind contemplates. To dispense with such entities is to eliminate rather than solve a number of vexing problems. For we cannot ask how such objects can represent the world if there are no such objects, nor can we be puzzled by the question how the mind can be directly acquainted with them.

What remains of the concept of subjectivity? So far as I can see, two features of the subjective as classically conceived remain in place. Thoughts are private, in the obvious but important sense in which property can be private, that is, belong to one person. And knowledge of thoughts is asymmetrical, in that the person who has a thought generally knows he has it in a way in which others cannot. But this is all there is to the subjective. So far from constituting a preserve so insulated that it is a problem how it can yield knowledge of an outside world, or be known to others, thought is necessarily part of a common public world. Not only can others often learn what we think by noting the causal dependencies that give our thoughts their content, but the very possibility of thought demands shared standards of truth and objectivity.

4 *What is Present to the Mind?*

There is a sense in which anything we think about is, while we are thinking about it, before the mind. But there is another sense, well known to philosophers, in which only some of the things we can think about are said to be before the mind. Some are before the mind when we think about anything at all; others we do not have to think about for them to be before the mind. Both of these are things supposed to be so directly before the mind that it is impossible to misidentify them, or we can misidentify them only if we do not know what we think; in this they differ from ordinary physical objects or indeed any other objects at all, all of which are easy to misidentify. We cannot mistake these entities for others simply because it is these objects that fix the contents of our thoughts. It is things of this second sort I want to discuss.

Some things of this second sort are the objects, so called, of desires, beliefs, intentions, worries, and hopes; they are the propositions to which we have the various attitudes, the thoughts (as Frege named them) which our sentences express. We must also include the constituents of propositions, such things as properties and relations.

The objects I have mentioned have a special relation to the mind: it is only through the mind that we can know them. Since they are abstract, they cannot be accessed by the senses. They have no causal powers, and so cannot act on, or be acted on by, our minds, our brains, or us.

This raises the question what sort of relations we or our minds are thought to have to these objects when we say they are before the mind. We have many words to express our relations to propositions: we grasp them when we understand a sentence, we entertain them, reject them, wish they were true, hope they aren't, or intend to make them true. But what sort of relations are these? They sound like psychological relations, as if there were some sort of mental transaction between us and these entities. But what kind of business can be transacted with an abstract object?

The propositional objects of the mind and their constituents are supposed, then, to have these two properties: they *identify* a thought by fixing its content; and they *constitute* an essential aspect of the psychology of the thought by being grasped or otherwise known by the person with the thought. It is a problem how these two properties can be reconciled. My thesis is that they cannot.

Here is the main difficulty. I take for granted that for the most part we do know what we think, even though there are departures from total self-knowledge. (I use 'think' to cover all the propositional attitudes.) But if a thought is constituted the thought it is by the mind's knowledge of the identifying object, then someone knows what thought she is thinking only if she knows which object she has in mind. Yet there seems to be no clear meaning to the idea of knowing which object one has in mind. The trouble is that ignorance of even one property of an object can, under appropriate circumstances, count as not knowing which object it is. This is the reason philosophers who have wanted to found knowledge on infallible identification of objects have sought objects that, like Hume's impressions and ideas, 'Are what they seem and seem what they are'—that is, have all and only the properties we think they have. Alas, there are no such objects. Every object has an infinity of logically independent properties, even those objects, like numbers, all of whose 'essential' properties we specify.[1]

---

[1] In *The Interpretation of Frege's Philosophy*, 50, Michael Dummett describes this feature of Fregean senses: 'A sense cannot have any features not discernible by reflection on or deduction from what is involved in expressing or in grasping it. Only that belongs to the sense of an expression which is relevant to the determination of the truth value of the sentence in which it occurs; if we fail to grasp some features of its contribution to the truth-conditions of certain sentences, then we fail fully to grasp its sense, while, on the other hand, any aspect of its meaning that does not bear on the truth-conditions of the sentences containing it is no part of its sense. It cannot be, therefore, that the sense has all sorts of other features not detectable by us . . . A thought is transparent in the sense that, if you grasp it, you thereby know everything to be known about it as it is in itself.' Dummett limits the features of senses we cannot fail to detect to their 'internal properties', but it is not clear on what non-question-begging principle such properties are to be told from others.

Steve Yablo asks (in a private communication) why we couldn't pay attention to some only of the properties of the objects, perhaps the 'essential' properties. No, not if we are to stick to the idea that the contents of the thought are individuated by the object. For if two objects have the same 'essential' properties, but differ in some other property, they are different objects, and so the thoughts must differ.

So perhaps it isn't the *object* that is before the mind, but only some *aspect* of it. We might get the object wrong, but it wouldn't matter. But then the aspect is the object of thought, not the object of which it is the aspect; and the same difficulties arise anew.

Recent discussion of *de re* belief brings out the point. If we agree with Russell that a person cannot form a judgement about an object unless he knows which object it is, or (to put it in another way that Russell favored) it is an object with which the person is acquainted, and that this demands, in the case of propositions, that this special relation hold between the judge and each part of the proposition judged, then there is a problem about attitudes like the following: There is a recipe for making corn bread that Joan believes is easy. The truth of this attribution not only demands that there be a recipe for making corn bread, but it also seems to require that Joan know which recipe it is—or be somehow acquainted with it. When Quine first emphasized the distinction between *de re* and *de dicto* belief sentences in modern terms, he was inclined to see *de re* reference as an island of clarity in the opaque sea of intensionality.[2] Subsequent developments led to a change of mind. In 'Intensions Revisited' he wrote, 'The notion of knowing or believing who or what someone or something is, is utterly dependent on context.'[3] What led to the change of mind was the difficulty in explaining the relation between a person and an object that would justify the claim that the person knew which object it was. A number of attempts have been made to clarify the relation: Føllesdal declared only 'genuine' names could enter into it; Kripke spoke of 'rigid designators'; David Kaplan called the elect names 'vivid'.[4] Gareth Evans studied the problem in depth; he thought, with others, that the only psychological relation that could count as providing the requisite sort of 'fundamental iden-tification' of an object was demonstrative identification. In such a case alone could one say that the object was part of the proposition entertained. Following Russell, Evans concluded that when a person thinks he is entertaining a singular thought, but is using a nonrefer-ring name, there is no proposition for him to contemplate, and there-fore no thought that he has. If he uses a sentence containing a non-referring name, he expresses no thought.[5] If, like me, you have trouble feeling confidence in the criteria for genuine cases of 'funda-mental identification', you will appreciate why Russell limited such cases to situations in which the mind is directly acquainted with its

[2] W. V. Quine, 'Quantifiers and Propositional Attitudes'.

[3] W. V. Quine, 'Intensions Revisited', 121.

[4] Dagfinn Føllesdal, 'Knowledge, Identity, and Existence'; Saul Kripke, 'Naming and Necessity'; David Kaplan, 'Quantifying In'.

[5] Gareth Evans, *The Varieties of Reference*.

objects, something he thought was possible only with sense data (and perhaps with oneself).

What lies behind some of these attempts to characterize the special relation between the mind and its objects is, of course, the Cartesian drive to identify a sort of knowledge which is guaranteed against failure. If this search is combined with the assumption that all knowledge consists in the mind being in psychological contact with an object, then objects must be found about which error is impossible—objects that must be what they seem and seem what they are.

There simply are no such objects. Not even appearances are everything we think they are. Nor can the 'aspects' of sense data, if they really are objects, be protected from one or another sort of misidentification. The reason Quine is right in thinking we cannot pick out 'the' relation that constitutes knowing which object some object is is simply that *any* property of an object may, under suitable conditions, be considered the relevant identifier.

I have dwelt briefly on the problem as it has been studied in relation to proper names because it is there that philosophers seem to have come closest to appreciating the nature of the difficulty. But if my diagnosis is correct, the problem really has nothing special to do with proper names; it is a perfectly general problem about the objects of the mind. If the mind can think only by getting into the right relation to some object which it can for certain distinguish from all others, then thought is impossible. If a mind can know what it thinks only by flawlessly identifying the objects before it, then we must very often not know what we think.

Why, if they make so much trouble, do we suppose there *are* propositional objects of thought? Well, for one thing we certainly talk as if there were such entities: we think deep thoughts, share thoughts, discard and embrace beliefs, entertain, consider, reflect on, contemplate ideas and propositions—one could go on for a long time. These are the sort of remarks we have been taught, with reason, to view with ontological suspicion. But it is much harder to take lightly the problem we get into when we attempt to give a systematic account of what certain sentences mean—the ones we use to attribute thoughts to thinkers. For it is difficult to see how ordinary sentences like 'Paul believes that the Koh-i-noor diamond is one of the crown jewels' can be analyzed except as relating Paul to some entity picked out by the phrase 'that the Koh-i-noor diamond is one of the crown jewels', or perhaps by the sentence 'The Koh-i-noor diamond is one of the crown jewels'. Plenty of attempts have been made to avoid taking 'believes' as a relational term, that is, as relating two objects, a believer and something else, but none of these attempts is, as far as I know, successful.

One proposal is to treat the rest of the sentence after 'believes' as a complex adverb. The reading might be something like: 'Paul believes in a that-the-Koh-i- noor-diamond-is-one-of-the-crown-jewels fashion'. But this is an unsatisfactory suggestion, since no one has any idea how to derive the meaning of such an adverbial modifier from the meanings of the constituent words. Yet it is intuitively obvious that we understand the sentences that follow the 'that' in belief sentences because we understand the constituent words. If the meanings of such contained sentences (which give the 'contents' of propositional attitudes) are not constructed from the meanings of their parts, they must have to be learned independently—as if they were new, often very long, words. It seems clear that this is a wrong idea, and probably an impossible one, since any declarative sentence can feature as a content–sentence, and there is an unlimited, and so presumably unlearnable, totality of these.

Other suggestions along similar lines have been made fairly often, but no one has ever shown how to implement such suggestions by incorporating them in a developed semantic theory.[6] The governing principle seems clear: apart from sentences, whenever we recognize a grammatical category to which we must assign an infinity of expressions, ontology is required. There must be an infinity of objects that can be referred to either indexically or by means of descriptions; these are the two devices available to enable a finite vocabulary to cope with any of a potential infinity of objects. Objects allow us to manage adjectives; events do the same for at least some adverbs. Numbers do the job when we want to measure.[7]

There is, then, no plausible alternative to taking belief sentences as relational, and therefore no alternative to taking the content sentence ('The Koh-i-noor diamond is one of the crown jewels' plus, perhaps, the word 'that' when it is present) as a singular term

---

[6] For a discussion of a number of attempts to eliminate the ontological commitment to 'objects of thought' in the analysis of belief sentences, and other sentences that attribute propositional attitudes, see essay 7 in *Inquiries into Truth and Interpretation*.

[7] See W. V. Quine, 'Events and Reification'.

which, by referring to an appropriate entity, specifies the relevant belief.[8]

Apparently we have a dilemma. On the one hand, there is the fact that to have a belief or other propositional attitude is to be related to an object of some sort; on the other hand, there is the fact that there seems to be no satisfactory account of the psychological relation a person must be in to the appropriate object in order to have the attitude. The difficulty in giving such an account hinges on the idea that since a person generally knows what he thinks, he must be directly acquainted with, or be able in some special way to identify or individuate, the object or objects that define (give the contents of) his thought.

If we rid ourselves of preconceptions, I think it is easy to see where we have gone wrong. It does not follow, from the facts that a thinker knows what he thinks and that what he thinks can be fixed by relating him to a certain object, that the thinker is acquainted with, or indeed knows anything at all about, the object. Someone who attributes a thought to another must, I have argued, relate that person to some object, and so the attributer must, of course, identify an appropriate object, either by pointing to it or by describing it. But there is no reason why the attributer must stand in any special relation to the identifying object; all he has to do is refer to it in the way he refers to anything else.

We specify the subjective state of the thinker by relating him to an object, but there is no reason to say that this object itself has a subjective status, that it is 'known' by the thinker, or is 'before the mind' of the thinker. This consequence was already implicit in some analyses of sentences about propositional attitudes, for example the suggestion once entertained by Carnap, and discussed by Quine, that belief sentences be taken to relate a believer to a sentence of the attributer. Thus Quine, who holds that a cat can have a belief, points out that there is no reason to suppose a cat is acquainted with the sentence 'Food's on' just because it can correctly be said that the cat believes that food's on. For those who doubt that cats have propositional attitudes, the

---

[8] Stephen Schiffer rightly emphasizes that the possibility of 'compositional semantics' (the idea that the meanings of complex expressions must be seen as a function of the meanings of the expressions of which they are composed) depends crucially on the relational analysis of sentences that are used to attribute attitudes. He despairs of finding a satisfactory analysis for reasons I do not share, and so abandons hope for a compositional semantics. Stephen Schiffer, *Remnants of Meaning*.

same point can be made by remarking that we may identify a belief of Sebastian's by saying he believes that Naples is north of San Francisco, though he doesn't know a word of English. My point here isn't that belief sentences relate believers to sentences, but that this familiar proposal assumes that the objects used to identify a belief may not be within the ken of the believer. Once we grant this possibility, we are free to divorce the semantic need for content-specifying objects from the idea that there must be any objects at all with which someone who has an attitude is in psychic touch.

Here is an analogy: consider weight. Some things weigh more than others; some things weigh nothing; occasionally two things weigh the same. One thing may weigh twice what another does. These relations among objects are what we wish to report when we assign weights to them. Introducing a standard does not alter the situation. Thus a monetary pound in the time of William I weighed the same as 12 ounces; it took 20 pennies to weigh an ounce; and a penny weighed the same as 32 grains of wheat taken from the middle of the ear. Thus a pound weighed the same as 7,680 grains of wheat. All that we wish to say about how much things weigh can be put in terms of these comparisons: for example, the Koh-i-noor diamond in its present condition weighs about the same as $15^1/_3$ pennies, or 490 grains of wheat.

All these comparisons can be tedious, and in any case we make the relevant comparisons perspicuously by using numbers. So the convenient thing is to settle on a way of representing the relations among objects with respect to weight by using numbers directly. Thus we say the Koh-i-noor diamond weighs 109 carats or 345 grams. But talk of this sort does not require us to include carats or grams in our ontology. The only objects we need are the numbers and the things that have weight. To say the weight in carats of the Koh-i-noor diamond is 109 does not commit us to *weights* as objects: it is just to assign the number 109 to the diamond as a way of relating it to other objects on the carat scale.

Seen this way, talk of how much things weigh is relational: it relates objects to numbers, and so to one another. But no one supposes the numbers are in any sense intrinsic to the objects that have weight, or are somehow 'part' of them. What are basic are certain *relations* among objects: we conveniently keep track of these relations by assigning numbers to the objects, and remembering how the relations among the objects are reflected in the numbers.

One important aspect of numerical measurement is that typically some only of the properties of numbers are relevant to their use in reporting relative weights. Thus it *is* relevant that whatever numbers we use to keep track of weights preserve ratios: if one thing weighs twice as many grams as another, it must also weigh twice as many pounds. On the other hand, the absolute size of the number is irrelevant: measurement in pounds, grains of wheat, and grams yields different numbers, but the same *relative* weights when compared to other objects.[9]

The analogy with beliefs is this. Just as in measuring weight we need a collection of entities which have a structure in which we can reflect the relations between weighty objects, so in attributing states of belief (and other propositional attitudes) we need a collection of entities related in ways that will allow us to keep track of the relevant properties of and relations among the various psychological states.

In thinking and talking of the weights of physical objects we do not need to suppose there are such things as weights for objects to have. Similarly, in thinking and talking about the beliefs of people we needn't suppose there are such entities as beliefs. Nor do we have to invent objects to serve as the 'objects of belief' or what is before the mind, or in the brain. Such invention is unnecessary because the entities we mention to help specify a state of mind do not have to play any *psychological* or epistemological role for the person in that state, just as numbers play no physical role. As a consequence, there is no reason to conclude, from the thinker's lack of knowledge of the entities we use to track his thoughts, that *he* may not know what he thinks.

The suggestion I am proposing about the nature of the propositional attitudes applies directly to a problem that has troubled a number of philosophers in recent years. There are convincing arguments to show that the correct determination of the contents of beliefs (and meanings and other propositional attitudes) depends in part on causal connections between the believer and events and objects in the world of which he may be ignorant. A now familiar example is Putnam's Twin Earth case.[10] We are invited to imagine

---

[9] A comparison between how we attribute beliefs and numerical measurement has been made by Paul Churchland in *Scientific Realism and the Plasticity of Mind*, 105. But he makes the mistake of supposing we can take a phrase like '345 grams' in 'The Koh-i-noor diamond weighs 345 grams' as an *adverb* of 'weighs', and thus get rid of the ontological problem (he would say the same about the sentence that follows 'believes'). But as we have seen, this suggestion cannot be supported by a serious semantics.

[10] Hilary Putnam, 'The Meaning of "Meaning" '.

that there is a twin to our Earth which is, in all immediately discernible respects, identical with our Earth. On Twearth is my doppelgänger, molecule for molecule the same (that is, similar in 'relevant respects'), having been exposed to the same conditioning, and having exactly the same linguistic dispositions, as I have. Yet one of us believes it is water he sees before him (me) when the other believes it is twater. The explanation is that where there is water on Earth, there is twater on Twearth, though no one has yet detected the difference. Putnam argues that there is no inner, or psychological, difference between me and my twin. Neither of us has any reason to say he believes one thing rather than the other. Therefore (Putnam continues) neither of us knows what he believes. (I don't know whether I believe this is water or twater.) So there may be, and perhaps always are, nonsubjective factors, factors unknown to the thinker, which decide what the 'object of thought' is. If the identity of the 'object of thought' is partly dependent on factors of which the person who has the thought is ignorant, doesn't it follow that the person may not know what he thinks?

The answer is that it doesn't follow. It would follow if the object used to identify my thought were something I had to be able to discriminate in order to know what I think. But this is the assumption I have urged we should abandon. What I see before me I believe to be water; I am in no danger of thinking it is twater, since I do not know what twater is. If I am on Earth, I also believe I think I am seeing water, and in this I am right. If I were without my knowledge transferred to Twearth I would believe twater was water—a mistake. In both cases I would know what I believed. Of course my twin on Twearth refers to twater by the word 'water'. He refers to twater by using the word 'water' because he thinks it is twater. This is also what he thinks he thinks. So neither of us would be wrong about what he thought. The possibility of error, or of failure to distinguish one's own state of mind, due solely to the external elements that help determine that state of mind, is intelligible only on the supposition that having a thought requires a special psychological relation to the object used to identify the state of mind.[11]

The point of this exercise may surprise us. It is that subjective states are not supervenient on the state of the brain or nervous

[11] For further discussion of this point, see Essay 2.

system: two people may be in similar physical states[12] and yet be in dissimilar psychological states. This does not mean, of course, that mental states are not supervenient on physical states, for there must be a physical difference *somewhere* if psychological states are different. But the interesting physical difference may not be in the person; like the difference between water and twater, it may be (we are supposing) elsewhere.

Many philosophers faced with this result have decided that beliefs and other so-called propositional attitudes, as we usually identify them, are not quite as subjective as they were thought to be. Thus Jerry Fodor, in recommending 'methodological solipsism' to the psychologist, thinks he is recommending that the psychologist deal with *truly* subjective states, states whose identities are determined only by what is in the head. David Kaplan and Daniel Dennett have made similar suggestions.[13] Stephen Stich's idea is along the same lines, but more portentous, since he thinks we must give up folk psychology entirely if we want to have a serious science of human behavior.[14] I agree that the concepts of belief, desire, intention, and the like are not suited to a science like the physical sciences, and I agree that one of the reasons is that mental states are partly identified on the basis of their causes and effects. But since the same is true of human actions as we normally identify them, there seems to be no chance of more 'scientific' explanations in this area (assuming that what we mean by a 'scientific' explanation is the kind of explanation we hope for from physics).

But whatever we think about the scientific future of folk psychology, there is no good reason for claiming that beliefs and the other propositional attitudes are not truly subjective states. We have discovered no reason for saying that thinkers don't generally know what they think, or that there isn't always a presumption in favor of their being right when they disagree with others about what is on their minds. And this seems to be as good a test of subjectivity as we have.

There are two important points I have left hanging, and I shall devote a few remarks to them. First, I have not said anything about

---

[12] Not, of course, *identical* physical states, as is often erroneously said. For physical states cannot in the relevant sense be identical unless they inhere in the same object.

[13] Jerry Fodor, 'Methodological Solipsism Considered as a Research Strategy in Cognitive Psychology'; David Kaplan, 'Quantifying In'; Daniel Dennett, 'Beyond Belief'.

[14] Stephen Stich, *From Folk Psychology to Cognitive Science*.

what the objects are to which we refer when we want to specify what someone believes. And, second, I have argued that the discovery that what is believed is partly settled by facts of which the believer may be ignorant does not show he doesn't know what he believes. But this is only a negative point; it does not even hint at *why* there is a presumption—usually correct—that he does know. These two points are closely related.

First, then, what are the objects we name or describe in order to characterize states of mind? Well, what do we *say*? We say things like 'Paul believes the Koh-i-noor diamond is one of the crown jewels'. The words 'believes that the Koh-i-noor diamond is one of the crown jewels' characterize an aspect of Paul's state of mind. The relational word is 'believes', and what follows names the object, not of thought, I have insisted, but the object which in some regular way indicates Paul's state of mind. I have in the past suggested that we take the word 'that' in such sentences as a demonstrative that picks out or refers to the next utterance of the speaker who is doing the attributing. The following gives the idea: Paul believes what I would believe if I were sincerely to assert what I say next.

The Koh-i-noor diamond is one of the crown jewels.

Since I am not trying to make subtle semantic points, you may take as the 'object' either my actual utterance, or the sentence of which it is an utterance (relativized to a time and a speaker). If you wish, you even may take the object to be a proposition. Since utterances, sentences, and propositions are so closely related, the chances are if one choice will serve, the others can be made to serve. But utterances have certain prima facie advantages, since they are non-abstract, and so come with a speaker, a time, and a context attached. So I will assume we have settled on utterances, the very utterances that are produced in attributing attitudes, as the objects that serve to individuate and identify the various states of mind.

Such objects serve very well in their role of characterizing states of mind. There certainly are as many different utterances (or potential utterances) at our disposal as there are states of mind we are able to distinguish in attributing them—more, in fact. Even the special difficulties having to do with demonstrative or indexical expressions are not insoluble if we give up the idea that we are trying to identify objects with which those who have attitudes are in mysterious psychic touch.

Utterances are related to each other in much the same way beliefs are: by relations of entailment and evidential support. Utterances, like beliefs, are true and false. Aside from complications due to indexical elements, we identify a belief by uttering a sentence that has the same truth conditions as the belief it is used to identify. Nor is any of this surprising since we often express our beliefs by uttering sentences with the truth conditions of the belief we are expressing.

At this point you may think I am coming dangerously close to restoring the very theory that made all the trouble in the first place. For why not go on to say that since utterances have determinate meanings, and it is meanings that match up with belief states, the objects we are naming when we utter content sentences in the context of attributing beliefs just are the meanings of those content sentences, that is, propositions. This would fix it so that when a Frenchman attributed the same state of mind to Paul as I did, we would both be naming the same object: this would not be the case on the theory I was just considering, for the Frenchman's relevant sentence was not mine.

I have only marginal objections in the present context to taking this step, for it is not the step that makes the trouble. (It may make some other kind of trouble, meanings and propositions being the tricky things they are.) The trouble we have been concerned with here sprang from the identification of the object used to characterize a state of mind with an object that the mind 'knows' or is 'acquainted with', an 'object of thought'. If we avoid this identification, we can stay out of the difficulties I have been exploring. But if we avoid this identification, neither do we gain anything by the steps from utterances to sentences to meanings or propositions. So as a help in keeping my main point in mind, it is well to stick to utterances. There will then be no danger of supposing that in general the believer is acquainted with the objects used to characterize his states of mind. It should not bother us that the Frenchman and I use different utterances to characterize the same state of Paul's mind: this is like measuring weight in carats or ounces: different sets of numbers do the same work.

This last point directs our attention to a larger issue. When we use numbers to keep track of the relations among weights and lengths and temperatures, we are not apt to respond to the fact that different sets of numbers do as well as others in keeping track of all that is relevant empirically by complaining that weights or lengths or temperatures are not 'real'. We know there is no contradiction between saying that the temperature of the air is 32° Fahrenheit and saying that it is 0° Celsius; there is nothing in this 'relativism' to show that the properties being measured are not real. Curiously, though, this conclusion has repeatedly been drawn. John Searle, for example, finds it incomprehensible that either of two quite different interpretations might correctly be put on the same thought (or utterance) of a person.[15] Yet in the light of the considerations put forward here, this amounts merely to the recognition that more than a single set of one person's utterances might be equally successful in capturing the contents of someone else's thoughts or speech. Just as numbers can capture all the empirically significant relations among weights or temperatures in infinitely many different ways, so one person's utterances can capture all the significant features of another person's thoughts and speech in different ways. This fact does not challenge the reality of the attitudes or meanings thus variously reported. Jerry Fodor is another philosopher who thinks that holism, or the indeterminacy of translation that is associated with it, threatens realism with respect to the propositional attitudes.[16] This is the same mistake. Indeterminacy of translation means that different sets of utterances (or sentences, as Quine has it) do equally well in interpreting a speaker's language (or thoughts); this does not suggest that the states of mind of the speaker or thinker thus captured are somehow vague or unreal. Holism maintains that the contents of speech and thought depend on the relations among meanings and among thoughts. But again there is nothing in this claim to threaten the reality of the states that are related in these ways. The threat to the reality of thoughts and meanings that Searle and Fodor think they detect is in fact a quite different threat, a threat to the assumption that the entities used to identify thoughts and meanings are somehow 'grasped' by the mind, and so, if the entities are different, the thoughts themselves must be different. It is as if the 'difference' between being a yard long and 36 inches long in a yardstick were a difference in the yardstick itself.

I come now to the last question: given that a correct view of the way in which the 'objects of thought' determine the identity of the various states of mind does not threaten first person authority, what accounts for that authority?

[15] John Searle, 'Indeterminacy and the First Person'.
[16] Jerry Fodor, *Psychosemantics*.

One difficulty was created by grammar and false inferences from it: these led to the idea of an inner object known in a privileged way. This obstacle was removed by showing that there was no reason to suppose there are such objects. A second difficulty sprang from the conviction that the truly subjective—that of which the person has privileged knowledge—can owe none of its subjective quality to connections with the outside world. I have argued that though an interpreter must, if he is to get things right, look to relations between the mind he is interpreting and its environment, this does not prejudice the self-knowledge of the knower.

Having removed the obstacles, there is little left to say about how we know what we think. In the interesting, and originally puzzling cases, there *is* no *way* we know—for there is no evidence to be sought, no inner object to be scrutinized, no competing hypothesis to be weighed. The point comes out if we consider this situation: suppose I say, 'I believe the Koh-i-noor diamond is a crown jewel'. Or don't just suppose it, for I do say this. And suppose, as is the case, that I know what the words I have just uttered mean, and that I am making a sincere assertion. Finally, let us suppose that both you and I agree on these points, namely that I did utter those words and that in doing so I was sincerely uttering words I understood. From these suppositions it follows that I know what I believe, but it does not follow that you know what I believe. The reason is simple: you may not know what I mean. Your knowledge of what my words mean has to be based on evidence and inference: you probably assume you have it right, and you probably do. Nevertheless, it is a hypothesis. Of course, I may not know what I mean by those words either. But there is a *presumption* that I do, since it does not make sense to suppose I am *generally* mistaken about what my words mean; the presumption that I am not generally mistaken about what I mean is essential to my having a language—to my being interpretable at all. To appeal to a familiar, though often misunderstood, point: I can do no better, in stating the truth conditions for my utterance of the sentence 'The Koh-i-noor diamond is a crown jewel' than to say it is true if and only if the Koh-i-noor diamond is a crown jewel. If I say this, I utter a tautology, but if you give the truth conditions of my utterance in the same words, you are making an empirical claim, though probably a true one.[17]

---

[17] This paragraph summarizes the conclusion of Essay 1 in this volume.

According to Dummett, Brentano 'refused to admit that a mental act . . . had any inner object distinct from the external one, namely a mental representation . . . by which the external object was presented to the mind'.[18] Dummett points out that this leaves Brentano with the problem of thoughts (or apparent thoughts) about objects that don't exist, a problem, Dummett remarks, Brentano 'did not succeed in resolving'. But the problem is easily solved if we give up the idea that there are inner objects or mental representations in the required sense. There is no need to suppose that if there are no such inner objects, only outer objects remain to help us identify the various states of mind. The simple fact is that we have the resources needed to identify states of mind, even if those states of mind are, as we like to say, directed to nonexistent objects, for we can do this without supposing there are any objects whatever before the mind.

[18] Michael Dummett, *The Interpretation of Frege's Philosophy*, 57. Dummett refers us to Franz Brentano's *Psychology from an Empirical Standpoint*, 79.

5 Indeterminism and Antirealism

Antirealism is a manifestation of the irrepressible urge in Western philosophy to insure that whatever is real can be known: antirealism attempts to achieve this by reading out of existence whatever it decrees lies beyond the scope of human knowledge. So Parmenides should be counted an early and extreme antirealist, since he declared that the globular, homogeneous, changeless One was all that was real on the ground that it was the only possible object of knowledge. Plato must, of course, be counted an antirealist, since he held that the physical world, and all in it, is less than real because it cannot be known. Most reductive isms should count as forms of antirealism: idealism, pragmatism, empiricism, materialism, behaviorism, verificationism. Each tries to trim reality down to fit within its epistemology. Each of these positions offers consolations: ordinary objects like tables and dinnerware are real, we are told, but exist only in the mind; physical objects are nothing but permanent possibilities of sensation; mental states are nothing but patterns of behavior; intentional phenomena are nothing but physical events and objects; etc. We are allowed the terminology of our old ontology as long as we agree to accept only what can be cobbled together out of entities or experiences we can for certain know. But these sops to skepticism should not deceive us; antirealisms remain sour grape philosophies. Their motto is: if you can't grasp the grapes (in some approved sense), they aren't just sour; they were never there in the first place. For reasons I shall mention presently, some antirealisms are better expressed in terms of epistemic limitations on the concept of truth. Thus it may be held that when our epistemic faculties are deficient with respect to determining the truth or falsity of some sentence, we should rule that the sentence has no truth value, or that we should employ some reduced sense of truth. The outcome is the same: the real or the true is cut down to the size of a favored form of knowledge. I do not see realism as the alternative to antirealism. We can reject one or another version of antirealism on the grounds that the arguments for it fail without having to endorse some vague position called realism. One common characterization of realism is this: there is something in or about the world that makes our utterances or assertions or thoughts true when they are true, whether or not we have the power to determine their truth. Most criticisms of this formulation fasten, understandably, on the difficulty in spelling out what 'power' and 'determine' mean in this context. But I don't think we need to get in this deep, since I do not think we understand the prior claim that there is something in or about the world that makes our thoughts or assertions true when they are true. The fact is that no one has ever been able to say in a nontrivial way what sort of 'thing' it is that makes a sentence (or other truth bearer) true. Some sentences or utterances or beliefs are true, and there are a lot of things in the world, but it explains nothing to say that the things 'make' the truth vehicles true. The result is that realists are left holding the concept of truth, but can't explain how reality accounts for it. The failure of correspondence theories to give substance to the concept of truth at the same time demonstrates the vacuity of characterizations of realism in terms of correspondence.

Here I discuss those versions of antirealism that throw doubt on the reality of mental states and events in the light of the indeterminacy of translation or interpretation. I am equally concerned with those who argue that *if* we accept the indeterminacy of interpretation, then we must be in doubt about the status of propositional attitudes— or at least the status of attributions of propositional attitudes. Since I accept the thesis of the indeterminacy of interpretation, I would be aggrieved to find that it entails some sort of antirealism. But I do not think it does, as I shall try to explain. I think neither that indeterminism shows that propositional attitudes are less than fully real (whatever that may mean) nor that we must modify the concept of truth when we come to talk of propositional attitudes. In other words, many of our beliefs and statements about what people believe, intend, desire, and hope for are true, and they are true because people have those attitudes.

Three considerations seem to stand in the way of accepting this thesis. The first is a form of scientism. The propositional attitudes do not seem suited to incorporation into a unified scientific view of the world. Thus Quine has said that 'the essentially dramatic idiom of propositional attitudes' has no place in serious science,[1] or that our mentalistic vocabulary is 'stubbornly at variance with scientific patterns'. I think Quine is right in holding that the mentalistic vocabulary cannot be reduced to or incorporated into the vocabulary of physics, or of any of the other 'hard' sciences. One reason for this irreducibility springs from the fact that any correct account of an agent's beliefs and other attitudes must recognize the normative element inherent in cognitive contents. One attitude has logical relations with others; these relations, though distorted and deranged by the limits of our powers, nevertheless serve to locate, and thus identify, the contents of our thoughts. When we treat the world as mindless, as in the natural sciences, nothing corresponds to this dimension of the mental. A less often noticed property that sets our talk of mental states apart from the vocabulary of the advanced sciences is its dependence on causal concepts. Ordinary physical talk, like psychological talk, is full of causal concepts: the notion of a catalyst is as causal as the notion of an intentional action. The difference lies in the promise, intrinsic to physics, but irrelevant to psychology, that the causal concept can, with time and research, be supplanted by an account of the mechanism which will explain what the clumsy causal notion merely finessed. The laws of physics may, if we please, be called causal. The point is that they do not employ causal concepts. The concentration of psychology on the causal role of reasons rules out any hope that the basic mental concepts can be fitted into a closed system of laws. There is one more (much debated) consideration which militates against the nomological or definitional reduction of mental concepts to those of physics, namely, the fact that propositional attitudes and related events and states are in part identified in terms of their causal and other relations to events extraneous in time and place to the agent they characterize. Thus it is held, correctly in my opinion, that the history of an individual's learning and use of words and concepts is in central cases necessarily a factor in determining what the words mean, and the contents of the concepts. I also think interpersonal communication plays a necessary role in the possibility and nature of thought. If externalisms of these sorts are indeed dominant and unavoidable

---

[1] *Word and Object*, 219.

features of the mental, the impossibility of incorporating psychology into a unified scientific theory of the world is clear.

These remarks are no more than reminders of why many philosophers, including me, are convinced that psychology, as long as it is taken to include the concepts of intentional action, belief, perception, and the affective attitudes, cannot be made part of physics or any other 'natural' science. The question here is whether the definitional and nomological irreducibility of the propositional attitudes is a reason to doubt the objective status of the propositional attitudes.

Quine has said that he agrees with my token–token version of monism, which holds that each object or event identified in mental terms is identical with an object or event identifiable in physical terms, though the *classes* staked out by the mental vocabulary cannot be equated by definition or strict laws with classes definable in the physical vocabulary. This position, which I call anomalous monism, comes close to reconciling most, though not all, of Quine's declarations about propositional attitudes. Anomalous monism makes sense of the claim that attitudes are dispositions to behave in certain ways, which are in turn physiological states, which finally are physical states, as well as the claim that intentional descriptions are not reducible to behavioral or physical descriptions, and so are not suited to incorporation into any strict system of laws. The mental vocabulary is practical and indispensable, but it is not made for the most precise science. Anomalous monism does not suggest that mental events and states are merely projected by the attributer onto an agent; on the contrary, it holds that mental events are as real as physical events, being identical with them, and attributions of states are as objective. Quine's description of attitude attributions as dramatic portrayals does not imply that there is nothing to portray.

The fact that the mental vocabulary is not fit for inclusion in sciences like physics or physiology cannot in itself be taken as impugning the reality of the states, events, and objects it is used to describe. A perfected physics must comprehend every object and event, but this is an ontological and nomological requirement that defines the aim of physics: physics does not speak to the interests that demand other ways of characterizing things.

I have not yet touched directly on the issue of the indeterminacy of translation or interpretation. If the thesis of indeterminacy holds, doesn't this imply that propositional attitudes are less than real? Quine may be thought to hint as much when he says 'Brentano's thesis of the irreducibility of intentional idioms is of a piece with the thesis of indeterminacy of translation' since '[to] accept intentional usage at face value is . . . to postulate translation relations as somehow objectively valid though indeterminate in principle relative to the totality of speech dispositions'.[2] Doesn't this say that accepting the mental idiom means postulating something for which there is no empirical evidence—something that we therefore have no reason to believe exists?

In any case, whether or not Quine's views entail that there is something unreal about the propositional attitudes, it is an idea common to a number of philosophers that indeterminism does undermine the reality of mental states. Fodor and others have thought this constitutes a reductio of indeterminism. Daniel Dennett, on the other hand, endorses indeterminism, but agrees that it subtracts from the reality of mental states. I argue against the inference. I see no way around indeterminism, but think it leaves the reality of the mental untouched.

First, let me defend the passages from Quine which I just quoted, and which seem to aver that 'intentional usage' has no empirical content. There is a confusion here that may in part be Quine's fault, but it is easy to resolve. If by 'intentional usage' Quine means talk of meanings and propositions as hypostatized by philosophers, it is true that he rejects these as without empirical or explanatory content. But it does not follow that ordinary attributions of attitudes, including interpretations of speech, are empty. Indeed, how could they be if mental talk is, as Quine allows, something we cannot do without?

There are, I think, two things that above all tempt us to suppose that there cannot be any indeterminacy about what we mean by our words or what we think. One is first person authority, the fact that there is a presumption that we know what we think in a way no one else can. The other is engendered by the semantics of the sentences that are used to attribute attitudes. Let me take the second point first, and let me stick to belief sentences for simplicity. It is obvious that there is a potential infinity in the number of beliefs that might be assigned to someone, and it is clear that there is a potential infinity of sentences available, for we can create a well-formed sentence by putting any of an infinity of sentences after the words 'Agnes believes that . . .'. But the only viable semantic devices we have

---

[2] Ibid. 221.

available to accommodate this situation involve taking 'believes' (or 'believes that') as a relational verb, and treating what follows as a singular term or description. The singular terms can't all be unstructured proper names; there aren't enough such. So if what follows 'believes' or 'believes that' is a singular term, a demonstrative device must be at work; otherwise we must have descriptions. But in either case, there must be an infinite store of *entities* to be picked out. Once we have picked the appropriate entity, though, we have, as attitude attributers, assigned a content to the belief.

It is natural, perhaps, to suppose that the entity we refer to in order to specify the content of a belief is the *object* of the belief, an entity which the believer entertains or grasps, the *thing* the believer believes. Given the relational semantics of sentences about beliefs (and, of course, the other attitudes), and the natural assumption that the entity that identifies the belief is the object grasped by the believer, we are virtually forced to conclude that the entity designated must be unique. For if more than one entity would do equally well in specifying the same state of belief, which entity should we say the believer grasps, or how can we say that the believer knows what he believes?

This conundrum can be solved by giving up the idea of treating the grammatical objects in belief sentences as terms that name psychologically real objects, objects known to or entertained by or grasped by the believer. The only *object* required for the existence of a belief is a believer. Having a belief is not like having a favorite cat, it is being in a state; and being in a state does not require that there be an entity called a state that one is in. All that is necessary for the truth of an attitude attribution is that the predicate employed be true of the person with the attitude.

Dummett deserves credit for characterizing antirealism in terms of truth rather than of reference, in terms of sentences rather than of names or descriptions. For the real issue about sentences that attribute mental states is not ontological; beliefs are not entities, nor do the 'objects of belief' have to be objects. The real issue is whether or not attributions of attitudes are objectively true or false.[3]

The attribution of attitudes is analogous in many ways to the

---

[3] There is, to be sure, the question whether meanings and propositions exist, but this I see as a matter for decision. If they exist, they are abstract entities, and need no more than defining. Once defined, it remains to be shown whether they do useful explanatory or descriptive work.

measurement of various magnitudes. We can assign numbers to keep track of the sizes, weights, and speeds of objects provided the objects exhibit a pattern of the appropriate kind. We do not suppose there are empirical entities called weights or sizes or speeds that objects have. As Carnap pointed out long ago, we should not think of the sentence 'This box weighs 8 pounds' as identifying two entities called 'the weight of this box' and '8 pounds', but rather as equating the weight of the box in pounds with the number 8. Thus the ontology required consists of the objects that have weights, and the numbers. The numbers are not part of the weighty objects; they belong not to the empirical world but to us who need them in order to keep track of certain relations among objects. In the same way, the entities to which we relate thinkers when we attribute beliefs and other propositional attitudes to them are not in the thinkers—not in their minds, or before their minds. Having a belief is just exemplifying a property, having a certain predicate true of one; but in order to have enough predicates for all the beliefs we may wish to distinguish, we must construct the predicates by using a relational verb and filling in one of the places with a reference to an object drawn from some potentially infinite store. One such predicate is 'x believes that snow is white'.

One virtue of this analogy is that it makes clear why different assignments of objects can capture all the relevant information about a situation without compromising the truth or 'reality' of the situation. No one thinks the fact that we can register weight in either pounds or kilograms shows that there is something unreal about the weight of an object: different sets of numbers can be used to keep track of exactly the same facts. Suppose the fact is that A weighs the same as B; then the number assigned to measure the weights of A and B is the same number, whether we measure weight in pounds or kilos. Suppose the fact is that C weighs twice what D does; then the number assigned to measure the weight of C must be twice the number assigned to measure the weight of D, whether the weights are given in pounds or kilos. All that is necessary is that the entities we use to keep track of how much things weigh have a structure in which certain features of the objects weighed can be represented, and numbers can do this in endless ways.

Another virtue of the analogy is that it makes clear why Quine is justified when he insists, against Chomsky and others, that the indeterminacy of translation is distinct from the underdetermination of theories by all possible evidence. There is a question, to be sure, whether underdetermination in Quine's sense can occur, for it requires that there be empirically equivalent, but incompatible, theories.[4] Indeterminacy is not like this: the empirically equivalent theories it accepts as equally good for understanding an agent are not incompatible, any more than the measurement of weight in pounds or kilos involves incompatible theories of weight.

What objects can we use to keep track of the attitudes? Clearly they must constitute approximately as complexly figured a field as the individual attitudes themselves. The most conspicuous features of the individual attitudes are their basically rational structures (if someone believes that everything is white, that person has a belief that entails that snow is white), and their relations to the world (the belief that snow is white is true if and only if snow is white).[5]

Entities that have these required properties are our *sentences*, and it is not clear that any other set of entities will do as well (except utterances[6]). In any case, there is a sense in which our standard attributions of attitude do use the sentences of the attributer to specify the contents of the attributed attitude. By this I mean no more than that we must use a sentence of our own after such words as 'Joan believes that . . .' to identify Joan's belief. Now we must ask which properties of the sentence are relevant to the identification of the belief, just as we ask which properties of numbers are essential to their role in recording weights. It is obvious that the property of having a truth value is not enough. The syntax would be more than enough if it were not for the fact that the same sentence can be used to mean quite different things, depending on the interpretation (the same sentence may belong to different languages or idiolects, or it may be ambiguous). Because of this difficulty, I have suggested that we take the actual *utterance* (or inscription) provided by the attributer as the object to which he is referring to give the content of an attitude. So I proposed a paratactic account of attitude-attributing sentences, in which the 'that' of 'Joan believes that . . .' is to be

[4] Quine has changed his mind on the issue more than once. See W. V. Quine, *Pursuit of Truth*, 97 ff.

[5] It should not be thought that by speaking of the relations between the attitudes and the world I am embracing a correspondence theory. A theory of truth of the sort I have in mind does depend on setting up a relation between certain words and objects (Tarski's relation of 'satisfaction'), but it makes no use of objects to which sentences might correspond.

[6] See Essay 4.

taken as a demonstrative referring to the utterance that follows. The utterance has a unique syntax, and can be taken to resolve the question of the appropriate language and idiolect, to have eliminated ambiguities, and to have provided the parameters needed to fix indexical references. As a rough equivalent of the paratactic account, we could think of the content sentence as enclosed in quotation marks, with the language and other features of the speaker and context understood or made explicit. This second idea does better at capturing the intuition that attitude-attributing expressions are single sentences, but it is more complicated.

It should not surprise us that what we can say and understand about the propositional attitudes of others should be what we can capture by matching up our own sentences (or utterances; I shall not bother to distinguish) to those attitudes. This does not mean, of course, that someone else may not think things I cannot; but then that is bound to be something the content of which I cannot express either. I do not want, either, to rule out altogether propositional thoughts I have but cannot express. It is enough for my argument that when we can express a thought, our own or that of another, we must fall back on the basic device of representing it in the fabric of our sentences. Our sentences provide the only measure of the mental.

What follows for indeterminacy? Everyone is apt to agree that sometimes quite distinct sentences of the same reporter may be used to attribute exactly the same thought, so some degree of indeterminacy comes automatically with the redundancy of language. But the indeterminacies of which Quine speaks, and most of which I accept, are another matter, for they suggest that sentences that no one would take to be even roughly synonymous may nevertheless be used to specify the same thought.

Let me say briefly where Quine and I differ and agree on these matters. Both of us take as the basic evidence for interpretation a person's attitudes towards various utterances and the circumstances that cause these attitudes. Quine takes certain patterns of assent and dissent to yield the interpretation of the truth-functional sentential functions, and so do I; but I go on, as Quine does not, to use the same method to locate the devices for quantification and cross-reference. Thus I do not, like Quine, see the internal structure of the simplest sentences as indeterminate. We both assume that the observed range of phenomena which prompt assent and dissent to certain sentences allow us to connect those sentences to events and objects in the world. As for sentences less directly tied to the readily observable, I think we can often do better than Quine believes, because I hold that we can use our ability to detect degrees of evidential support between sentences as a key to correct interpretation. There remain two important kinds of indeterminacy on which we agree: indeterminacy due to what Quine calls the inscrutability of reference, and indeterminacy that results from the blurring of the distinction between the analytic and the synthetic.

The thesis of the inscrutability of reference says there is no way to tell which way of connecting words with things is the right way; if one way works, there will be countless others that do as well. From a technical point of view, this means that for the standard satisfaction relation (satisfaction is a sophisticated form of reference) we can substitute endless other relations without altering the truth conditions of any sentence or the logical relations among sentences. Since all the evidence for interpreting language must come at the sentential level (for only sentences have a use in communication), the result is that there can be no evidence that one of the satisfaction (or reference) relations is the right one.

Here is an example. Suppose satisfaction relation s maps the word 'Rome' onto Rome, and the predicate 'is a city in Italy' onto cities in Italy. Then the truth definition will show that the sentence 'Rome is a city in Italy' is true if and only if Rome is a city in Italy. Now consider another satisfaction relation s' which maps the word 'Rome' onto an area 100 miles to the south of Rome, and the predicate 'is a city in Italy' onto areas 100 miles south of cities in Italy. The truth definition will now say that the sentence 'Rome is a city in Italy' is true if and only if the area 100 miles south of Rome is an area 100 miles south of a city in Italy. The truth conditions are clearly equivalent. The thesis of the inscrutability of reference contends that there can be no evidence that s is any better than s' for interpreting the sentence 'Rome is a city in Italy'. There is no telling what a sentence is 'about', or what someone is thinking about.

How can this be? Surely Rome and an area 100 miles to its south are not the same entity. True enough. However, any differences we conventionally think of as differences in the reference of names or the extensions of predicates will be preserved by any correct satisfaction relation. The fact that there is no empirical difference between the interpretations yielded by s and by s' doesn't entail that the person being interpreted can't tell the difference between Rome and an area 100 miles to the south; but it does entail that there is no saying which one his word 'Rome' refers to. Correct interpretation keeps track of a complex pattern, and locates particular sentences and attitudes within it. But the counters we use to represent this pattern, namely our sentences, can represent it in more than one way.

If the two interpretations of someone's utterance of 'Rome is a city in Italy' are equally correct, why is it that we feel that one is the right one? The complete answer is, I think, pretty complicated, but the simple answer is that we accept the standard, and in this case easiest, method of word-for-word translation. Of course, when the homophonic translation manual is one of the available manuals, we will use it; and in interpreting a language for which no homophonic manual is available, we will use the conventional, and for the most part shortest, available method. This does not mean that other interpretations are wrong: *s'* provides as correct an interpretation of 'Rome is a city in Italy' as *s*.

To someone who objects, 'But "Rome" doesn't *mean* "an area 100 miles south of Rome" ', the right answer is: individual words don't have meanings. They have a *role* in determining the truth conditions of sentences, and this role is captured by *s'* as surely as it is by *s*.

Still, this answer leaves something out, which is the necessity, in assigning contents to an agent's speech or attitudes, of sticking to some one method of interpretation. It will falsify 'Rome is a city in Italy' to interpret it as true if and only if Rome is in an area 100 miles south of a city in Italy; and it will destroy the entailment relations among sentences to use one method of interpretation for one sentence and another method for another sentence. Just as we must indicate whether the numbers we are using to measure temperature place the temperature on the Fahrenheit or the centigrade scale, so we must indicate which method of interpretation we are using (*s* or *s'*, for example). One of the conveniences of sticking to the same method is that we can leave the indication of the method tacit. (Somewhat similarly, if I say 'It must be 70 in this room', you will naturally understand me to be using the Fahrenheit scale.)

There is a further objection which many people feel is fatal to the thesis of indeterminacy. The claim is that indeterminacy undermines first person authority. Such people want to say, 'Maybe Quine's empirical criteria can't rule out the use of alternative methods of interpretation for others, but *I* know that I mean Rome by my word "Rome" and not the area 100 miles south of Rome'. This remark is correct, but it doesn't conflict with indeterminism. The reason it is correct is that the speaker does not identify Rome and an area 100 miles to the south of Rome. When a person is making such self-attributions, we know that words in the metalanguage play the same roles as those words do in the object language, for object language and metalanguage are one and the same. First person interpretations are necessarily tied to the homophonic translation manual (which is to say, translation, or interpretation, has no place here).

It should not be concluded from the fact that a person is restricted to a unique way of interpreting himself (if this can be called interpretation: it would be better to say that aside from pathological cases, our way of interpreting others has no application to ourselves) that therefore his words have unique reference. All that the agent has discovered in our example is that his phrases 'Rome' and 'the area 100 miles south of Rome' cannot be substituted for one another in his language, and this does not fix the reference of either expression. By the same token, the fact that the reference of his words is not fixed doesn't show that he doesn't know what he means or thinks. The different ways of interpreting his speech, or of representing his thoughts, mark no difference in the contents of his attitudes, so there is nothing he fails to know if he doesn't know which way of representing his thoughts is the right way; since there is no one right way; there is nothing more for him to know.

Not all cases of indeterminacy depend on the possibility of systematically altering the satisfaction relation in ways that do not affect the truth conditions of sentences; there can be indeterminacies that affect truth values. These indeterminacies arise if one accepts Quine's claim (as I do) that there is no principled way to make a clear distinction between the analytic and the synthetic. Here it is easy to give examples. I find that I very often disagree with other people over whether to call the color of some object green or blue. The disagreement is consistent: there is a fairly definite range of cases where I say green and they say blue. We can account for this difference in two ways: it may be that I (or most other people) are wrong about the color of certain objects, or it may be that I don't use the words 'blue' and 'green' in quite the way others do. There may be no way to decide between these two accounts; by making compensatory adjustments elsewhere in one's interpretation of my sentences and beliefs one can accommodate either story. But on one account certain of my pronouncements about colors are false, while on the other they are true. And on both accounts, I know what I think: I think the things I call green are green and the things I call blue are blue; neither account of what I mean and think threatens this first person knowledge.

Where the criticisms I have been discussing suggest that if one accepts indeterminism one is treating meanings and mental states as less than totally real, Daniel Dennett has refreshingly complained that on my view intentional states are *too* real.[7] Dennett sees clearly why my view, which compares rival theories of interpretation to different ways of representing length or temperature in the numbers, can't in itself call into question the reality of what is represented. But he thinks two different systems of belief attribution to an individual may differ substantially, even to the point of yielding different predictions of behavior, and yet nothing would establish that one system and not the other described the person's real beliefs.

Here I think the issue of prediction is something of a red herring. No system of attitude attribution, no matter how complete, yields any prediction of actions without a theory, and it is certainly possible to differ on predictive theories in psychology. It is clear that no plausible predictions will be forthcoming without a quantitative description that specifies degrees of belief (subjective probabilities) and the relative strength of desires. But even supposing we could give a complete description of all the attitudes and their strengths for a given individual at a time, there is no reason to suppose that there exist strict laws to predict what the individual will do next—and good reasons to suppose there are no such laws. What sort of evidence can Dennett appeal to, then, to show that equally justified systems for attributing attitudes are incompatible? The fact that different systems result in different predictions proves nothing, since the same system can be used to support different predictions.

Dennett's idea is that what is real is behavior, and intentional states are patterns in this behavior. The patterns aren't defined in terms of the behavior—they are perceived by an observer when the observer takes the 'intensional stance'. The value of the patterns is that they reduce a vast, by us indescribably complex, physical situation to something we can grasp, and something on the basis of which we can make rough predictions. The patterns are in some (reduced) sense real, though abstract; and different people may

----

[7] Daniel Dennett, 'Real Patterns'.

perceive different patterns in the same behavioral field. Some of these patterns may do better at predicting or understanding some phenomena; other patterns do better at predicting or understanding other phenomena. All these patterns are 'real', but when they are different, there is no saying which one represents the real attitudes of the targeted agent.

It is not easy to see how to judge this suggestion, and harder to grasp how it relates to the issue of realism. Surely not *every* pattern one perceives in behavior is a pattern of propositional attitudes. But is any? Patterns, Dennett tells us, are abstractions, like centers of gravity. But then can they be beliefs and desires? Beliefs and desires, we like to think, are states of a physical body which can have causal consequences; abstractions, I assume, have no causal relations. Forces act not on centers of gravity, but on the things that have centers of gravity; but forces certainly alter my beliefs and intentions. Do we perceive patterns? It seems to me not: what we perceive is something that *has* a certain pattern, and with luck (and the right stance) we may perceive *that* it has that pattern. So the question isn't whether patterns are real. Being no nominalist, I think patterns, like shapes and numbers, are as real as can be. But I do not see how the propositional attitudes of a person can *be* patterns. If we ask what exhibits the pattern, we can say it is the person, or we can say it is the observable behavior of the person. But in either case no issue concerning the ontological status of attitudes is at stake. If people or their behavior really do exhibit the patterns Dennett says they do, and for someone to have a propositional attitude is for that person to exhibit that pattern, then there is nothing ontologically or epistemically second-grade about the attitudes.

It seems to me Dennett has confused two issues. One is whether the attitudes are entities, and here I think the answer is no, unless you suppose that states are entities. Otherwise one should simply talk of people having attitudes, which means that certain predicates are true of them. The second issue is whether there is a correct answer to the question whether or not someone has a certain attitude. This I take to be, not a question about vagueness or borderline cases, but a question whether there are objective grounds for choosing among conflicting hypotheses. Dennett has urged that the answer to the second question is that there are no such grounds; but I do not think he has given any reason to accept this answer.

Are there objective grounds for choosing among conflicting

hypotheses? Especially in this case we have to ask what makes grounds 'objective'. The ultimate source (not ground) of objectivity is, in my opinion, intersubjectivity. If we were not in communication with others, there would be nothing on which to base the *idea* of being wrong, or, therefore, of being right, either in what we say or in what we think. The possibility of thought as well as of communication depends, in my view, on the fact that two or more creatures are responding, more or less simultaneously, to input from a shared world, and from each other. We are apt to say that someone responds in 'the same way' to, say, wolves. But of course, 'same' here means 'similar'. Our grounds for claiming that a person finds one wolf similar to another is the fact that the person responds in similar ways to wolves. This prompts the next question: what makes the reactions similar? The only answer is, someone else finds both wolves and the reactions of the first person similar. This of course only puts the basic question off once more. Nevertheless, it is this triangular nexus of causal relations involving the reactions of two (or more) creatures to each other and to shared stimuli in the world that supplies the conditions necessary for the concept of truth to have application. Without a second person there is, as Wittgenstein powerfully suggests, no basis for a judgement that a reaction is wrong or, therefore, right.[8]

This brings me to my last point. The analogy I proposed between measurement in the physical sciences and the assignment of contents to the words and thoughts of others is imperfect in an essential respect. In the case of ordinary measurement, we use the numbers to keep track of the facts that interest us. In the case of the propositional attitudes we use our sentences or utterances. But there is this difference: we can mutually specify the properties of the numbers. The numbers, like the objects we apply them to, lie, as it were, halfway between ourselves and others. This is what it means to say that they are objective or that they are objects. It cannot be this way with our sentences. You and I cannot come to agree on the interpretation of our sentences as a preliminary to using them to interpret others, for the process of coming to such an agreement involves interpretation of the very sort we thought to prepare for. It makes no sense to ask for a common standard of interpretation, for mutual interpretation provides the only standard we have.

---

[8] For more on the subject of this and the concluding paragraphs, see Essay 14.

We should not despair because we cannot provide a standard by which to judge the standard, a test for whether the standard meter bar is actually a meter long. Our conclusion should rather be: if our judgements of the propositional attitudes of others are not objective, no judgements are, and the concept of objectivity has no application.

6 *The Irreducibility of the Concept of the Self*

In his gentle, probing way Dieter Henrich often asked me whether I thought the idea of the self was an irreducible or primitive concept. I replied that I did think so, but so far as I remember, I never said why. I remain in doubt what an adequate response calls for, but here I shall try to list some of the considerations that may be relevant to a fuller answer.

A concept is irreducible only relative to specified resources. When it comes to the large, grand concepts that concern philosophers, like the good, truth, belief, knowledge, physical object, cause, and event, I think of a concept as irreducible if it cannot be defined in terms that are as general as the concept to be reduced, at least as clear, and that do not lead in a circle. With respect to the concepts I have listed, I think the search for such a definition or analysis is doomed. The question is, is the concept of the self another of the essential, and therefore irreplaceable, conceptual building blocks of our thought and languages?

I had better confess at once that I see no way to address this question directly, since the phrase 'the self' doesn't play any clear role in ordinary speech. Philosophers introduce it when they want to discuss such topics as self-consciousness, or the question what unites the various experiences of a person. So my approach will of necessity be oblique.

Thomas Nagel asks us (in 'The Objective Self') to imagine a description of the universe that tells when and where everything happens relative to some objectively given space-time framework; the description names each person with his or her mental states along with the positions and properties of all other objects. The description includes a complete history of Nagel himself, all from a third person point of view. The one thing it doesn't contain, Nagel says, is the information that *he* is a particular one of the people described. Of course, since he may not know his name is Nagel, the only way he can with certainty locate himself in that world is by using the word 'I'. Thus the personal pronoun allows him to express knowledge that cannot be expressed in any other way. Clearly, there is something irreducible, irreplaceable, embodied in the use of the first person pronouns—all the first person pronouns. In fact, all sentences containing indexicals depend, for their interpretation and their truth value, on who utters them. But if I utter them, I know without observation that it is I who uttered them. In this way, I relate myself to places, objects, times, and other people, by my use of 'there' ('here', 'behind me'), 'that' ('this'), 'now' ('tomorrow', all tensed verbs), 'you'. There is no substitute for this way of placing myself in the public world.

A less obvious, but equally important, function of indexicals is to provide an early and essential step into the domain of thought and language. For what we learn first is to associate what in the end turn out to be one-word sentences ('Mama', 'No', 'Dog', 'Blue') with situations, events, objects, and their features. Soon the child learns the magical power of making sounds adults find appropriate and hence reward. These are only preliminaries to fully fledged talk and thought, for in the beginning the child lacks awareness of the distinction between what is believed and what is the case, what is asked or demanded and what is answered or done. But though only preliminaries, these primitive relations between two people in the presence of stimuli from a shared world contain the kernel of ostensive learning, and it is only in the context of such interactions that we come to grasp the propositional contents of beliefs, desires, intentions, and speech.

I am not, of course, trying to establish the truth of these claims here; I have argued for them elsewhere. But if I am right, this view of the origin and nature of rational thought point to another sense in which the outlook on the world of each person differs irreducibly from that of any other person. The full force and meaning of this statement will emerge presently. But this much should be clear: the basic triangle of two people and a common world is one of which we must be aware if we have any thoughts at all. If I can think, I know that there are others with minds like my own, and that we inhabit a public time and space filled with objects and events many of which are (through the ostensions which made such thoughts available to us) known to others. In particular I, like every other rational creature, have three kinds of knowledge: knowledge of the objective world (without numerous successful ostensions, I would have no thoughts); knowledge of the minds of others; and knowledge of the contents of my own mind. None of these three sorts of knowledge is reducible to either of the other two, or to any other two in combination. It does indeed *follow* from the fact that I have any one of these sorts of knowledge that I have the other two since the basic triangle is a condition of thought, but none is conceptually or temporally prior to the others.

If my knowledge were exclusively of the contents of minds, perhaps of my own and that of others, there is no way I could construct my knowledge of the world we live in, for that requires the causal connections with the world provided by perception. Of course, if I had knowledge of the contents either of my own mind or of another mind, I would have knowledge of the public world, and would know that I did. But this does not mean I could *construct* such knowledge from my knowledge of the contents of minds.

My knowledge of another mind is not reducible to my knowledge of the contents of my own mind and of the natural world, though my knowledge of the minds of others is dependent on my perceptual knowledge of the movements of their bodies. But to suppose that mental states can be *defined* in terms drawn exclusively from the natural sciences (as some behaviorists once held) is to suppose that the intentional is reducible to the extensional, and such reduction is surely not in the cards.

That knowledge of the contents of my own mind is special, and basic to all my knowledge, is, of course, part of the Cartesian and empiricist dreams. And this much is correct: such knowledge is basic in the sense that without it I would know nothing (though self-knowledge is not sufficient for the rest), and special in that it is irreducibly different from other sorts of knowledge.

What unites the three varieties of knowledge, and makes their interdependence the grounding of all thought, is best illustrated by describing the process of ostension. Consider the case of two people both of whom have developed languages. One asks, pointing, 'What's that?' 'A cormorant', the other answers. More questions and pointings may be needed before the learner gets it right, but astonishingly often shared habits of generalization do the work at one try.

Here we have the three mature forms of knowledge at work. The learner and teacher each know what is in the other's mind, and a vital element in this understanding depends on the shared perceptual stimulus. More important, however, is the way this triangular set of relations reveals the basis of the objectivity of thought, its ability to latch on to something in the public world. In our imagined scenario, both participants already have the concept of objective content and of truth; they know what a physical object is, and what it is for a belief to be true or false. Nevertheless, at the start of the ostension, the learner has nothing but a wordless, conceptless stimulus to connect with a concept and a word. The learner has, we are supposing, plenty of concepts available; but which is the right one? Only the teacher can determine this. It takes two to triangulate the location of the distal stimulus, two to provide an objective test of correctness and failure. If this is so, it must be so from the start, before the learner has the idea of objectivity and is learning, by way of ostensions which are, to begin with, no more than ways of establishing associations, what it is to *judge* that a response is right or wrong. The possibility of thought comes with company. Thus the gearing of verbal (and other) responses to situations, events, and objects through the prompting and perception of others plays a key role both in the acquisition of a first language, or the learning of a second language in the absence of an interpreter or bilingual dictionary.

Learning a first and learning a second language are, of course, very different enterprises. The former is a matter of entering the domain of thought for the first time, the latter is a matter of someone already at home in the realm of thought entering into the thought of someone else. Both, however, depend on similar mechanisms and similar cues. Furthermore, the contrast is weakened by the realization that in the case of the child initiate, the two forms of learning mesh, for in absorbing the idea of an objective world, the child is simultaneously learning to communicate with others, which requires insight into the thoughts and intentions of those others.

Making sense of the verbal and nonverbal behavior of others is not an enterprise limited to the special cases of learning first or further languages or adding new words to one's own. Or we might say, treating the notion of a language more strictly than it is treated in ordinary talk, that all these are matters of learning a new language, since any addition to or alteration in our verbal resources makes ours a different, a new, language. If we look at the fine detail, no two idiolects are identical, nor is any person's language apt to remain unaltered for long. We are as interpreters constantly working out (often automatically) what others mean by what they say. We are also, both because of the interdependence of thought and speech and for obvious further reasons, constantly deciding what others think, intend, and want. Much of the time we assume we have things right enough for the purposes at hand, and most of the time what small adjustments are needed come so easily that we are aware of no mental effort. It is only now and then that we realize we are coping with old words used in ways new to us, or that some piece of grammar cannot be treated as familiar. In such cases we become conscious that our interpretive skills are being tested. It is here that the unique contribution of the first person point of view—the 'self'—becomes most apparent.

The conceptually developed thinker has two basic interpretive resources at his or her disposal in coming to understand the utterances and actions of others: the assumption of sufficient rationality to make these actions intelligible, and knowledge of how perception yields the contents of belief. In the case of speech, this is easy to illustrate, and the lesson carries over to the propositional attitudes. Sentences, or rather the attitudes they express, owe their content, that is their meaning, to two things: their relations to other sentences or attitudes, and their relations, direct or indirect, to the world through perception. It is therefore impossible for an interpreter wholly to disregard the logical relations among a speaker's sentences or attitudes. This is not a matter of an effort on the part of agents to be consistent; it is a matter of their speech and behavior having the meaning they do because of how they hang together. Unless there is sufficient coherence, it is impossible to assign propositional contents to their speech, beliefs, desires, or intentions. The interpreter's assumption of a degree of rationality on the part of those she wishes to understand is thus no more than a condition of understanding them at all.

The fundamental role of ostension in learning and interpreting speech guarantees that an interpreter cannot go wrong in generally supposing that a speaker's utterances reliably touched off by evident features of the observable world are true and about those features. Mistakes on the part of speaker or interpreter are to be expected, but these cannot be the rule, since errors take their content from a background of veridical thought and honest assertion. The crucial difference between the predominant, mostly banal, run-of-the-mill but on-target beliefs and assumptions and the occasional deviation is this: errors, confusions, irrationalities have particular explanations; getting things right, aside from hard cases, is to be expected.

I have said little about knowledge of the contents of our own minds. Like all knowledge, it cannot exist in isolation from its social beginnings; the concept of oneself as an independent entity depends on the realization of the existence of others, a realization that comes into its own with communication. But the vocabulary of the attitudes applies equally to oneself and to others, and the contents of the attitudes so attributed is likewise expressed in concepts that are in the public domain. My thought that Shakespeare was a woman is mine, but anyone can think as I do. What, then, is so special about my knowledge of my own mind?

I not only know what I think. I also know an infinity of things that I can express and which I know someone else might believe or doubt or wonder about; the list is in a sense as large as the list of things expressible in my language, in concepts I command. These are the propositional contents to which I advert when I attribute attitudes to myself or to others. This rich reservoir of conceptual resources is what I must use in interpreting the utterances or actions of those around me. When I speak of 'using' these resources, I do not mean it generally takes reflection or effort. It is done without notice, automatically. Even your slips of tongue, omissions, fragmented grammar, accidental substitutions of one name for another, I silently, and often unconsciously, correct. Most of the time, your words strike my ear and I understand them without any conscious intermediate mental process. But my understanding proves that a process, however inarticulate or far from introspective investigation, has taken place, a process that deserves to be called, if not interpretation, then something much like it. It is interpretation in which conscious reasoning and explicit recourse to evidence and induction have been reduced to zero.

Interpretation in this etiolated sense can be described in terms, not of the observed process, but of the transition from input to outcome, for this transition is after all the same as the transition accomplished by conscious interpretation. Here the elements are as before: the search for coherence based on the assumption of rationality, and the perception of external cues which are within the ken of the speaker or actor. My interest here is not in the details of the process, but in a fact so obvious it may escape notice: that the standards of rationality and reality on which I depend in understanding others are my own, and there can be no appeal beyond them. This is not to deny that what standards I have would not exist if it were not for a history of communication and experience. Nor is it to suppose I cannot reflect on my own reasoning and consult with others for greater clarity, wisdom, and information. But insofar as I seek information directly by experiment and observation, I again can do no better or more than employ my own resources. And if I wonder whether the norms of rationality I employ in trying to comprehend others are correct, I can, of course, ask Sebastian whether I am as objective or reasonable as I should be in my account of Basil's thoughts and actions. But my understanding of Sebastian's reply will be one more exercise of my own standards and methods. There is another obvious indication of the irreducible singularity of my direct acquaintance with the contents of my own mind, and this is that such knowledge is unique in that it is, aside from unusual cases, unsupported by observation, evidence, or reasons. This is due, at least in part, to the fact that here interpretation has no application. Drawing on my store of potential thoughts will yield nothing but tautologies when applied to those same thoughts. Self-consciousness of this kind can direct attention inward and promote self-criticism, but it can lead from insight to action only indirectly.

I do not think that, because the ultimate court of appeal is personal, therefore my judgements are arbitrary or subjective, for they were formed in a social nexus that assures the objectivity if not the correctness of my beliefs. Intersubjectivity is the root of objectivity, not because what people agree on is necessarily true, but because intersubjectivity depends on interaction with the world. Though we could not have been at the point of comparing notes without prior interaction, it is private notes that in the end get compared. It is here that each person, each mind or self, reveals itself as part of a community of free selves. There would be no thought if individuals did not play the indispensable, and ultimately unavoidably creative, role of final arbiter.

INTERSUBJECTIVE

7 *Rational Animals*

Neither an infant 1 week old nor a snail is a rational creature. If the infant survives long enough, he or she will probably become rational, while this is not true of the snail. If we like, we may say of the infant from the start that he is a rational creature because he will probably become rational if he survives, or because he belongs to a species with this capacity. Whichever way we talk, there remains the difference, with respect to rationality, between the infant and the snail on one hand, and the normal adult person on the other.

The difference consists in having propositional attitudes such as belief, desire, intention, and shame. This raises the question how to tell when a creature has propositional attitudes; snails, we may agree, do not, but how about dogs or chimpanzees? The question is not entirely empirical, for there is the philosophical question what evidence is relevant to deciding when a creature has propositional attitudes.

Some animals think and reason; they consider, test, reject, and accept hypotheses; they act on reasons, sometimes after deliberating, imagining consequences, and weighing probabilities; they have desires, hopes, and hates, sometimes for good reasons. They also make errors in calculation, act against their own best judgement, or accept doctrines on inadequate evidence. Any one of these accomplishments, activities, actions, or errors is enough to show that such an animal is a rational animal, for to be a rational animal is just to have propositional attitudes, no matter how confused, contradictory, absurd, unjustified, or erroneous those attitudes may be. This, I propose, is the answer.

The question is: what animals are rational? Of course I do not intend to name names, even names of species or other groups. I shall not try to decide whether dolphins, apes, human embryos, or politicians are rational, or even whether all that prevents computers from being rational is their genesis. My question is what makes an animal (or anything else, if one wants) rational.

The propositional attitudes provide an interesting criterion of rationality because they come only as a matched set. Obviously a rich pattern of beliefs, desires, and intentions suffices for rationality; yet it may seem far too stringent to make this a necessary condition. But in fact the stringency lies in the nature of the propositional attitudes, since to have one is to have a large complement. One belief requires many beliefs, and beliefs demand other basic attitudes such as intentions, desires, and, if I am right, the gift of tongues. This does not mean that there are not borderline cases. Nevertheless, the intrinsically holistic character of the propositional attitudes makes the distinction between having any and having none dramatic.

To make the distinction so strong, and to make it depend on language, invites an accusation of anthropocentrism. The complaint is just, but it ought not to be leveled against me. I merely describe a feature of certain concepts. After all, it is not surprising that our human language is rich in resources for distinguishing men and women from other creatures, just as the Inuit are said to have a vocabulary convenient for picking out varieties of snow (this is now said to be a myth). We connive with our language to make it, and us, seem special.

I promised not to discuss the question whether particular species are rational, but it will be impossible to avoid the appearance of talking of the feats and abilities of beasts because so much discussion of the nature of thought has by tradition centered on the mental powers of nonhuman animals. I consider this approach as just a colorful (and sometimes emotionally laden) way of thinking about the nature of thought.[1]

Norman Malcolm tells this story, which is intended to show that dogs think:

---

[1] My records tell me that before this essay was written I gave no less than ten talks, from Valdosta, Georgia, to Auckland, with the title 'Why Animals can't Think'. The title was tendentious, since what I argued for (as here) was that only creatures with a language can think. I happen to believe, however, that men and women are alone in having language, or anything enough like a language to justify attributing propositional thoughts to them. On the moral issue how we should treat dumb creatures, I see no reason to be less kind to those without thoughts or language than to those with; on the contrary.

Suppose our dog is chasing the neighbor's cat. The latter runs full tilt toward the oak tree, but suddenly swerves at the last moment and disappears up a nearby maple. The dog doesn't see this maneuver and on arriving at the oak tree he rears up on his hind feet, paws at the trunk as if trying to scale it, and barks excitedly into the branches above. We who observe this whole episode from a window say, 'He thinks that the cat went up that oak tree'.[2]

(Malcolm added, we would say the dog was barking up the wrong tree.) Malcolm claims that under the circumstances someone who attributed that belief to the dog might well—almost surely would— be right; he would have exactly the sort of evidence needed to justify such an attribution.

Let me give a preliminary argument designed to put Malcolm's claim in doubt. It's clear that the evidence for the dog's 'belief' depends on taking belief as a determinant of action and emotional response. We are asked to infer from what we see that the dog wants to catch the cat, that he runs where he does because of this desire and a belief about where the cat has gone, and that he is venting his frustration at not being able to follow the cat up the tree by barking, pawing the ground, and so forth. The details do not need to be right, of course. The point is so far obvious: if we are justified in inferring beliefs, we are also justified in inferring intentions and desires (and perhaps much more).

But how about the dog's supposed belief that the cat went up that oak tree? That oak tree, as it happens, is the oldest tree in sight. Does the dog think that the cat went up the oldest tree in sight? Or that the cat went up the same tree it went up the last time the dog chased it? It is hard to make sense of the questions. But then it does not seem possible to distinguish between quite different things the dog might be said to believe.

One way of telling that we are attributing a propositional attitude is by noting that the sentences we use to do the attributing may change from true to false if, in the words that pick out the object of the attitude, we substitute for some referring expression another expression that refers to the same thing. The belief that the cat went up that oak tree is not the same belief as the belief that the cat went up the oldest tree in sight. If we use words like 'believe', 'think', and 'intend', while dropping the feature of semantic opacity, there is a question whether we are using those words to attribute propositional

2 Norman Malcolm, 'Thoughtless Brutes', 13.

attitudes. For it has long been recognized that semantic opacity distinguishes talk about propositional attitudes from talk of other things.

Someone may suggest that the position occupied by the expression 'that oak tree' in the sentence 'The dog thinks the cat went up that oak tree' is, in Quine's terminology, transparent. The right way to put the dog's belief (the suggestion continues) is 'The dog thinks, with respect to that oak tree, that the cat went up it' or 'That oak tree is the one the dog thinks the cat went up'. But such constructions, while they may relieve the attributer of the need to produce a description of the object that the believer would accept, nevertheless imply that there is some such description; the *de re* description picks out an object the believer could somehow pick out. In a popular if misleading idiom, the dog must believe, under some description of the tree, that the cat went up that tree. But what kind of description would suit the dog? For example, can the dog believe of an object that it is a tree? This would seem impossible unless we suppose the dog has many general beliefs about trees: that they are growing things, that they need soil and water, that they have leaves or needles, that they burn. There is no fixed list of things someone with the concept of a tree must believe, but without many general beliefs, there would be no reason to identify a belief as a belief about a tree, much less an oak tree. Similar considerations apply to the dog's supposed thinking about the cat.

We identify thoughts, distinguish among them, describe them for what they are, only as they can be located within a dense network of related beliefs. If we really can intelligibly ascribe single beliefs to a dog, we must be able to imagine how we would decide whether the dog has many other beliefs of the kind necessary for making sense of the first. It seems to me that no matter where we start, we very soon come to beliefs such that we have no idea at all how to tell whether a dog has them, and yet such that, without them, our confident first attribution looks shaky.

Not only does each belief require a world of further beliefs to give it content and identity, but every other propositional attitude depends for its particularity on a similar world of beliefs. In order to believe the cat went up the oak tree I must have many true beliefs about cats and trees, this cat and this tree, the place, appearance, and habits of cats and trees, and so on; but the same holds if I wonder whether the cat went up the oak tree, fear that it did, hope that it did, wish that it had, or intend to make it do so. Belief—indeed, true belief—plays a central role among the propositional attitudes. So let me speak of all the propositional attitudes as thoughts.

As remarked above, there may be no fixed list of beliefs on which any particular thought depends. Nevertheless, much true belief is necessary. Some beliefs of the sort required are general, but plausibly empirical, such as that cats can scratch or climb trees. Others are particular, such as that the cat seen running a moment ago is still in the neighborhood. Some are logical. Thoughts, like propositions, have logical relations. Since the identity of a thought cannot be divorced from its place in the logical network of other thoughts, it cannot be relocated in the network without becoming a different thought. Radical incoherence in belief is therefore impossible. To have a single propositional attitude is to have a largely correct logic, in the sense of having a pattern of beliefs that logically cohere. This is one reason why to have propositional attitudes is to be a rational creature. The point extends to intentional action. Intentional action is action that can be explained in terms of beliefs and desires whose propositional contents rationalize the action. Similarly, an emotion like being pleased that one has stopped smoking must be an emotion that is rational in the light of beliefs and values one has.

This is not to deny the existence of irrational beliefs, actions, and emotions, needless to say. An action one has reasons to perform may be an action one has better reasons to avoid. A belief may be reasonable in the light of some but not the totality of one's other beliefs; and so on. The point is that the possibility of irrationality depends on a large degree of rationality. Irrationality is not mere lack of reason but a disease or perturbation of reason.

I assume that an observer can under favorable circumstances tell what beliefs, desires, and intentions an agent has. Indeed, I appealed to this assumption when I urged that if a creature cannot speak, it is unclear that intensionality can be maintained in the descriptions of its purported beliefs and other attitudes. Similarly, I wondered whether, in the absence of speech, there could be adequate grounds for attributing the general beliefs needed for making sense of any thought. Without defending the assumption that we can know other minds, let me distinguish this assumption from other stronger assumptions. Merely to claim that an observer can under favorable conditions tell what someone else is thinking is not to embrace verificationism, even with respect to thoughts. For the observability assumption does not imply that it is possible to state explicitly what evidence is necessary or sufficient to determine the presence of a particular thought; there is no suggestion that thinking can somehow be reduced definitionally to something else. Nor does the observability assumption imply that the only way to determine the existence of a thought is by observing. On the contrary, it is clear that people normally know without observation or evidence what they believe, want, and intend.

Nor does the observability assumption amount to behaviorism. Propositional attitudes can be discovered by an observer who witnesses nothing but behavior without the attitudes being in any way reducible to behavior. There are conceptual ties between the attitudes and behavior which are sufficient, given enough information about actual and potential behavior, to allow correct inferences to the attitudes.

From what has been said about the dependence of beliefs on other beliefs, and of other propositional attitudes on beliefs, it is clear that a very complex pattern of behavior must be observed to justify the attribution of a single thought. Or, more accurately, there has to be good reason to believe there is such a complex pattern of behavior. And unless there is actually such a complex pattern of behavior, there is no thought.

I think there is such a pattern only if the agent has language. If this is right, then Malcolm was justified in attributing thought to his dog only if he believed, on good evidence, that his dog had language.

The view that thought—belief, desire, intention, and the like—requires language is controversial, but certainly not new. The version of the thesis which I want to promote needs to be distinguished from various related versions. I don't, for example, believe that thinking can be reduced to linguistic activity. I find no plausibility in the idea that thoughts can be nomologically identified with, or correlated with, phenomena characterized in physical or neurological terms. Nor do I see any reason to maintain that what we can't say we can't think. My thesis is not, then, that each thought depends for its existence on the existence of a sentence that expresses that thought. My thesis is rather that a creature cannot have a thought unless it has language. In order to be a thinking, rational creature, the creature must be able to express many thoughts, and above all, be able to interpret the speech and thoughts of others.

As I remarked above, this has often been claimed; but on what grounds? Given the popularity of the idea, from the rationalists through the American pragmatists, and even among contemporary analytic philosophers, there is a remarkable dearth of arguments. So far, I have pointed to the dubious applicability of the intensionality test where dumb animals are concerned, and the requirement, if thought is to be present, that there be a rich supply of general (and true) beliefs. These considerations point in the direction of language, but they do not amount to a demonstration that language is necessary to thought. Indeed, what these considerations suggest is only that there probably can't be much thought without language.

Against the dependence of thought on language is the plain observation that we succeed in explaining, and sometimes predicting, the behavior of languageless animals by attributing beliefs and desires and intentions to them. This method works for dogs and frogs much as it does for people. And, it may be added, we have no general and practical alternative framework for explaining animal behavior. Don't these facts amount to a *justification* of the application of the method?[3]

No doubt they do. But there could remain a clear sense in which it would be wrong to conclude that dumb (= incapable of interpreting or engaging in linguistic communication) animals have propositional attitudes. To see this it is only necessary to reflect that someone might easily have no better or alternative way of explaining the movements of a heat-seeking missile than to suppose the missile wanted to destroy an airplane and believed it could by moving in the way it was observed to move. This uninformed observer might be justified in attributing a desire and beliefs to the missile; but he would be wrong. I know better, for example, not because I know how the missile is designed, but because I know that it moves as it does because it was designed and built by people who had the very desire and beliefs my ignorant friend assigned to the missile. My explanation, while still teleological, and dependent on the existence of propositional attitudes, is a better explanation because it does not attribute to the missile the potentiality for the rich range of behavior that a thinking creature must have.

The case of a languageless creature differs from the case of the missile in two respects: many animals are far more like humans in the range of their behavior than missiles are; and we often do not

---

[3] This is the position stressed by Jonathan Bennett, *Linguistic Behavior.*

have a better way of explaining their behavior than by appropriating propositional attitudes. What we need, then, in order to make a case, is a characterization of what it is that language supplies that is necessary for thought. For if there is such a necessary condition, we can continue to explain the behavior of speechless creatures by attributing propositional attitudes to them while at the same time recognizing that such creatures do not actually have propositional attitudes. We will be bound to acknowledge that we are applying a pattern of explanation that is far stronger than the observed behavior requires, and to which the observed behavior is not subtle enough to give point.

In the rest of this essay I state the condition for thought that I believe only language can supply, and I marshal considerations in favor of my view. Although I present these considerations as an argument, it will be clear that my reasoning can be challenged at several points.

The 'argument' has two steps. I think I have shown that all the propositional attitudes require a background of beliefs, so I shall concentrate on conditions for belief. Without belief there are no other propositional attitudes, and so no rationality as I have characterized it.

First, I argue that in order to have a belief, it is necessary to have the concept of belief.

Second, I argue that in order to have the concept of belief one must have language.

Norman Malcolm, in the article mentioned above, makes a distinction similar to the one I want between having a belief and having the concept of a belief, but his terminology differs from mine. I have been using the word 'thought' to cover all the propositional attitudes. Malclom, however, restricts the application of 'thought' to a higher level of thinking. In his view, the dog can believe the cat went up that oak tree, but it cannot have the thought that the cat has gone up that oak tree. The latter, but not the former, Malcolm holds, requires language. Malcolm makes the distinction by saying a creature merely thinks (believes) that p if it is aware that p, but it has the thought that p if it is aware that it is aware that p. This is close to the distinction I have in mind between believing that p and believing that one believes that p. The second is a belief about a belief, and so requires the concept of belief. To make a rough comparison:

Malcolm holds that language draws a line between creatures that merely think and creatures that have the concept of a thought; I hold that in order to think one must have the concept of a thought, and so language is required in both cases.

Donald Weiss takes issue with Malcolm: Weiss thinks it is possible to make sensible attributions of awareness to speechless creatures.[4] Since I think his example may strike a responsive chord in others, let me paraphrase and then quote him at some length. Here is the story. Arthur is not a dog, but, let us say, a superdog from another planet. Arthur arrives on earth unaccompanied, and here he hatches. He has no commerce with, or knowledge of, other creatures—he is observed through one-way mirrors. He has no language. According to Weiss, we become convinced he has reflective intelligence when we witness this scene:

One day Arthur comes upon a shiny metal, puts it in the fire, tries to hammer it out—but discovers that it is apparently no more malleable than it was when cold. He tries again more slowly and more methodically—but again the same result. The regularity in which Arthur believed—we whisper among ourselves—is not entirely universal. Arthur has discovered an instance that does not conform to the general rule.

Arthur proceeds to walk agitatedly around his living space. He abruptly sits down; just as abruptly he gets up again; he paces forward and back. Once more he sits down, but this time he remains seated. Fifteen minutes pass without change of posture; Arthur's eyes are focused straight ahead. Then suddenly he leaps up and immediately proceeds to pile a large quantity of wood onto his fire . . . He then plunges his newly discovered metal into the fire, and, after a time, withdraws it. He again attempts to hammer it out—and this time he meets with success. Thus apparently satisfied . . . he proceeds in a leisurely manner to cook himself a meal.[5]

Weiss says we now have strong evidence Arthur has reflected upon his own beliefs; he is particularly impressed by the fact that Arthur in response to his state of befuddlement, sits wide-eyed and stock-still, and then veritably leaps to perform the acts that constitute the solution to his problem.[6]

I will ignore the question-begging vocabulary Weiss uses in describing Arthur's movements, for I think Weiss is barking up a right tree: it is essential that we be able to describe Arthur as being surprised. What I think is clear is that if he is surprised, he does have reflective thoughts, and, of course, beliefs.

---

[4] Donald Weiss, 'Professor Malcolm on Animal Intelligence'.
[5] Ibid., 91–2.   [6] Ibid.

This is not to claim that all thinking is self-conscious, or that whenever we think that *p* we must be aware that *p*, or believe that we believe that *p*, or think that we think that *p*. My claim is rather this: in order to have any propositional attitude at all, it is necessary to have the concept of a belief, to have a belief about some belief. But what is required in order to have the concept of a belief? Here I turn for help to the phenomenon of surprise, since I think that surprise requires the concept of a belief.

Suppose I believe there is a coin in my pocket. I empty my pocket and find no coin. I am surprised. Clearly enough I could not be surprised (though I could be startled) if I did not have beliefs in the first place. And perhaps it is equally clear that having a belief, at least one of the sort I have taken for my example, entails the possibility of surprise. If I believe I have a coin in my pocket, something might happen that would change my mind. But surprise involves a further step. It is not enough that I first believe there is a coin in my pocket, and after emptying my pocket I no longer have this belief. Surprise requires that I be aware of a contrast between what I did believe and what I come to believe. Such awareness, however, is a belief about a belief: if I am surprised, then among other things I come to believe that my original belief was false. I do not need to insist that every case of surprise involves a belief that a prior belief was false (though I am inclined to think so). What I do want to claim is that one cannot have a general stock of beliefs of the sort necessary for having any beliefs at all without being subject to surprises that involve beliefs about the correctness of one's own beliefs. Surprise about some things is a necessary and sufficient condition of thought in general. This concludes the first part of my 'argument'.

Much of the point of the concept of belief is that it is the concept of a state of an organism which can be true or false, correct or incorrect. To have the concept of belief is therefore to have the concept of objective truth. If I believe there is a coin in my pocket, I may be right or wrong; I'm right only if there is a coin in my pocket. If I am surprised to find there is no coin in my pocket, I come to believe that my former belief did not correspond with the state of my finances. I have the idea of an objective reality which is independent of my belief.

A creature may interact with the world in complex ways without entertaining any propositions. It may discriminate among colors, tastes, sounds, and shapes. It may learn, that is change its behaviour, in ways that preserve its life or increase its food intake. It may 'generalize', in the sense of reacting to new stimuli as it has come to react to prior stimuli. Yet none of this, no matter how successful by my standards, shows that the creature commands the contrast between what is believed and what is the case, as required by belief.

What *would* show command of this contrast? Clearly linguistic communication suffices. To understand the speech of another, I must be able to think of the same things she does; I must share her world. I don't have to agree with her in all matters, but in order to disagree we must entertain the same propositions, with the same subject matter, and the same concept of truth. Communication depends on each communicator having, and correctly thinking that the other has, the concept of a shared world, an intersubjective world. But the concept of an intersubjective world is the concept of an objective world, a world about which each communicator can have beliefs.

I suggest, then, that the concept of intersubjective truth suffices as a basis for belief and hence for thoughts generally. And perhaps it is plausible enough that having the concept of intersubjective truth depends on communication in the full linguistic sense. To complete the 'argument', however, I need to show that the *only* way one could come to have the belief–truth contrast is through having the concept of intersubjective truth. I confess I do not know how to show this. But neither do I have any idea how else one could arrive at the concept of an objective truth. In place of an argument for the first step, I offer the following analogy.

If I were bolted to the earth, I would have no way of determining the distance from me of many objects. I would only know they were on some line drawn from me towards them. I might interact successfully with objects, but I could have no way of giving content to the question where they were. Not being bolted down, I am free to triangulate. Our sense of objectivity is the consequence of another sort of triangulation, one that requires two creatures. Each interacts with an object, but what gives each the concept of the way things are objectively is the base line formed between the creatures by language. The fact that they share a concept of truth alone makes sense of the claim that they have beliefs, that they are able to assign objects a place in the public world.

The conclusion of these considerations is that rationality is a social trait. Only communicators have it.

8 *The Second Person*

... meaning something is like going up to someone.

(Wittgenstein, *Philosophical Investigations*, §457)

How many competent speakers of a language must there be if anyone can be said to speak or understand a language? Since this is a matter governed by the crooked course of evolution, I have no idea what the answer is; perhaps it takes quite a crowd. But as philosophers we can ask the question in a more theoretical vein. In this essay I shall be concentrating on the role—the role in principle—of the second person. My subject is not, I should perhaps add, the grammatical second person, the 'you' or 'thou', the 'tú' or 'vosotros'; I shall be writing about real second people, not the words used to address them.

A language may be viewed as a complex abstract object, defined by giving a finite list of expressions (words), rules for constructing meaningful concatenations of expressions (sentences), and a semantic interpretation of the meaningful expressions based on the semantic features of individual words. I shall not be concerned in this essay with the details of how such objects should be described or defined.

Thought of this way, a language is abstract in the obvious sense that it is unobservable, changeless, and its components are also unobservable and changeless. Expressions may, if we wish, be viewed as acoustical or two-dimensional geometric shapes that could, on occasion, inform actual utterances or inscriptions, but expressions themselves would remain abstract and their existence independent of exemplification.[1] The functions that interpret some expressions by

---

[1] Or, to take equally abstract entities, expressions may be thought of as classes of utterances or inscriptions. But if we take expressions to be classes of utterances or inscriptions, all unuttered and unwritten expressions, and hence all expressions of unused languages, will be identical. In some cases there are awkward ways around this. (See W. V. Quine and

mapping them on to objects or classes of objects are also, of course, abstract. The only concrete particulars that enter into the characterization of a language are some of the objects on to which some expressions are mapped (for example, by the naming relation, or, at another remove, by Tarski's satisfaction relation).

The abstract character of language is nothing to wonder at. The concept of a language is of a sort with, and depends on, concepts like name, predicate, sentence, reference, meaning, with observation. These are all theoretical concepts, and the items to which they apply are abstract objects. We don't need them in order to use or learn a language; obviously they are not available to us when we are learning a first language. Where we want these concepts is in talking about speech behavior. Philosophers, psychologists, and linguists need these theoretical terms if they want to describe, theorize about, and explain verbal activities. The rest of us also have occasion to talk about talk, or write about writing, so these theoretical concepts have their place in the loose informal 'theories' we all have about language. Indeed, we all talk so freely about language, or languages, that we tend to forget that there are no such things in the world; there are only people and their various written and acoustical products. This point, obvious in itself, is nevertheless easy to forget, and it has consequences that are not universally recognized.

A feature of the concept of a language as I have described it is, then, that there must be an infinity of 'languages' no one ever has spoken or ever will speak. To say someone speaks a particular language, say French, is just to say that his or her datable utterances and writings are tokens of French expressions. To be the token of a French sentence an utterance or inscription must instantiate a French sentence, that is, have one of the shapes defined to be a French sentence; and the utterance must have the semantic features the definition of French assigns to the shape. (Other, probably unspoken, languages will assign other semantic features to these same shapes.) The existence of the French language does not depend on anyone's speaking it, any more than the existence of shapes depends on there being objects with those shapes.[2]

Nelson Goodman, 'Steps toward a Constructive Nominalism'.) For our purposes it will be better to take expressions to be shapes, i.e. properties that utterances and inscriptions can have.

[2] This concept of a language is essentially that of David Lewis, 'Languages and Language'.

It follows that there is nothing about the existence of a particular language that imbues it with anything more than the sort of interest any abstract object may have; as logicians we can study it as one example among countless others of a formal pattern. Such research pays dividends of various sorts, but it is unrelated to our normal concern with understanding the speech of others, or learning to make ourselves understood by them. Our practical, as opposed to our purely theoretical, interest in linguistic phenomena is this: we want to understand the actual utterances of others, and we want our utterances to be understood. What has language to do with this interest?

The answer is that it is only by employing such concepts as word and sentence that we can give a systematic description of the linguistic aspects of linguistic behavior and aptitudes. We could not, for example, say what we have learned when we learn that 'demain' means tomorrow in French if we could not speak of words—those mysterious abstract (acoustical) shapes which utterances of the word 'demain' share. Thus an utterance of the word 'demain' refers to the day after the day of the utterance. There is no easy way we could specify which utterances constitute utterances of sentences, and therefore constitute intelligible utterances, if we could not refer to words and sentences.

The main point of the concept of a language, then, and its attendant concepts like those of predicate, sentence, and reference, is to enable us to give a coherent description of the behavior of speakers, and of what speakers and their interpreters know that allows them to communicate. I do not suggest that speakers and those who understand them must themselves be able to provide such descriptions of their abilities and behavior. To illustrate: a competent speaker of a language (and a competent interpreter) knows the truth conditions of an indefinitely large number of sentences. So most English speakers know that an utterance of the sentence 'Montreal is in Canada' is true if and only if Montreal is in Canada; and the speaker knows an analogous fact about endless other sentences. The speaker doesn't need to put this knowledge into words. But *we* cannot describe the totality of this knowledge possessed by the speaker or interpreter of the language without ourselves having a theory—a theory of truth, or something like it—which is part of the description of English. (This description of what an English speaker knows does not have to be stated in English, and if it is not, it does not sound so trivial.)

To return now to the question with which I began: how many

speakers or interpreters of a language must there be for there to be one speaker? Let me start with an apparent difficulty. To speak a language, one's utterances must be consistent with the definition of some language. The trouble is that utterances are finite in number, while the definition of a language assigns meanings to an infinite number of sentences. There will therefore be endless different languages which agree with all of a speaker's actual utterances, but differ with respect to unspoken sentences. What makes the speaker a speaker of one of these languages rather than another? And the problem may be worse still. For even if a speaker were (impossibly) to utter every sentence in some one language, many other languages would be consistent with all his behavior and internal states, as Quine has maintained; and I agree.

The fact that all the publicly available evidence with regard to a speaker or group of speakers, even if imagined to exhaust all possible such evidence, might be consistent with many different languages (in the sense of 'language' we have temporarily ordained) ought not in itself to worry us, for we can agree that it is enough to know that a speaker speaks any one of a set of empirically equivalent languages, as long as the empirical constraints clearly define the set. So let us henceforth simply call any language in this set 'the language' of a speaker.[3] This strategy is good enough for empirically equivalent languages if the evidence is imagined to contain an utterance of every sentence we would count as belonging to the language. But of course such evidence is never available. So there will be endless languages consistent with all the actual utterances of a speaker none of which is 'the' language the speaker is speaking.

The problem can be stated in a temporal mode, and addressed to an interpreter. If you (the interpreter) do not know how a speaker is going to go on, you do not know what language she speaks, no matter how much she has said up until now. It will not help to mention that the speaker has performed according to expectation so far, or that she went to the same school you did, or belongs to the same culture or community, for the question concerns not the past but the future. Nor can we appeal to the idea that the speaker has mastered a set of

---

[3] I regard the existence of empirically equivalent languages (that is, languages equally consistent with all possible empirical evidence) as no more threatening to the reality or objectivity of the correct interpretation of utterances and their accompanying mental states than the existence of various scales for recording temperatures or lengths is to the reality or objectivity of temperature or length. (See Essay 5.)

conventions (which conventions?), or has learned a set of rules (which ones?). The concepts of conventions or rules, like the concept of a language, cannot be called on to justify or explain linguistic behavior; at best these concepts help describe (i.e. define) linguistic behavior.

This difficulty, though it may have troubled Wittgenstein, and certainly troubled Kripke,[4] seems to me to have a relatively simple answer. The longer we interpret a speaker with apparent success as speaking a particular language, the greater our legitimate confidence that the speaker is speaking that language—that is, that she will continue to be interpretable as speaking that language. Our strengthening expectations are as well founded as our evidence and ordinary induction make them. These expectations are in the main conditional. We do not usually know what someone will say, but we are prepared to interpret any of a very large number of things that person might say. Our dispositions to interpret and a speaker's dispositions to go on in certain ways are not shadowy or mysterious: they are real features of brains and muscles. Of course our beliefs about what is true of another person, and therefore what we expect that person to mean by what he does or might say, may easily be wrong. I think such beliefs are frequently wrong. But far more often they are right, and the things we are right about usually put us in a position to correct our understanding of an utterance which does not belong to a language we thought was being spoken. To the extent that we are right about what is in someone's head, and therefore are right about what he would mean by endless things he does not say, we are right about 'the' language he speaks.

This very partial answer to the question what reasons an interpreter can have for believing that a speaker is speaking one language rather than another language that is equally compatible with the speech behavior that the interpreter has observed does not depend heavily on the details of how we explain successful interpretation. The point of the answer is that there are not *two* questions, one about reasons for believing a speaker is speaking one language rather than another, and a second question about how we naturally form expectations; the first question is simply a case of the second.

There is another aspect of interpretation, however, that is essential to our concerns: an interpreter (correctly) interprets an utterance of a

---

[4] Saul Kripke, *Wittgenstein on Rules and Private Language*.

speaker only if he knows that the speaker intends the interpreter to assign certain truth conditions to his (the speaker's) utterance.[5] A full account of this thesis would require an explanation of the idea of 'assigning truth conditions' to an utterance, and this idea is no doubt as difficult to understand in relevant respects as the concept of meaning itself. But my aim here is not to solve that problem. It is only to emphasize, following Grice, the central importance of intention in communication. If, with Grice, we were sure that in order to mean something a speaker must intend to have a certain effect on a specific hearer or hearers, then language might already have been shown to be social to the extent of requiring the existence of at least two people (since it is arguable that one could not intend to have an effect on a specific other person unless such a person existed). I shall not take this direct and tempting line here. Nevertheless, we are in a position to say that if communication succeeds, there must be these intentions on the part of the speaker, and therefore *if* successful communication is essential to meaning, these intentions are essential to meaning. The presence of intentions is important, since it gives content to an attribution of error by allowing for the possibility of a discrepancy between intention and accomplishment. Intention, like belief and expectation, does not require attention or reflection, and intentions are not usually arrived at by conscious reasoning. Intentions are not normally attended by any special feelings, nor is our knowledge of our own intentions arrived at (usually) by inference or resort to observation. Yet intention has an indefinitely large scope, for intentions depend on the belief that one can do what one intends, and this requires that one believe nothing will prevent the intended action. Thus intention would seem to have just the properties needed to make sense of the idea that a speaker has failed to go on as before.[6]

The view I have just sketched deals only with interpretation, and so presupposes a social environment rather than providing an argu-

---

[5] This is clearly inadequate as it stands. It can be improved by adding the Gricean condition that the speaker intends the interpreter to arrive at the right truth conditions through the interpreter's recognition of the speaker's intention to be so interpreted. I do not argue here for the assumption that knowledge of truth conditions is adequate for interpretation.

[6] Essentially these points about intention are made by Crispin Wright in attempting, like me, to defuse Kripke's view that he has extracted an essentially insoluble 'skeptical paradox' from Wittgenstein's treatment of meaning. See Crispin Wright, 'Kripke's Account of the Argument against Private Language'.

ment for it. Nevertheless, it will be useful at this point to consider certain aspects of the view I think Kripke attributes to Wittgenstein. (For expository purposes I shall call this Kripke's view. In fact Kripke does not clearly say he endorses it; and I am uncertain that it is Wittgenstein's view. So perhaps it is no one's view.) Kripke concentrates on the idea of following a rule. According to this idea, to speak a language is to follow rules. The rules specify what it is to go on 'in the same way'; how, for example, to use a word. There is, however, no inner mental act or process of 'grasping' or of 'following' the rule, so no study or knowledge of what is inside the speaker will reveal whether she is following one set of rules or another. Interpreters simply judge that a speaker is following the same rule they (her interpreters) are if the speaker goes on as they would. Put in terms of meaning: we judge that a speaker means what we would if we were to utter the same words if she goes on as we would.[7]

We ought to question the appropriateness of the ordinary concept of following a rule for describing what is involved in speaking a language. When we talk of rules of language, we usually have in mind grammarians' or linguists' descriptions (generalized and idealized) of actual practice, or prescriptions grammarians wish we would follow. Rules can be a help in learning a language, but their aid is available only in the acquisition of a second language. Most learning of how to use words is accomplished without explicitly learning any rules at all.[8] Wittgenstein does, of course, treat meaning something in much the same way he does following some procedure, such as adding in arithmetic. But there is a clear distinction between the cases, which explains why we normally use the word 'rule' in one

---

[7] '. . . what do I mean when I say that the teacher judges that, for certain cases, the pupil must give the "right" answer? I mean that the teacher judges that the child has given the same answer that he himself would give . . . if, in enough concrete cases, Jones's inclinations agree with Smith's, Smith will judge that Jones is indeed following the rule' (Kripke, *Wittgenstein on Rules and Private Language*, 90–1). The following from Wittgenstein may bear out this interpretation: 'a person goes by [is guided by] a sign-post only in so far as there exists a regular use of sign-posts, a custom. . . . Is what we call "obeying a rule" something that it would be possible for only *one* man to do, and to do only *once* in his life? . . .—To obey a rule, to make a report, to give an order, to play a game of chess, are *customs* (uses, institutions)' (*Philosophical Investigations*, §§198, 199). I have ignored a very important aspect of Kripke's discussion, his claim that Wittgenstein's 'solution' to the problem of meaning is 'skeptical'.

[8] It should be obvious that the claim that there are internalized or genetically implanted rules of *grammar* is irrelevant here; Wittgenstein's and Kripke's 'rules' concern what the words of particular languages mean.

case and not in the other. In the case of adding, there is an explicit procedure for arriving at an answer; we can learn and describe the procedure, and it is appropriate to call the procedure or its description a rule. We normally follow no procedure in speaking; nothing in normal speaking corresponds to adding a column of numbers. If the concept of following a rule is not quite appropriate to describe meaning something by saying something, it is also questionable whether, even if we agree that the use of a language requires a social setting, we should accept without question the idea that meaning something demands (as opposed to sometimes involving) a convention, custom, or institution.[9]

A more important question concerns the idea that linguistic communication requires that a speaker go on in the same way as others do—that to mean something in speaking, one must mean the same thing by the same words as others do. The account I gave above of the sort of expectations that must be satisfied if one person is to understand another did not suggest that those people would have to speak the same language. Nor is it clear why this is necessary. Perhaps language would never have come into existence unless it could depend on the natural tendency of animals to imitate each other. This may be so, though I have my doubts, but surely it could have been otherwise. If you and I were the only speakers in the world, and you spoke Sherpa while I spoke English, we could understand one another, though each of us followed different 'rules' (regularities). What would matter, of course, is that we should each provide the other with something understandable as a language. This is an intention speakers must have; but carrying out this intention, while it may require a degree of what the other perceives as consistency, does not involve following shared rules or conventions. It might even be that because of differences in our vocal chords we couldn't make the same sounds, and therefore couldn't speak the same language. I know of no argument that shows that under such circumstances communication could not take place. So, while it may be true that speaking a language requires that there be an interpreter, it doesn't follow that more than one person must speak the same language. This is fortunate, since if we are precise about what consti-

---

[9] I have expressed my skepticism about the explanatory power of the concepts of rule-following and convention in the study of language at greater length in 'Communication and Convention', essay 18 in *Inquiries into Truth and Interpretation*.

tutes a language, it is probably the case that no two people actually do speak the same language. I conclude that Kripke's criterion for speaking a language cannot be right; speaking a language cannot depend on speaking as someone else does (or as many others do).[10]

Let us suppose, then, that the test for speaking a language is modified to accommodate this point: speaking a language, we will now claim, does not depend on two or more speakers speaking in the same way; it merely requires that each speaker intentionally make himself interpretable to the other (the speaker must 'go on' more or less as the other expects, or at least is equipped to interpret).

This is certainly a necessary condition for successful *communication*. But why is it a condition that must be satisfied in order to speak a language at all? Why couldn't someone go on in the same way— satisfy all the conditions for being *interpretable*—without actually being interpreted?[11]

It is true that our evidence that someone speaks a particular language is mainly based on the fact that he goes on as we expect a speaker of that language to go on. There are, of course, many other sorts of evidence; the speaker's clothes, his companions, his location on the face of the earth, may all be clues to his language. Still, we can agree that pinning matters down must in the end depend on the details of speech behavior. The trouble is that the original question concerned neither the conditions for communication nor the question what evidence one person could have that another was speaking a particular language; the issue was why a speaker's sole or first language could not be private.

---

[10] My mother kept a record, as fond mothers will, of the language I spoke when I was 3 years old. It certainly was not the language spoken by others in the family—or by anyone else, I imagine. But she claims, rightly, that she understood me and I her. And it is common for people who cannot or will not speak or write French to answer letters written in French in English.

I have argued in 'A Nice Derangement of Epitaphs' that communication does not demand that languages be shared. The same position is endorsed by Noam Chomsky, *Language and Problems of Knowledge*, 36–7. For a more extended treatment of this subject directly aimed at Kripke, see Chomsky, *Knowledge of Language: Its Nature, Origin and Use*, 223–37.

[11] Kripke seems to allow that Robinson Crusoe might be judged to be speaking a language, as long as he *could* be included in a society, even if he is not in fact (ever?) in a social setting. There would still have to be a society (or at least another person) legitimately to judge that Robinson Crusoe meant something by his noises. Chomsky thinks that by allowing the Robinson Crusoe case Kripke contradicts his main thesis. Perhaps so; but I think Chomsky is wrong in thinking the pure Robinson Crusoe case possible. By the pure case, I mean a Robinson Crusoe who has never been in communication with others.

Our discussion has led to a modification or elucidation of the concept of a private language: I am taking this to mean, not a language only one person speaks, but a language only one person understands. The question now is, why can't there be a language only one person understands?[12] The answer Wittgenstein seems to offer in the passage at the head of this essay is: without an interpreter no substance can be given to the claim that the speaker has gone wrong—that he has failed to go on in the same way.

But haven't we, by eliminating the condition that the speaker must go on as the interpreter (or others) would, at the same time inadvertently destroyed all chance of characterizing linguistic error? If there is no social practice with which to compare the speaker's performance, won't whatever the speaker says be, as Wittgenstein remarks, in accord with some rule (i.e. in accord with some language)? If the speech behavior of others doesn't provide the norm for the speaker, what can? The answer is that the intention of the speaker to be interpreted in a certain way provides the 'norm'; the speaker falls short of his intention if he fails to speak in such a way as to be understood as he intended. Under usual circumstances a speaker knows he is most apt to be understood if he speaks as his listeners would, and so he will intend to speak as he thinks they would. He will then fail in one of his intentions if he does not speak as others do. This simple fact helps explain, I think, why many philosophers have tied the meaning of a speaker's utterances to what others mean by the same words (whether 'others' refers to a linguistic community, experts, or an élite of one sort or another[13]). On my account, this tie is neither essential nor direct; it comes into play only when the speaker intends to be interpreted as (certain) others would be. When this intention is absent, the correct understanding of a speaker is unaffected by usage beyond the intended reach of his voice. (A failed intention to speak 'correctly', unless it foils the intention to be interpreted in a certain way, does not matter to what the speaker means.[14])

What these considerations show, if they are right, is that there is a

---

[12] Of course there can be a 'language' only one person understands, for example a secret code used in a diary. The question is whether a first language can be private.

[13] For examples, see Hilary Putnam, 'The Meaning of "Meaning" '; Tyler Burge, 'Individualism and the Mental'; Michael Dummett, 'The Social Character of Meaning', in *Truth and Other Enigmas*, and ' "A Nice Derangement of Epitaphs": Some Comments on Davidson and Hacking', in Ernest Lepore (ed.), *Truth and Interpretation: Perspectives on the Philosophy of Donald Davidson*.

[14] This issue is also discussed in Essay 2.

weaker and more plausible alternative to Kripke's proposed account
of what is required in order to mean something by what one says. For
while Kripke's account makes the test of whether a speaker means
something depend on his doing what others do, the same distinction
between thinking one means something and actually meaning it can
be made in terms of the success of the speaker's intention to be interpreted in a certain way. Both ways of making the distinction depend
on a social setting, but the second makes different demands on the
speaker.[15]

Have we now shown that there cannot be a private language?
Surely not. If we assume that Kripke's proposal is correct, then it is
true that one way of distinguishing between thinking one means
something and actually meaning it requires that language be public;
the same can be said for the alternative I have suggested. But nothing definitive has been said to show there may not be some other way
of drawing the distinction, a way that does not depend on a social
environment.

If we are to establish the essentially public character of language,
we need an entirely different sort of argument. In the remainder of
this essay I suggest such an argument, an argument that applies not
only to speech but also to belief, intention, and the rest of the propositional attitudes. The argument that follows does not start with a
skeptical doubt to which an answer is sought, but it does end with
what may be Wittgenstein's conclusion: language is necessarily a
social affair.

Consider first a primitive learning situation. Some creature is
taught, or anyway learns, to respond in a specific way to a stimulus or
a class of stimuli. The dog hears a bell and is fed; presently it salivates
when it hears the bell. The child babbles, and when it produces a
sound like 'table' in the evident presence of a table, it is rewarded; the
process is repeated and presently the child says 'table' in the presence
of tables. The phenomenon of generalization, of perceived similarity,
plays an essential role in the process. One ring of the bell is enough
like another to provoke similar responses in the dog, just as one

---

[15] There is a point here that I have not accommodated. A speaker fails in an intention if
he is not interpreted as he intends. But it would be wrong to say that such a failure is necessarily a failure to give the meaning to his words that he intended the interpreter to catch.
The latter failure depends (in ways that ordinary usage may not definitively settle) on such
questions as whether the speaker was justified in believing his interpreter could, or would,
interpret him as he intended.

presentation of food is enough like another to engender salivation. If some such discriminative mechanisms were not in our genes, none could be learned. The same goes for the child: we can class the child's stimuli by the similarity of the responses those stimuli elicit in the child.[16]

This seems straightforward, but as psychologists have noticed, there is a problem about the stimulus. In the case of the dog, why say the stimulus is the ringing of the bell? Why couldn't it be the vibration of the air close to the ears of the dog—or even the stimulation of its nerve endings? Certainly if the air were made to vibrate, in the same way the bell makes it vibrate, it would make no difference to the response of the dog. And if the right nerve endings were activated in the right way, there still would be no difference. In fact, if we must choose, it seems that the proximal cause of the behavior has the best claim to be called the stimulus, since the more distant an event is causally from its perceiver, the more chance there is that the causal chain will be broken. Why not say the same about the child: that its responses are not to tables but to patterns of stimulation at its surfaces, since those patterns of stimulation always produce the response, while tables produce it only under favorable conditions?

What explains the fact that it seems so natural to say the dog is responding to the bell, the child to tables? It seems natural to us because it *is* natural—to us. Just as the dog and the child respond in similar ways to certain stimuli, so do we. It is we who find it natural to group together the various salivations of the dog; and the events in the world that we effortlessly notice and group together that are causally linked to the dog's behavior are ringings of the bell. We find the child's mouthings of 'table' similar, and the objects in the world we naturally class together that accompany those mouthings is a class of tables. The acoustical and visual patterns that speed at their various rates between bell and dog ears, tables and child eyes, we cannot easily observe, and if we could we might have a hard time saying what made them similar. (Except by cheating, of course: they are the patterns characteristic of bells ringing, of tables viewed.) Nor do we observe the stimulation of nerve endings of other people and animals, and if we did we might find it impossible to describe in a

---

[16] Nothing here depends on the amateur psychology involving babbling, differential rewards, or preverbal induction. All that matters is the fact that generalization takes place in one way rather than another, and in similar ways in different people.

noncircular way what made the patterns relevantly similar from trial
to trial. The problem would be much the same as the (insoluble)
problem of defining tables and bell-ringings in terms of sense data
without mentioning tables or bells.

Involved in our picture there are now not two but three similarity
patterns. The child finds tables similar; we find tables similar; and
we find the child's responses in the presence of tables similar. It now
makes sense for us to call the responses of the child responses to
tables. Given these three patterns of response we can assign a location to the stimuli that elicit the child's responses. The relevant stimuli are the objects or events we naturally find similar (tables) which
are correlated with responses of the child we find similar. It is a form
of triangulation: one line goes from the child in the direction of the
table, one line goes from us in the direction of the table, and the third
line goes between us and the child. Where the lines from child to
table and us to table converge, 'the' stimulus is located. Given our
view of child and world, we can pick out 'the' cause of the child's
responses. It is the common cause of our response and the child's
response.[17]

Enough features are in place to give a meaning to the idea that the
stimulus has an objective location in a common space; but nothing in
this picture shows that either we, the observers, or our subjects, the
dog and the child, have this idea. Nevertheless, we have come a good
distance. For if I am right, the kind of triangulation I have described,
while not sufficient to establish that a creature has a concept of a
particular object or kind of object, is necessary if there is to be any
answer at all to the question what its concepts are concepts of. If we
consider a single creature by itself, its responses, no matter how
complex, cannot show that it is reacting to, or thinking about, events
a certain distance away rather than, say, on its skin. The solipsist's
world can be any size; which is to say, from the solipsist's point of
view it has no size, it is not a world.

The problem is not, I should stress, one of verifying what objects
or events a creature is responding to; the point is that without a
second creature responding to the first, there can be no answer to the
question. And of course if there is no answer to this question, there

[17] The triangulation metaphor is introduced in Essay 7. The idea of the 'common cause'
is developed in Essay 10. That thought is a social phenomenon is stressed in 'Thought and
Talk', essay 11 in *Inquiries into Truth and Interpretation*, and in Essay 7 in this volume.

is no answer to the question what language a creature speaks, since to designate a language as one being spoken requires that utterances be matched up with objects and events in the world (and not, in general, events on the surface of the skin). So we can say, as a preliminary to answering the question with which we began, that before anyone can speak a language, there must be another creature interacting with the speaker. Of course this cannot be enough, since mere interaction does not show how the interaction matters to the creatures involved. Unless the creatures concerned can be said to react to the interaction, there is no way *they* can take cognitive advantage of the three-way relation which gives content to *our* idea that they are reacting to one thing rather than another.

Here is part, I think, of what is required. The interaction must be made available to the interacting creatures. Thus the child, learning the word 'table', has already in effect noted that the teacher's responses are similar (rewarding) when its own responses (mouthing 'table') are similar. The teacher on his part is training the child to make similar responses to what he (the teacher) perceives as similar stimuli. For this to work, it is clear that the innate similarity responses of child and teacher—what they naturally group together—must be much alike; otherwise the child will respond to what the teacher takes to be similar stimuli in ways the teacher does not find similar. A condition for being a speaker is that there must be others enough like oneself.

So far I have left out of explicit account the concepts of belief and intention which are clearly essential to speaking a language. I have no thought of trying to introduce these concepts in terms of the simple conditioning situations I have been describing; the concept of thought is not reducible to anything else, much less to these simple concepts. All I have tried to show is that interaction among similar creatures is a necessary condition for speaking a language.

Now to put two points together. First, if someone is the speaker of a language, there must be another sentient being whose innate similarity responses are sufficiently like his own to provide an answer to the question, what is the stimulus to which the speaker is responding? And second, if the speaker's responses are linguistic, they must be knowingly and intentionally responses to specific stimuli. The speaker must have the concept of the stimulus—of the bell, or of tables. Since the bell or a table is identified only by the intersection of two (or more) sets of similarity responses (lines of thought, we might almost say), to have the concept of a table or a bell is to recognize the existence of a triangle, one apex of which is oneself, the second apex another a creature similar to oneself, and the third an object (table or bell) located in a space thus made common.

The only way of knowing that the second apex of the triangle—the second creature or person—is reacting to the same object as oneself is to know that the other person has the same object in mind. But then the second person must also know that the first person constitutes an apex of the same triangle another apex of which the second person occupies. For two people to know of each other that they are so related, that their thoughts are so related, requires that they be in communication. Each of them must speak to the other and be understood by the other. They don't, as I said, have to mean the same thing by the same words, but they must each be an interpreter of the other.

The hasty remarks of the last two paragraphs indicate the sort of work that would be necessary to give an account of meaningful speech. But such an account was not my aim; I was looking only to find an argument why a first language cannot be private.

The argument shows that one's first language cannot be a private language, that is, a language understood by only one creature, and to this extent it is in agreement with Kripke's Wittgenstein. But the argument takes a different course, and the flavor it gives the social aspect of language is different. Kripke depends on the second person, or a community, to embody a routine which the speaker can share. In contrast, the argument I have outlined does not require (though of course it allows) a shared routine, but it does depend on the interaction of at least two speaker-interpreters, for if I am right, there would be no saying what a speaker was talking or thinking about, no basis for claiming he could locate objects in an objective space and time, without interaction with a second person.

The considerations I have put forward do not apply to language only; they apply equally to thought in general. Belief, intention, and the other propositional attitudes are all social in that they are states a creature cannot be in without having the concept of intersubjective truth, and this is a concept one cannot have without sharing, and knowing that one shares, a world, and a way of thinking about the world, with someone else.

9 *The Emergence of Thought*

According to the Bible, the Word was there from the beginning, but it seems more plausible that words and thought emerged rather recently. What does it mean, though, to say some aspect of the world 'emerged'?

Emergence makes sense only as seen from a point of view, from within a set of concepts. Given *our* set of concepts, we can appreciate the idea that different concepts were instantiated at different times. The concepts of quantum physics were instantiated very early; the concepts of the various elements were instantiated over a longer subsequent period. The concept of life was instantiated quite recently, and the concepts of thought and language were filled out only moments ago, with the coming of the higher mammals. This doesn't mean the laws of physics changed, but it does mean that in order to describe and explain thought we need concepts that can't be defined in the vocabulary of physics (or any of the natural sciences). Thus, in a clear sense, emergence is relative to a set of concepts. Concepts themselves are abstractions and so timeless, of course, but it can happen that certain concepts are instantiated only as time goes on. The universe is, needless to say, indifferent to our concepts. But we care very much about the instantiation of the concepts on which the concept of thought depends: such concepts as belief, desire, intention, intentional action, memory, perception, and all the rest of our human attitudes and attributes.

Let me begin by saying why it is that in my view to try to say anything interesting and deep about the emergence of thought is so difficult. The reason is that there are so many concepts that we must have in order to talk about or describe thinking, acting on a reason, believing, or doubting, all of which depend on each other. This is the *holism of the mental*, the interdependence of various aspects of mentality. Within any one dimension of mentality, such as belief, it seems clear that it is impossible to take an atomistic approach, because it is impossible to make sense of the idea of having only one or two beliefs. Beliefs do not come one at a time: what identifies a belief and makes it the belief that it is is the relationship (among other factors) to other beliefs. One cannot believe that he or she is seeing a cat without believing many other things: one must know what a cat is, what seeing is, and above all, one must recognize the possibility, however remote, that one may be wrong. Some people suppose that a dog might have such an isolated belief, but it seems to me, for the very reasons I am now rehearsing, that dogs do not have beliefs, or any other propositional attitudes. They do not form judgements.

The reason neither a dog nor any other creature can have a single belief, such as that it is seeing a cat, is that what identifies a belief is what we loosely call its *propositional content*. Thus, to have a belief about a cat, one must have mastery of the concepts that are involved in this judgement or belief. A creature does not have the concept of a cat merely because it can discriminate cats from other things in its environment. Mice are very good at telling cats apart from trees, lions, and snakes. But being able to discriminate cats is not the same thing as having the concept of a cat. You have the concept of a cat only if you can make sense of the idea of *misapplying* the concept, of believing or judging that something is a cat which is not a cat. To have the concept of a cat, you must have the concept of an animal, or at least of a continuing physical object, the concept of an object that moves in certain ways, something that can move freely in its environment, something that has sensations. There is no fixed list of things you have to know about, or associate with, felinity; but unless you have a lot of beliefs about what a cat is, you don't have the concept of a cat.

Because of the fact that beliefs are individuated and identified by their relations to other beliefs, one must have a large number of beliefs if one is to have any. Beliefs support one another, and give each other content. Beliefs also have logical relations to one another. As a result, unless one's beliefs are roughly consistent with each other, there is no identifying the contents of beliefs. A degree of rationality or consistency is therefore a condition for having beliefs.

This is not to say everyone is perfectly rational; anyone is capable of making a mistake in logic, or of entertaining beliefs that are inconsistent with each other. (Both Frege and Quine, for example, wrote books based on inconsistent logics.) But there is a limit to how inconsistent a person can be and still be credited with clearly defined attitudes. Each belief must be involved with other beliefs with which it is consistent if it is to be identified as having a clear content. Inconsistency, or other forms of irrationality, can occur only within the space of reasons; inconsistencies are perturbations of rationality, not mere absence of rationality.

I am insisting, then, that one must have a quite fully developed set of basic concepts in order to have any concepts at all. And I have hardly begun to sketch the degree of interdependence among beliefs. For there are, in addition to the logical relations, relations of evidential support. While few concepts can be defined in terms of their empirical content, belief in some factual matters must count in favor of the truth of others; such relations of evidential or inductive support are essential to the identity of many beliefs.

In addition to the relations among beliefs, there are the relations between beliefs on the one hand and evaluative attitudes on the other. It is doubtful that a creature could be credited with beliefs if it did not also have desires, for it is an essential aspect of beliefs that they affect, and are evidenced by, behavior. Evaluative attitudes, including desires, intentions, moral convictions, views about duties, and obligations, are also propositional attitudes. This is not always obvious from the grammar of the expressions we use to attribute such attitudes. We speak, for example, of wanting an apple. If someone says, 'I want an apple', it may be rude but it would always be appropriate to ask, 'And what do you want it for?' It makes no sense to say, 'I just want the apple, not for anything or in any particular way'. I might reply, 'All right, you've got it. There it is in the tree. What more do you want?' The answer could be, 'I want it in my hand; or in my basket; or detached from the tree and in my stomach, etc.'. Wants and desires are directed to propositional contents. What one wants is *that* it be true that one has the apple in hand, or ready to eat. Similarly for intentions. Someone who intends to go to the opera intends to make it the case *that* he is at the opera.

Beliefs and desires conspire to cause, rationalize, and explain intentional actions. We act intentionally for reasons, and our reasons always include both values and beliefs. We would not act unless there were some value or end we hoped to achieve (or some supposed evil we hoped to avoid), and we believed our course of action was a way of realizing our aim. Decision theory is a way of systematizing the relations among beliefs, desires, and actions. It does this by imposing a complex, but clearly defined, pattern on the way in which people's beliefs and desires interact. Decision theory is often derided as a false description of how people actually act; great ingenuity has gone into tricking subjects into making a series of choices inconsistent according to the theory. As a description of actual behavior, decision theory seems false because there is no completely satisfactory way to test it; the test always depends on exactly how the theory is given empirical application. Nevertheless, the theory answers to our intuitions about how actual decisions are made; in effect it simply spells out our commonsense apparatus for explaining intentional action. For we all, whether we think about it or not, make our decisions in terms of how we weigh the values of various possible outcomes of our actions, and how likely we think one or another course of action is to attain those values. We understand why someone acts as he does only by supposing that he or she values to various degrees the possible results of action, and how probable he or she thinks a given action is to produce one or another result. So although not capable of precise predictions of actual choices, decision theory nevertheless corresponds to our intuitions about how actual decisions are made, and so is part of our commonsense apparatus for explaining intentional behavior.

In these remarks, I am emphasizing the holism of the mental, the extent to which various aspects of the mental depend on each other. There are, as I have argued, no beliefs without many related beliefs, no beliefs without desires, no desires without beliefs, no intentions without both beliefs and desires. Conceptually, actions themselves belong to the realm of the mental, for a piece of behavior counts as an action only if there is some description under which it is intentional, and so can be explained as done for a reason. Of course, any action will be unintentional under many descriptions. Like any object or event, actions can be described in endless ways. Thus if I intentionally sit down, I unintentionally move some air molecules out of the way; I unintentionally depress the cushion on which I sit; I unintentionally change the center of gravity of the earth, the solar system, and our home galaxy. Even our failures are intentional. Not that we intend to fail, of course; the point is that in failing there nevertheless is something we are doing on purpose. If my return of serve goes long, an intention failed; still, I did intentionally strike the ball.

You will see my strategy. I am enlarging the field of the mental aspects of life all of which must emerge together. Intentional action cannot emerge before belief and desire, for an intentional action is one explained by beliefs and desires that caused it; beliefs can't emerge one at a time, since the content of each belief depends on its place in the nexus of further beliefs; and so on. It is the holism of the mental that makes its emergence so difficult to describe. There cannot be a sequence of emerging features of the mental, not if those features are to be described in the usual mentalistic vocabulary. Of course, everything in the universe and its history can in principle be described in the language of physics, and so each stage in the emergence of thought can be described in physical terms. But this will fail as an explanation of the emergence of the mental since we do not have, and cannot expect to find, a way of mapping events described in the physical vocabulary onto events described in the mental vocabulary.

The difficulty in describing the emergence of mental phenomena is a conceptual problem: it is the difficulty of describing the early stages in the maturing of reason, the stages that precede the situation in which concepts like intention, belief, and desire have clear application. In both the evolution of thought in the history of mankind, and the evolution of thought in an individual, there is a stage at which there is no thought followed by a subsequent stage at which there is thought. To describe the emergence of thought would be to describe the process which leads from the first to the second of these stages. What we lack is a satisfactory vocabulary for describing the intermediate steps. We are able to describe what a preverbal child does by employing the language of neurology, or in crude behavioristic terms we can describe movements and the sounds emitted. You can deceive yourself into thinking that the child is talking if it makes sounds which, if made by a genuine language user, would have a definite meaning. (It is even possible to do this with chimpanzees.) But words, like thoughts, have a familiar meaning, a propositional content, only if they occur in a rich context, for such a context is required to give the words or thoughts a location and a meaningful function. If a mouse had vocal cords of the right sort, you could train it to say 'Cheese'. But that word would not have a meaning when uttered by the mouse, nor would the mouse understand what it 'said'. Infants utter words in this way; if they did not, they would never come to have a language. But if you want to describe what is going on in the head of the child when it has a few words which it utters in appropriate situations, you will fail for lack of the right sort of words of your own. We have many vocabularies for describing nature when we regard it as mindless, and we have a mentalistic vocabulary for describing thought and intentional action; what we lack is a way of describing what is in between. This is particularly evident when we speak of the 'intentions' and 'desires' of simple animals. We have no better way to explain what they do.

It is not that we have a clear idea what sort of language we could use to describe half-formed minds; there may be a very deep conceptual difficulty or impossibility involved. That means there is a perhaps insuperable problem in giving a full description of the emergence of thought. I am thankful that I am not in the field of developmental psychology.

Despite these pessimistic remarks, I do have some suggestions about how we might approach the problem of saying something intelligible about the emergence of thought. There is a prelinguistic, precognitive situation which seems to me to constitute a necessary condition for thought and language, a condition that can exist independent of thought, and can therefore precede it. Both in the case of nonhuman animals and in the case of small children, it is a condition that can be observed to obtain. The basic situation is one that involves two or more creatures simultaneously in interaction with each other and with the world they share; it is what I call *triangulation*. It is the result of a threefold interaction, an interaction which is twofold from the point of view of each of the two agents: each is interacting simultaneously with the world and with the other agent. To put this in a slightly different way, each creature learns to correlate the reactions of other creatures with changes or objects in the world to which it also reacts. One sees this in its simplest form in a school of fish, where each fish reacts almost instantaneously to the motions of the others. This is apparently a reaction that is wired in. A learned reaction can be observed in certain monkeys which make three distinguishable sounds depending on whether they see a snake, an eagle, or a lion approaching; the other monkeys, perhaps without seeing the threat themselves, react to the warning sounds in ways appropriate to the different dangers, by climbing trees, running, or hiding. But on reflection we realize that the behavior of these primates, complex and purposeful as it is, cannot be due to propositional beliefs, desires, or intentions, nor does their mode of communication constitute a language.

Nevertheless, the triangle I have indicated is essential to the existence, and hence to the emergence, of thought. For without the triangle, there are two aspects of thought for which we cannot account. These two aspects are the objectivity of thought and the empirical content of thoughts about the external world.

Thought, propositional thought, is objective in the sense that it has a content which is true or false independent (with rare exceptions) of the existence of the thought or the thinker. Furthermore, this is a fact of which a thinker must be aware; one cannot believe something, or doubt it, without knowing that what one believes or doubts may be either true or false and that one may be wrong. Where do we get the idea that we may be mistaken, that things may not be as we think they are? Wittgenstein has suggested, or at least I take him to have suggested, that we would not have the concept of getting things wrong or right if it were not for our interactions with other people. The triangle I have described stands for the simplest interpersonal situation. In it two (or more) creatures each correlate their own reactions to external phenomena with the reactions of the other. Once these correlations are set up, each creature is in a position to expect the external phenomenon when it perceives the associated reaction of the other. What introduces the possibility of error is the occasional failure of the expectation; the reactions do not correlate. Wittgenstein expresses this idea when he talks of the difference between following a rule and merely thinking one is following a rule; he says that following the rule (getting things right) is at bottom a matter of doing as others do.[1] Of course, the others may sometimes be wrong. The point isn't that consensus defines the concept of truth but that it creates the space for its application. If this is right, then thought as well as language is necessarily social.

Social interaction, triangulation, also gives us the only account of how experience gives a specific content to our thoughts. Without other people with whom to share responses to a mutual environment, there is no answer to the question what it is in the world to which we are responding. The reason has to do with the ambiguity of the concept of cause. It is essential to resolve these ambiguities, since it is, in the simplest cases, what causes a belief that gives it its content. In the present case, the cause is doubly indeterminate: with respect to width, and with respect to distance. The first ambiguity concerns

---

[1] But see the caveats of Essay 8.

how much of the total cause of a belief is relevant to content. The brief answer is that it is the part or aspect of the total cause that typically causes relevantly similar responses. What makes the responses relevantly similar in turn is the fact that others find those responses similar; once more it is the social sharing of reactions that makes the objectivity of content available. The second problem has to do with the ambiguity of the relevant stimulus, whether it is proximal (at the skin, say) or distal. What makes the distal stimulus the relevant determiner of content is again its social character; it is the cause that is shared. The stimulus is thus triangulated; it is where causes converge in the world.

The triangular relationship between agents and an environment to which they mutually react is, I have argued, necessary to thought. It is not sufficient, as is shown by the fact that it can exist in animals we do not credit with judgement. For this reason we are in a position to say something about a situation that must exist if thought does, but it is a situation that can exist independently, and so can precede thought in the order of things. It can exist first, and it surely does. Thus we can say that a certain kind of primitive social interaction is part of the story of how thought emerged.

What more is needed for thought? I think the answer is language. In itself, this is not much help, since it is obvious that a creature that has a language can think; language is an instrument for the expression of propositional contents. Still, we can ask why language is essential to thought. The reason, stated briefly, is that unless the base line of the triangle, the line between the two agents, is strengthened to the point where it can implement the communication of propositional contents, there is no way the agents can make use of the triangular situation to form judgements about the world. Only when language is in place can creatures appreciate the concept of objective truth. There is much more that can be said about the deep relationship between language as a means of interpersonal communication and thought, but I shall here assume this relationship, and make use of it to say something more about the emergence of thought. Language offers us the opportunity to make relatively sharp comparisons among various linguistic and prelinguistic symbol systems, and various ways of describing them.

For this purpose, I suggest that we think of formal semantic theories in analogy with theories of fundamental measurement. In a theory of fundamental measurement, there are one or more primitive concepts; in the case of the measurement of weight, for example, these may be the relation of one thing being *at least as heavy as* another and the operation of *adding* one thing to another (this is a function that maps two things on to their sum). These concepts are not defined, but before the theory can be applied to, or tested against, some collection of objects, a method for giving an empirical content to the primitives must be indicated. (Thus *a* is at least as heavy as *b* if *a* does not go up in the pan of an equal-arm balance which holds *b* in the other pan.) A set of *axioms* then specifies the logical properties of the primitives and the entities to be measured. (So the axioms for weight will specify that the relation of being at least as heavy as is transitive, and that the sum of *a* and *b* is at least as heavy as the sum of *b* and *a*.)

The aim of the theory is to describe in precise terms the sort of structure a set of entities must have if we are to assign weights to them. If weights are to have the properties we intuitively expect, the axioms must be proven sufficient to account for these properties. One of the things we want to prove (*about* the theory, not *in* the theory) is a representation theorem, which states that numbers can be assigned to the objects covered by the theory in a way that keeps track of the relations in weight among the different objects. The second thing to be proven is a uniqueness theorem, which states that if one set of numbers represents the weights of objects, then any other set of numbers that is related to the first set by a certain kind of transformation will represent the weights just as well. In the case of weight, multiplication by any positive constant will transform one measure into another; weights in pounds are as good as weights in kilos.

Now let me compare a semantic theory for some speaker or group of speakers. Tarski's truth definitions, when modified to apply to natural languages, may be viewed as such theories. Like a theory for the measurement of weight, a semantic theory will place restrictions on one or more primitive concepts. The most important primitive is that of truth. (Here I deviate from Tarski's interests and intentions. Where he *defined* truth for particular languages, I have in mind axiomatizations of a general, and hence indefinable, concept of truth. This course risks what Tarski sought to avoid, namely inconsistency.) The theory imposes a certain structure on any language it can describe; in giving the truth conditions of all the sentences of a language, it necessarily defines the logical relations among sentences.

We can think of such a theory as saying what is needed in order to understand a language; it describes what a speaker intuitively knows about his own language, and it can serve to interpret what such a speaker says. The adequacy of the theory for these purposes can be shown by demonstrating that one can represent the properties of the object language in some language one understands. Thus the theory serves to validate a translation manual. Just as we use numbers as a convenient way of keeping track of the weights of objects, we keep track of the semantic features of a language by using sentences we understand. What makes the numbers so suited to this job is that we know exactly what structure they have. In much the same way, the sentences of a language we understand have a known structure which we can use to understand other speakers.

Different forms of measurement make use of different properties of the numbers; roughly speaking, the more properties of the numbers they use, the more powerful or informative the mode of measurement. For example, when numbers are used to keep track of the members of a team, their only significance is that one number is different from another. The Mohs hardness scale makes use of the fact that one number is larger than another: any other ten numbers (besides those actually used, 1–10), as long as ordered in ascending magnitude, would do as well. Any linear transformation of the Fahrenheit temperature scale would serve, while the more powerful weight and distance scales allow only multiplication by a positive constant. In the case of temperature, two numbers are arbitrary, the zero point, and the numerical value of an interval; as a result, it makes no sense to say one body is twice as warm as another. On the other hand, one body can weigh twice as much as another.

This gives us a way of thinking about the relative expressive powers of languages. It is intuitively clear that many sentences are equivalent in what they convey. Thus it makes sense to ask: in how many different ways could we assign our own sentences to the sentences of another language and still capture the same information (that is, how many of these ways would constitute equally satisfactory translation manuals?). Of course, a translation manual doesn't translate one sentence at a time; the manual is a function that maps all of the sentences of one language onto the sentences of another. (Just as you can't compare weights in pounds with weights in kilos, so you can't change translation manuals without notice, for this would destroy the relations among sentences.) What we must consider, then, are total systems of translation. The claim that there are such empirically equivalent systems is Quine's thesis of the indeterminacy of translation: you could keep track of everything you could ever learn about what someone means by what they say, and therefore everything that they mean, in different ways.

What is clear is that the more different ways there are of representing another language in our own, the less expressive power that language has (from our point of view, of course). Let us consider some examples. All languages have a finite basic vocabulary. We can imagine a language with just proper names and predicates. Such a language must have a finite number of sentences, so our theory need do no more than match some sentence of our own to each of the sentences in the other language. The semantics of such a language are simple indeed: there is no need to break sentences down into parts, no reason to employ recursive devices, no grounds for attributing an ontology. If you consider how simple the semantics of such a language can be, you must wonder whether it ought to be called a language; after all, a 'language' that does not require that we find a relation between its parts ('words') and entities in the world barely merits the term.

We advance a step in complexity by introducing the truth-functional connectives like the signs of conjunction, negation, alternation, and the material conditional ('and', 'not', 'or', 'if . . . then . . .'). There now will be an infinity of sentences, since one can add negation to any sentence and get a sentence, or conjoin a sentence to any sentence and produce another sentence. This introduces the element of productivity, the possibility of producing and understanding new sentences on the basis of simple syntactic and semantic rules. The semantics remain elementary, however, since the semantics for our first, finite language still suffice to give the truth conditions of the atomic sentences, and the truth tables give the semantics of the molecular sentences. The only parts of speech that need to be distinguished are the simplest sentences and sentential connectives; ontology is still waiting in the wings.

The last stage requires a leap; it introduces quantification, the concepts expressed by the words 'some' and 'all'. Once we advance to this stage, we have arrived at languages that match, or begin to match, our own in complexity. The semantics must distinguish predicates of various orders, singular terms, and expressions that do the work of variables (pronouns and the like), and, of course, the quantifiers. For the first time, it is necessary to find structure in the simplest sentences, and to correlate predicates and singular terms with objects. It is here, in my opinion, that we reach the degree of expressive sophistication that we associate with thought, for it is only at this level that there is positive evidence that the speaker of the language can predicate properties of objects and events. It was Alfred Tarski who made this point clear, for it was he who first showed what was required if we are to characterize truth for languages with general quantification. He did this by introducing the concept of *satisfaction* which is a relation between predicates of any degree of complexity and objects in the world.[2]

It is not necessary to be dogmatic about where thought, or language, begins in order to appreciate the relative clarity that formal semantics and the analogy with measurement theory bring to our thinking about the emergence of thought. For however troubled and vague our attempts to describe the stages leading up to thought and language may be, semantics and measurement theory give us a platform from which to distinguish levels of development from an objective standpoint.

[2] Alfred Tarski, 'The Concept of Truth in Formalized Languages'.

OBJECTIVE

10 *A Coherence Theory of Truth and Knowledge*

In this essay I defend what may as well be called a coherence theory of truth and knowledge. The theory I defend is not in competition with a correspondence theory, but depends for its defense on an argument that purports to show that coherence yields correspondence.

The importance of the theme is obvious. If coherence is a test of truth, there is a direct connection with epistemology, for we have reason to believe many of our beliefs cohere with many others, and in that case we have reason to believe many of our beliefs are true. When the beliefs are true, then the primary conditions for knowledge would seem to be satisfied.

Someone might try to defend a coherence theory of truth without defending a coherence theory of knowledge, perhaps on the ground that the holder of a coherent set of beliefs might lack a reason to believe his beliefs coherent. This is not likely, but it may be that someone, though he has true beliefs, and good reasons for holding them, does not appreciate the relevance of reason to belief. Such a one may best be viewed as having knowledge he does not know he has: he thinks he is a skeptic. In a word, he is a philosopher.

Setting aside aberrant cases, what brings truth and knowledge together is meaning. If meanings are given by objective truth conditions, there is a question how we can know that the conditions are satisfied, for this would appear to require a confrontation between what we believe and reality; and the idea of such a confrontation is absurd. But if coherence is a test of truth, then coherence is a test for judging that objective truth conditions are satisfied, and we no longer need to explain meaning on the basis of possible confrontation. My slogan is: correspondence without confrontation. Given a correct epistemology, we can be realists in all departments. We can accept objective truth conditions as the key to meaning, a realist view of truth, and we can insist that knowledge is of an objective world independent of our thought or language.

Since there is not, as far as I know, a theory that deserves to be called 'the' coherence theory, let me characterize the sort of view I want to defend. It is obvious that not every consistent set of interpreted sentences contains only true sentences, since one such set might contain just the consistent sentence *s* and another just the negation of *s*. And adding more sentences, while maintaining consistency, will not help. We can imagine endless state-descriptions—maximal consistent descriptions—which do not describe our world.

My coherence theory concerns beliefs, or sentences held true by someone who understands them. I do not want to say, at this point, that every possible coherent set of beliefs is true (or contains mostly true beliefs). I shy away from this because it is so unclear what is possible. At one extreme, it might be held that the range of possible maximal sets of beliefs is as wide as the range of possible maximal sets of sentences, and then there would be no point to insisting that a defensible coherence theory concerns beliefs and not propositions or sentences. But there are other ways of conceiving what it is possible to believe which would justify saying not only that all actual coherent belief systems are largely correct but that all possible ones are also. The difference between the two notions of what it is possible to believe depends on what we suppose about the nature of belief, its interpretation, its causes, its holders, and its patterns. Beliefs for me are states of people with intentions, desires, sense organs; they are states that are caused by, and cause, events inside and outside the bodies of their entertainers. But even given all these constraints, there are many things people do believe, and many more that they could. For all such cases, the coherence theory applies.

Of course some beliefs are false. Much of the point of the concept of belief is the potential gap it introduces between what is held to be true and what is true. So mere coherence, no matter how strongly coherence is plausibly defined, cannot guarantee that what is believed is so. All that a coherence theory can maintain is that most of the beliefs in a coherent total set of beliefs are true.

This way of stating the position can at best be taken as a hint, since there is no useful way to count beliefs, and so no clear meaning to the idea that most of a person's beliefs are true. A somewhat better way to put the point is to say there is a presumption in favor of the truth of a belief that coheres with a significant mass of belief. Every belief in a coherent total set of beliefs is justified in the light of this presumption, much as every intentional action taken by a rational agent (one whose choices, beliefs, and desires cohere in the sense of Bayesian decision theory) is justified. So to repeat, if knowledge is justified true belief, then it would seem that all the true beliefs of a consistent believer constitute knowledge. This conclusion, though too vague and hasty to be right, contains an important core of truth, as I shall argue. Meanwhile I merely note the many problems asking for treatment: What exactly does coherence demand? How much of inductive practice should be included, how much of the true theory (if there is one) of evidential support must be in there? Since no person has a completely consistent body of convictions, coherence with *which* beliefs creates a presumption of truth? Some of these problems will be put in better perspective presently.

It should be clear that I do not hope to define truth in terms of coherence and belief. Truth is beautifully transparent compared to belief and coherence, and I take it as a primitive concept. Truth, as applied to utterances of sentences, shows the disquotational feature enshrined in Tarski's Convention T, and that is enough to fix its domain of application. Relative to a language or a speaker, of course, so there is more to truth than Convention T; there is whatever carries over from language to language or speaker to speaker. What Convention T, and the trite sentences it declares true, like ' "Grass is green", spoken by an English speaker, is true if and only if grass is green', reveal is that the truth of an utterance depends on just two things: what the words as spoken mean, and how the world is arranged. There is no further relativism to a conceptual scheme, a way of viewing things, or a perspective. Two interpreters, as unlike in culture, language, and point of view as you please, can disagree over whether an utterance is true, but only if they differ on how things are in the world they share, or what the utterance means.

I think we can draw two conclusions from these simple reflections. First, truth is correspondence with the way things are. (There is no straightforward and nonmisleading way to state this; to get things right, a detour is necessary through the concept of satisfaction in terms of which truth is characterized.[1]) So if a coherence theory of

---

[1] See my 'True to the Facts', essay 3 in *Inquiries into Truth and Interpretation*, and 'Afterthoughts' in this volume.

truth is acceptable, it must be consistent with a correspondence theory. Second, a theory of knowledge that allows that we can know the truth must be a nonrelativized, noninternal form of realism. So if a coherence theory of knowledge is acceptable, it must be consistent with such a form of realism. My form of realism seems to be neither Hilary Putnam's internal realism nor his metaphysical realism.[2] It is not internal realism because internal realism makes truth relative to a scheme, and this is an idea I do not think is intelligible.[3] A major reason, in fact, for accepting a coherence theory is the unintelligibility of the dualism of a conceptual scheme and a 'world' waiting to be coped with. But my realism is certainly not Putnam's metaphysical realism, for *it* is characterized by being 'radically non-epistemic', which implies that all our best-researched and -established thoughts and theories may be false. I think the independence of belief and truth requires only that *each* of our beliefs may be false. But of course a coherence theory cannot allow that all of them can be wrong.

But why not? Perhaps it is obvious that the coherence of a belief with a substantial body of belief enhances its chance of being true, provided there is reason to suppose the body of belief is true, or largely so. But how can coherence alone supply grounds for belief? Mayhap the best we can do to justify one belief is to appeal to other beliefs. But then the outcome would seem to be that we must accept philosophical skepticism, no matter how unshaken in practice our beliefs remain.

This is skepticism in one of its traditional garbs. It asks: why couldn't all my beliefs hang together and yet be comprehensively false about the actual world? Mere recognition of the fact that it is absurd or worse to try to *confront* our beliefs, one by one, or as a whole, with what they are about does not answer the question nor show the question unintelligible. In short, even a mild coherence theory like mine must provide a skeptic with a reason for supposing coherent beliefs are true. The partisan of a coherence theory can't allow assurance to come from outside the system of belief, while nothing inside can produce support except as it can be shown to rest, finally or at once, on something independently trustworthy.

---

[2] Hilary Putnam, *Meaning and the Moral Sciences*, 125.
[3] See my 'On the Very Idea of a Conceptual Scheme', essay 13 in *Inquiries into Truth and Interpretation*.

It is natural to distinguish coherence theories from others by reference to the question whether or not justification can or must come to an end. But this does not define the positions, it merely suggests a form the argument may take. For there are coherence theorists who hold that some beliefs can serve as the basis for the rest, while it would be possible to maintain that coherence is not enough, although giving reasons never comes to an end. What distinguishes a coherence theory is simply the claim that nothing can count as a reason for holding a belief except another belief. Its partisan rejects as unintelligible the request for a ground or source of justification of another ilk. As Rorty has put it, 'nothing counts as justification unless by reference to what we already accept, and there is no way to get outside our beliefs and our language so as to find some test other than coherence'.[4] About this I am, as you see, in agreement with Rorty. Where we differ, if we do, is on whether there remains a question how, given that we cannot 'get outside our beliefs and our language so as to find some test other than coherence', we nevertheless can have knowledge of, and talk about, an objective public world which is not of our own making. I think this question does remain, while I suspect that Rorty doesn't think so. If this is his view, then he must think I am making a mistake in trying to answer the question. Nevertheless, here goes.

It will promote matters at this point to review very hastily some of the reasons for abandoning the search for a basis for knowledge outside the scope of our beliefs. By 'basis' here I mean specifically an epistemological basis, a source of justification.

The attempts worth taking seriously attempt to ground belief in one way or another on the testimony of the senses: sensation, perception, the given, experience, sense data, the passing show. All such theories must explain at least these two things: what, exactly, is the relation between sensation and belief that allows the first to justify the second? and, why should we believe our sensations are reliable, that is, why should we trust our senses?

The simplest idea is to identify certain beliefs with sensations. Thus Hume seems not to have distinguished between perceiving a green spot and perceiving that a spot is green. (An ambiguity in the word 'idea' was a great help here.) Other philosophers noted Hume's confusion, but tried to attain the same results by reducing the gap

---

[4] Richard Rorty, *Philosophy and the Mirror of Nature*, 178.

between perception and judgement to zero by attempting to formulate judgements that do not go beyond stating that the perception or sensation or presentation exists (whatever that may mean). Such theories do not justify beliefs on the basis of sensations, but try to justify certain beliefs by claiming that they have exactly the same epistemic content as a sensation. There are two difficulties with such a view: first, if the basic beliefs do not exceed in content the corresponding sensation, they cannot support any inference to an objective world; and second, there are no such beliefs.

A more plausible line is to claim that we cannot be wrong about how things appear to us to be. If we believe we have a sensation, we do; this is held to be an analytic truth, or a fact about how language is used.

It is difficult to explain this supposed connection between sensations and some beliefs in a way that does not invite skepticism about other minds, and in the absence of an adequate explanation, there should be a doubt about the implications of the connection for justification. But in any case, it is unclear how, on this line, sensations justify the belief in those sensations. The point is rather that such beliefs require no justification, for the existence of the belief entails the existence of the sensation, and so the existence of the belief entails its own truth. Unless something further is added, we are back to another form of coherence theory.

Emphasis on sensation or perception in matters epistemological springs from the obvious thought: sensations are what connect the world and our beliefs, and they are candidates for justifiers because we often are aware of them. The trouble we have been running into is that the justification seems to depend on the awareness, which is just another belief.

Let us try a bolder tack. Suppose we say that sensations themselves, verbalized or not, justify certain beliefs that go beyond what is given in sensation. So, under certain conditions, having the sensation of seeing a green light flashing may justify the belief that a green light is flashing. The problem is to see how the sensation justifies the belief. Of course if someone has the sensation of seeing a green light flashing, it is likely, under certain circumstances, that a green light is flashing. *We* can say this, since we know of his sensation, but *he* can't say it, since we are supposing he is justified without having to depend on believing he has the sensation. Suppose he believed he didn't have the sensation. Would the sensation still justify him in the belief in an objective flashing green light?

The relation between a sensation and a belief cannot be logical, since sensations are not beliefs or other propositional attitudes. What then is the relation? The answer is, I think, obvious: the relation is causal. Sensations cause some beliefs and in *this* sense are the basis or ground of those beliefs. But a causal explanation of a belief does not show how or why the belief is justified.

The difficulty of transmuting a cause into a reason plagues the anticoherentist again if he tries to answer our second question: what justifies the belief that our senses do not systematically deceive us? For even if sensations justify belief in sensation, we do not yet see how they justify belief in external events and objects.

According to Quine, science tells us that 'our only source of information about the external world is through the impact of light rays and molecules upon our sensory surfaces'.[5] What worries me is how to read the words 'source' and 'information'. Certainly it is true that events and objects in the external world cause us to believe things about the external world, and much, if not all, of the causality takes a route through the sense organs. The notion of information, however, applies in a nonmetaphorical way only to the engendered beliefs. So 'source' has to be read simply as 'cause' and 'information' as 'true belief' or 'knowledge'. Justification of beliefs caused by our senses is not yet in sight.

The approach to the problem of justification we have been tracing must be wrong. We have been trying to see it this way: a person has all his beliefs about the world—that is, all his beliefs. How can he tell if they are true, or apt to be true? This is possible, we have been assuming, only by connecting his beliefs to the world, confronting

---

[5] W. V. Quine, 'The Nature of Natural Knowledge', 68. Many other passages in Quine suggest that he hopes to assimilate sensory causes to evidence. In *Word and Object*, 22, he writes that 'surface irritations . . . exhaust our clues to an external world'. In *Ontological Relativity*, 75, we find that 'The stimulation of his sensory receptors is all the evidence anybody has had to go on, ultimately, in arriving at his picture of the world.' On the same page: 'Two cardinal tenets of empiricism remain unassailable . . . One is that whatever evidence there *is* for science *is* sensory evidence. The other . . . is that all inculcation of meanings of words, must rest ultimately on sensory evidence.' In *The Roots of Reference*, 37–8, Quine says 'observations' are basic 'both in the support of theory and in the learning of language', and then goes on, 'What are observations? They are visual, auditory, tactual, olfactory. They are sensory, evidently, and thus subjective . . . Should we say then that the observation is not the sensation . . . ? No . . .'. Quine goes on to abandon talk of observations in favor of talk of observation sentences. But of course observation sentences, unlike observations, cannot play the role of evidence unless we have reason to believe they are true.

certain of his beliefs with the deliverances of the senses one by one, or perhaps confronting the totality of his beliefs with the tribunal of experience. No such confrontation makes sense, for of course we can't get outside our skins to find out what is causing the internal happening of which we are aware. Introducing intermediate steps or entities into the causal chain, like sensations or observations, serves only to make the epistemological problem more obvious. For if the intermediaries are merely causes, they don't justify the beliefs they cause, while if they deliver information, they may be lying. The moral is obvious. Since we can't swear intermediaries to truthfulness, we should allow no intermediaries between our beliefs and their objects in the world. Of course there are causal intermediaries. What we must guard against are epistemic intermediaries.

There are common views of language that encourage bad epistemology. This is no accident, of course, since theories of meaning are connected with epistemology through attempts to answer the question how one determines that a sentence is true. If knowing the meaning of a sentence (knowing how to give a correct interpretation of it) involves, or is, knowing how it could be recognized to be true, then the theory of meaning raises the same question we have been struggling with, for giving the meaning of a sentence will demand that we specify what would justify asserting it. Here the coherentist will hold that there is no use looking for a source of justification outside of other sentences held true, while the foundationalist will seek to anchor at least some words or sentences to non-verbal rocks. This view is held, I think, both by Quine and by Michael Dummett.

Dummett and Quine differ, to be sure. In particular, they disagree about holism, the claim that the truth of our sentences must be tested together rather than one by one. And they disagree also, and consequently, about whether there is a useful distinction between analytic and synthetic sentences, and about whether a satisfactory theory of meaning can allow the sort of indeterminacy Quine argues for. (On all these points, I am Quine's faithful student.)

But what concerns me here is that Quine and Dummett agree on a basic principle, which is that whatever there is to meaning must be traced back somehow to experience, the given, or patterns of sensory stimulation, something intermediate between belief and the usual objects our beliefs are about. Once we take this step, we open the door to skepticism, for we must then allow that a very great many—perhaps most—of the sentences we hold to be true may in fact be false. It is ironical. Trying to make meaning accessible has made truth inaccessible. When meaning goes epistemological in this way, truth and meaning are necessarily divorced. One can, of course, arrange a shotgun wedding by redefining truth as what we are justified in asserting. But this does not marry the original mates.

Take Quine's proposal that whatever there is to the meaning (information value) of an observation sentence is determined by the patterns of sensory stimulation that would cause a speaker to assent to or dissent from the sentence. This is a marvelously ingenious way of capturing what is appealing about verificationist theories without having to talk of meanings, sense data, or sensations; for the first time it made plausible the idea that one could, and should, do what I call the theory of meaning without need of what Quine calls meanings. But Quine's proposal, like other forms of verificationism, makes for skepticism. For clearly a person's sensory stimulations could be just as they are and yet the world outside very different. (Remember the brain in the vat.)

Quine's way of doing without meanings is subtle and complicated. He ties the meanings of some sentences directly to patterns of stimulation (which also constitute the evidence, Quine thinks, for assenting to the sentence), but the meanings of further sentences are determined by how they are conditioned to the original, or observation, sentences. The facts of such conditioning do not permit a sharp division between sentences held true by virtue of meaning and sentences held true on the basis of observation. Quine made this point by showing that if one way of interpreting a speaker's utterances was satisfactory, so were many others. This doctrine of the indeterminacy of translation, as Quine called it, should be viewed as neither mysterious nor threatening. It is no more mysterious than the fact that temperature can be measured in centigrade or Fahrenheit (or any linear transformation of those numbers). And it is not threatening because the very procedure that demonstrates the degree of indeterminacy at the same time demonstrates that what is determinate is all we need.

In my view, erasing the line between the analytic and synthetic saved philosophy of language as a serious subject by showing how it could be pursued without what there cannot be: determinate meanings. I now suggest also giving up the distinction between observation sentences and the rest. For the distinction between sentences belief in whose truth is justified by sensations and sentences belief in whose truth is justified only by appeal to other sentences held true is as anathema to the coherentist as the distinction between beliefs justified by sensations and beliefs justified only by appeal to further beliefs. Accordingly, I suggest we give up the idea that meaning or knowledge is grounded on something that counts as an ultimate source of evidence. No doubt meaning and knowledge depend on experience, and experience ultimately on sensation. But this is the 'depend' of causality, not of evidence or justification.

I have now stated my problem as well as I can. The search for an empirical foundation for meaning or knowledge leads to skepticism, while a coherence theory seems at a loss to provide any reason for a believer to believe that his beliefs, if coherent, are true. We are caught between a false answer to the skeptic, and no answer.

The dilemma is not a true one. What is needed to answer the skeptic is to show that someone with a (more or less) coherent set of beliefs has a reason to suppose his beliefs are not mistaken in the main. What we have shown is that it is absurd to look for a justifying ground for the totality of beliefs, something outside this totality which we can use to test or compare with our beliefs. The answer to our problem must then be to find a *reason* for supposing most of our beliefs are true that is not a form of *evidence*.

My argument has two parts. First I urge that a correct understanding of the speech, beliefs, desires, intentions, and other propositional attitudes of a person leads to the conclusion that most of a person's beliefs must be true, and so there is a legitimate presumption that any one of them, if it coheres with most of the rest, is true. Then I go on to claim that anyone with thoughts, and so in particular anyone who wonders whether he has any reason to suppose he is generally right about the nature of his environment, must know what a belief is, and how in general beliefs are to be detected and interpreted. These being perfectly general facts we cannot fail to use when we communicate with others, or when we try to communicate with others, or even when we merely think we are communicating with others, there is a pretty strong sense in which we can be said to know that there is a presumption in favor of the overall truthfulness of anyone's beliefs, including our own. So it is bootless for someone to ask for some *further* reassurance; that can only add to his stock of beliefs. All that is needed is that he recognize that belief is in its nature veridical.

Belief can be seen to be veridical by considering what determines the existence and contents of a belief. Belief, like the other so-called propositional attitudes, is supervenient on facts of various sorts, behavioral, neurophysiological, biological, and physical. The reason for pointing this out is not to encourage definitional or nomological reduction of psychological phenomena to something more basic, and certainly not to suggest epistemological priorities. The point is rather understanding. We gain one kind of insight into the nature of the propositional attitudes when we relate them systematically to one another and to phenomena on other levels. Since the propositional attitudes are deeply interlocked, we cannot learn the nature of one by first winning understanding of another. As interpreters, we work our way into the whole system, depending much on the pattern of inter-relationships.

Take, for example, the interdependence of belief and meaning. What a sentence means depends partly on the external circumstances that cause it to win some degree of conviction; and partly on the relations, grammatical or logical, that the sentence has to other sentences held true with varying degrees of conviction. Since these relations are themselves translated directly into beliefs, it is easy to see how meaning depends on belief. Belief, however, depends equally on meaning, for the only access to the fine structure and individuation of beliefs is through the sentences speakers and interpreters of speakers use to express and describe beliefs. If we want to illuminate the nature of meaning and belief, therefore, we need to start with something that assumes neither. Quine's suggestion, which I shall essentially follow, is to take *prompted assent* as basic, the causal relation between assenting to a sentence and the cause of such assent. This is a fair place to start the project of identifying beliefs and meanings, since a speaker's assent to a sentence depends both on what he means by the sentence and on what he believes about the world. Yet it is possible to know that a speaker assents to a sentence without knowing either what the sentence, as spoken by him, means, or what belief is expressed by it. Equally obvious is the fact that once an interpretation has been given for a sentence assented to, a belief has been attributed. If correct theories of interpretation are not unique (do not lead to uniquely correct interpretations), the same will go for attributions of belief, of course, as tied to acquiescence in particular sentences.

A speaker who wishes his words to be understood cannot systematically deceive his would-be interpreters about when he assents to sentences—that is, holds them true. As a matter of principle, then, meaning, and by its connection with meaning, belief also, are open to public determination. I shall take advantage of this fact in what follows and adopt the stance of a radical interpreter when asking about the nature of belief. What a fully informed interpreter could learn about what a speaker means is all there is to learn; the same goes for what the speaker believes.[6]

The interpreter's problem is that what he is assumed to know—the causes of assents to sentences of a speaker—is, as we have seen, the product of two things he is assumed not to know, meaning and belief. If he knew the meanings he would know the beliefs, and if he knew the beliefs expressed by sentences assented to, he would know the meanings. But how can he learn both at once, since each depends on the other?

The general lines of the solution, like the problem itself, are owed to Quine. I will, however, introduce some changes into Quine's solution, as I have into the statement of the problem. The changes are directly relevant to the issue of epistemological skepticism.

Radical interpretation (which is much, but not entirely, like Quine's radical translation) aims at producing a Tarski-style characterization of truth for the speaker's language, and a theory of his beliefs. (The second follows from the first plus the presupposed knowledge of sentences held true.) This adds little to Quine's program of translation, since translation of the speaker's language into one's own plus a theory of truth for one's own language add up to a theory of truth for the speaker. But the shift to the semantic notion of truth from the syntactic notion of translation puts the formal restrictions of a theory of truth in the foreground, and emphasizes one aspect of the close relation between truth and meaning.

The principle of charity plays a crucial role in Quine's method, and an even more crucial role in my variant. In either case, the principle directs the interpreter to translate or interpret so as to read some of his own standards of truth into the pattern of sentences held true by the speaker. The point of the principle is to make the speaker intelligible, since too great deviations from consistency and correctness leave no common ground on which to judge either conformity or difference. From a formal point of view, the principle of charity helps

---

[6] I now think it is essential, in doing radical interpretation, to include the desires of the speaker from the start, so that the springs of action and intention, both belief and desire, are related to meaning. But in the present essay it is not necessary to introduce this further factor.

solve the problem of the interaction of meaning and belief by restraining the degrees of freedom allowed belief while determining how to interpret words.

We have no choice, Quine has urged, but to read our own logic into the thoughts of a speaker; Quine says this for the sentential calculus, and I would add the same for first-order quantification theory. This leads directly to the identification of the logical constants, as well as to the assignment of a logical form to each sentence.

Something like charity operates in the interpretation of those sentences whose causes of assent come and go with time and place: when the interpreter finds a sentence of the speaker the speaker assents to regularly under conditions the interpreter recognizes, the interpreter takes those conditions to be the truth conditions of the speaker's sentence. This is only roughly right, as we shall see in a moment.

Sentences and predicates less directly geared to easily detected goings-on can, in Quine's canon, be interpreted at will, given only the constraints of interconnections with sentences conditioned directly to the world. Here I would extend the principle of charity to favor interpretations that as far as possible preserve truth: I think it makes for mutual understanding, and hence for better interpretation, to interpret what the speaker accepts as true as true when we can. In this matter, I have less choice than Quine, because I do not see how to draw the line between observation sentences and theoretical sentences at the start. There are several reasons for this, but the one most relevant to the present topic is that this distinction is ultimately based on an epistemological consideration of a sort I have renounced: observation sentences are directly based on something like sensation—patterns of sensory stimulation—and this is an idea I have been urging leads to skepticism. Without the direct tie to sensation or stimulation, the distinction between observation sentences and others can't be drawn on epistemologically significant grounds. The distinction between sentences whose causes to assent come and go with observable circumstances and those a speaker clings to through change remains, however, and offers the possibility of interpreting the words and sentences beyond the logical.

The details are not here to the point. What should be clear is that if the account I have given of how belief and meaning are related and understood by an interpreter is right, then most of the sentences a speaker holds to be true—especially the ones he holds to most stubbornly, the ones most central to the system of his beliefs—most of these sentences *are* true, at least in the opinion of the interpreter. For the only, and therefore unimpeachable, method available to the interpreter automatically puts the speaker's beliefs in accord with the standards of logic of the interpreter, and hence credits the speaker with the plain truths of logic. Needless to say, there are degrees of logical and other consistency, and perfect consistency is not to be expected. What needs emphasis is only the methodological necessity for finding consistency enough.

Analogously, it is impossible for an interpreter to understand a speaker and at the same time discover the speaker to be largely wrong about the world. For the interpreter interprets sentences held true (which is not to be distinguished from attributing beliefs) according to the events and objects in the outside world that cause the sentence to be held true.

What I take to be the important aspect of this approach is apt to be missed because the approach reverses our natural way of thinking of communication derived from situations in which understanding has already been secured. Once understanding has been secured, we are able, often, to learn what a person believes quite independently of what caused him to believe it. This may lead us to the crucial, indeed fatal, conclusion that we can in general fix what someone means independently of what he believes and independently of what caused the belief. But if I am right, we can't in general first identify beliefs and meanings and then ask what caused them. The causality plays an indispensable role in determining the content of what we say and believe. This is a fact we can be led to recognize by taking up, as we have, the interpreter's point of view.

It is an artifact of the interpreter's correct interpretation of a person's speech and attitudes that there is a large degree of truth and consistency in the thought and speech of an agent. But this is truth and consistency by the interpreter's standards. Why couldn't it happen that speaker and interpreter understand one another on the basis of shared but erroneous beliefs? This can, and no doubt often does, happen. But it cannot be the rule. For imagine for a moment an interpreter who is omniscient about the world, and about what does and would cause a speaker to assent to any sentence in his (potentially unlimited) repertoire. The omniscient interpreter, using the same method as the fallible interpreter, finds the fallible speaker largely consistent and correct. By his own standards, of course, but since these are objectively correct, the fallible speaker is seen to be largely correct and consistent by objective standards. We may also, if we want, let the omniscient interpreter turn his attention to the fallible interpreter of the fallible speaker. It turns out that the fallible interpreter can be wrong about some things, but not in general; and so he cannot share universal error with the agent he is interpreting. Once we agree to the general method of interpretation I have sketched, it becomes impossible correctly to hold that anyone could be mostly wrong about how things are.

There is, as I noted above, a key difference between the method of radical interpretation I am now recommending, and Quine's method of radical translation. The difference lies in the nature of the choice of causes that govern interpretation. Quine makes interpretation depend on patterns of sensory stimulation, while I make it depend on the external events and objects the sentence is interpreted as being about. Thus Quine's notion of meaning is tied to sensory criteria, something he thinks can be treated also as evidence. This leads Quine to give epistemic significance to the distinction between observation sentences and others, since observation sentences are supposed, by their direct conditioning to the senses, to have a kind of extralinguistic justification. This is the view against which I argued in the first part of my essay, urging that sensory stimulations are indeed part of the causal chain that leads to belief, but cannot, without confusion, be considered to be evidence, or a source of justification, for the stimulated beliefs.

What stands in the way of global skepticism of the senses is, in my view, the fact that we must, in the plainest and methodologically most basic cases, take the objects of a belief to be the causes of that belief. And what we, as interpreters, must take them to be is what they in fact are. Communication begins where causes converge: your utterance means what mine does if belief in its truth is systematically caused by the same events and objects.[7]

The difficulties in the way of this view are obvious, but I think they can be overcome. The method applies directly, at best, only to

---

[7] It is clear that the causal theory of meaning has little in common with the causal theories of reference of Kripke and Putnam. Those theories look to causal relations between names and objects of which speakers may well be ignorant. The chance of systematic error is thus increased. My causal theory does the reverse by connecting the cause of a belief with its object.

occasion sentences—the sentences assent to which is caused systematically by common changes in the world. Further sentences are interpreted by their conditioning to occasion sentences, and the appearance in them of words that appear also in occasion sentences. Among occasion sentences, some will vary in the credence they command not only in the face of environmental change, but also in the face of change of credence awarded related sentences. Criteria can be developed on this basis to distinguish degrees of observationality on internal grounds, without appeal to the concept of a basis for belief outside the circle of beliefs.

Related to these problems, and easier still to grasp, is the problem of error. For even in the simplest cases it is clear that the same cause (a rabbit scampers by) may engender different beliefs in speaker and observer, and so encourage assent to sentences which cannot bear the same interpretation. It is no doubt this fact that made Quine turn from rabbits to patterns of stimulation as the key to interpretation. Just as a matter of statistics, I'm not sure how much better one approach is than the other. Is the relative frequency with which identical patterns of stimulation will touch off assent to 'Gavagai' and 'Rabbit' greater than the relative frequency with which a rabbit touches off the same two responses in speaker and interpreter? Not an easy question to test in a convincing way. But let the imagined results speak for Quine's method. Then I must say, what I must say in any case, the problem of error cannot be met sentence by sentence, even at the simplest level. The best we can do is cope with error holistically, that is, we interpret so as to make an agent as intelligible as possible, given his actions, his utterances, and his place in the world. About some things we will find him wrong, as the necessary cost of finding him elsewhere right. As a rough approximation, finding him right means identifying the causes with the objects of his beliefs, giving special weight to the simplest cases, and countenancing error where it can be best explained.

Suppose I am right that an interpreter must so interpret as to make a speaker or agent largely correct about the world. How does this help the person himself who wonders what reason he has to think his beliefs are mostly true? How can he learn about the causal relations between the real world and his beliefs that lead the interpreter to interpret him as being on the right track?

The answer is contained in the question. In order to doubt or wonder about the provenance of his beliefs, an agent must know what belief is. This brings with it the concept of objective truth, for the notion of a belief is the notion of a state that may or may not jibe with reality. But beliefs are also identified, directly and indirectly, by their causes. What an omniscient interpreter knows a fallible interpreter gets right enough if he understands a speaker, and this is just the complicated causal truth that makes us the believers we are, and fixes the contents of our beliefs. The agent has only to reflect on what a belief is to appreciate that most of his basic beliefs are true, and among his beliefs, those most securely held and that cohere with the main body of his beliefs are the most apt to be true. The question 'how do I know my beliefs are generally true?' thus answers itself, simply because beliefs are by nature generally true. Rephrased or expanded, the question becomes, 'How can I tell whether my beliefs, which are by their nature generally true, are generally true?'

All beliefs are justified in this sense: they are supported by numerous other beliefs (otherwise they wouldn't be the beliefs they are), and have a presumption in favor of their truth. The presumption increases the larger and more significant the body of beliefs with which a belief coheres and, there being no such thing as an isolated belief, there is no belief without a presumption in its favor. In this respect, interpreter and interpreted differ. From the interpreter's point of view, methodology enforces a general presumption of truth for the body of beliefs as a whole, but the interpreter does not need to presume each particular belief of someone else is true. The general presumption applied to others does not make them globally right, as I have emphasized, but provides the background against which to accuse them of error. But from each person's own vantage point, there must be a graded presumption in favor of each of his own beliefs.

We cannot, alas, draw the picturesque and pleasant conclusion that all true beliefs constitute knowledge. For though all of a believer's beliefs are to some extent justified to him, some may not be justified enough, or in the right way, to constitute knowledge. The general presumption in favor of the truth of belief serves to rescue us from a standard form of skepticism by showing why it is impossible for all our beliefs to be false together. This leaves almost untouched the task of specifying the conditions of knowledge. I have not been concerned with the canons of evidential support (if such there be), but to show that all that counts as evidence or justification for a belief must come from the same totality of belief to which it belongs.

Afterthoughts

A few aging philosophes, which category may include Quine, Putnam, and Dummett, and certainly includes me, are still puzzling over the nature of truth and its connections or lack of connections with meaning and epistemology. Rorty thinks we should stop worrying; he believes philosophy has seen through or outgrown the puzzles and should turn to less heavy and more interesting matters. He is particularly impatient with me for not conceding that the old game is up because he finds in my work useful support for his enlightened stance; underneath my 'out-dated rhetoric' he detects the outlines of a largely correct attitude.

In 'Pragmatism, Davidson, and Truth' Rorty urges two things: that my view of truth amounts to a rejection of both coherence and correspondence theories and should properly be classed as belonging to the pragmatist tradition, and that I should not pretend that I am answering the skeptic when I am really telling him to get lost. I pretty much concur with him on both points.

In our 1983 discussion at the Pacific Division Meeting of the American Philosophical Association I agreed to stop calling my position either a coherence or a correspondence theory if he would give up the pragmatist theory of truth. He has done his part; he now explicitly rejects both James and Peirce on truth. I am glad to hold to my side of the bargain. If it had not already been published, I would now change the title of 'A Coherence Theory of Truth and Knowledge', and I would not describe the project as showing how 'coherence yields correspondence'. On internal evidence alone, as Rorty points out, my view cannot be called a correspondence theory. As long ago as 1969 ('True to the Facts'[8]) I argued that nothing can usefully and intelligibly be said to correspond to a sentence; and I repeated this in 'A Coherence Theory of Truth and Knowledge'. I thought then the fact that in characterizing truth for a language it is necessary to put words into relation with objects was enough to give some grip for the idea of correspondence; but this now seems to me a mistake. The mistake is in a way only a misnomer, but terminological infelicities have a way of breeding conceptual confusion, and so it is here. Correspondence theories have always been conceived as

---

[8] Repr. in *Inquiries into Truth and Interpretation*.

providing an explanation or analysis of truth, and this a Tarski-style theory of truth certainly does not do. I would also now reject the point generally made against correspondence theories that there is no way we could ever tell whether our sentences or beliefs correspond to reality. This criticism is at best misleading, since no one has ever explained in what such a correspondence could consist; and, worse, it is predicated on the false assumption that truth is transparently epistemic.

I also regret having called my view a 'coherence theory'. My emphasis on coherence was properly just a way of making a negative point, that 'all that counts as evidence or justification for a belief must come from the same totality of belief to which it belongs'. Of course this negative claim has typically led those philosophers who held it to conclude that reality and truth are constructs of thought; but it does not lead me to this conclusion, and for this reason if no other I ought not to have called my view a coherence theory. There is also a less weighty reason for not stressing coherence. Coherence is nothing but consistency. It is certainly in favor of a set of beliefs that they are consistent, but there is no chance that a person's beliefs will not tend to be consistent, since beliefs are individuated in part by their logical properties; what is not largely consistent with many other beliefs cannot be identified as a belief. The main thrust of 'A Coherence Theory of Truth and Knowledge' has little to do with consistency; the important thesis for which I argue is that belief is intrinsically veridical. This is the ground on which I maintain that while truth is not an epistemic concept, neither is it wholly severed from belief (as it is in different ways by both correspondence and coherence theories).

My emphasis on coherence was misplaced; calling my view a 'theory' was a plain blunder. In his paper Rorty stressed a minimalist attitude towards truth that he correctly thought we shared. It could be put this way: truth is as clear and basic a concept as we have. Tarski has given us an idea of how to apply the general concept (or try to apply it) to particular languages on the assumption that we already understand it; but of course he didn't show how to define it in general (he proved, rather, that this couldn't be done). Any further attempt to explain, define, analyze, or explicate the concept will be empty or wrong: correspondence theories, coherence theories, pragmatist theories, theories that identify truth with warranted assertability (perhaps under 'ideal' or 'optimum' conditions), theories that ask truth to explain the success of science, or serve as the ultimate outcome of science or the conversations of some élite, all such theories either add nothing to our understanding of truth or have obvious counterexamples. Why on earth should we expect to be able to reduce truth to something clearer or more fundamental? After all, the only concept Plato succeeded in defining was mud (dirt and water). Putnam's comparison of various attempts to characterize truth with the attempts to define 'good' in naturalistic terms seems to me, as it does to Rorty, apt. It also seems to apply to Putnam's identification of truth with idealized warranted assertability.[9]

A theory of truth for a speaker, or group of speakers, while not a definition of the general concept of truth, does give a firm sense of what the concept is good for; it allows us to say, in a compact and clear way, what someone who understands that speaker, or those speakers, knows. Such a theory also invites the question how an interpreter could confirm its truth—a question which without the theory could not be articulated. The answer will, as I try to show in 'A Coherence Theory of Truth and Knowledge', bring out essential relations among the concepts of meaning, truth, and belief. If I am right, each of these concepts requires the others, but none is subordinate to, much less definable in terms of, the others. Truth emerges not as wholly detached from belief (as a correspondence theory would make it) nor as dependent on human methods and powers of discovery (as epistemic theories of truth would make it). What saves truth from being 'radically non-epistemic' (in Putnam's words) is not that truth is epistemic but that belief, through its ties with meaning, is intrinsically veridical.

Finally, how about Rorty's admonition to stop trying to answer the skeptic, and tell him to get lost? A short response would be that the skeptic has been told this again and again over the millennia and never seems to listen; like the philosopher he is, he wants an argument. To spell this out a bit: there is perhaps the suggestion in Rorty's 'Pragmatism, Davidson, and Truth' that a 'naturalistic' approach to the problems of meaning and the propositional attitudes will automatically leave the skeptic no room for maneuver. This thought, whether or not it is Rorty's, is wrong. Quine's naturalized epistemology, because it is based on the empiricist premise that what we mean and what we think is conceptually (and not merely causally) founded

---

[9] Hilary Putnam, *Realism and Reason*, p. xviii.

on the testimony of the senses, is open to standard skeptical attack. I was much concerned in 'A Coherence Theory of Truth and Knowledge' to argue for an alternative approach to meaning and knowledge, and to show that if this alternative were right, skepticism could not get off the ground. I agree with Rorty to this extent; I set out not to 'refute' the skeptic, but to give a sketch of what I think to be a correct account of the foundations of linguistic communication and its implications for truth, belief, and knowledge. If one grants the correctness of this account, one can tell the skeptic to get lost.

Where Rorty and I differ, if we do, is in the importance we attach to the arguments that lead to the skeptic's undoing, and in the interest we find in the consequences for knowledge, belief, truth, and meaning. Rorty wants to dwell on where the arguments have led: to a position which allows us to dismiss the skeptic's doubts, and so to abandon the attempt to provide a general justification for knowledge claims—a justification that is neither possible nor needed. Rorty sees the history of Western philosophy as a confused and victorless battle between unintelligible skepticism and lame attempts to answer it. Epistemology from Descartes to Quine seems to me just one complex, and by no means unilluminating, chapter in the philosophical enterprise. If that chapter is coming to a close, it will be through recourse to modes of analysis and adherence to standards of clarity that have always distinguished the best philosophy, and will, with luck and enterprise, continue to do so.

11 *Empirical Content*

The dispute between Schlick and Neurath over the foundations of empirical knowledge illustrates the difficulties in trying to draw epistemological conclusions from a verificationist theory of meaning. It also shows how assuming the general correctness of science does not automatically avoid, or provide an easy answer to, skepticism. But while neither Schlick nor Neurath arrived at a satisfactory account of empirical knowledge, there are promising hints of a better theory in their writings. Following up these hints, and drawing on further ideas in Hempel, Carnap, and particularly Quine, I suggest the direction I think a naturalistic epistemology should take.

The logical positivists agreed that the empirical content of an interpreted sentence derives from its relations to a subset of sentences that report, or are based on, observation or experience. Two main sources of difficulty and dispute immediately became evident. One was the question how to characterize the relations between protocol sentences and other sentences. The history of the developments and changes in the views of the logical positivists and their followers on this problem has been masterfully recorded, as well as much contributed to, by Carl Hempel.[1] This is not my present subject.

The second question was how protocol sentences should be formulated, and what their relation to experience or observation is. This is the issue I wish to discuss, and on which Schlick and Neurath disagreed, Schlick endorsing a foundationalist epistemology and Neurath a coherence theory. The difference was expressed in fairly strong terms. Neurath described the foundationalist position as

---

[1] See Carl Hempel, 'Empiricist Criteria of Cognitive Significance: Problems and Changes', in *Aspects of Scientific Explanation*.

'related to the belief in *immediate experiences* which is current in traditional academic philosophy', and remarked that 'methodological solipsism' (Carnap's term for a view like Schlick's) does 'not become more serviceable because of the addition of the word "methodological" '.[2] Schlick in turn called Neurath's version of the coherence theory an 'astounding error'.[3]

Astounding error or not, Carnap and Hempel at one time seemed to agree with Neurath. In 1935 Hempel wrote, 'I think that there is no essential difference left between protocol statements and other statements,' and he concurred with Carnap in holding that once the question which sentences were basic was put in the 'formal mode', the answer became a matter for convention to decide. 'This insight', he concluded, echoing Carnap's words, 'eliminates from the Logical Positivist's theory of verification and truth a remainder of absolutism which is due to metaphysical tendencies'.[4] Schlick jeered at such conventionalism, saying it made truth as relative as 'all the measuring rods of physics'. In an ironic vein he added, 'and it is this view with its consequences that has been commended as banishing the last remnant of "absolutism" from philosophy'.[5]

It is not entirely clear, however, just where matters stood. Fifteen years later, in a quasi-historical article, Hempel asserted that 'The fundamental tenet of modern empiricism is the view that all non-analytic knowledge is based on experience.' He went on to explain what it means for knowledge to be based on experience: nonanalytic knowledge can be expressed by sentences that are confirmed (in a specified way) by observation sentences, which in turn are 'ascertained' to be true by direct observation.[6] This sounds more like Schlick, and indeed like the 'fatal confrontation of statements and facts' which Hempel had previously rejected.[7]

In a note added to a reprinting of 'Studies in the Logic of Confirmation'[8] Hempel suggests a way of partially reconciling the apparently opposed points of view. Truth, he and Carnap had come to

---

[2] Otto Neurath, 'Protocol Sentences'; quoted from Ayer (ed.), *Logical Positivism*, 204, 206. All subsequent page references from *Logical Positivism* are preceded by *LP*.

[3] Moritz Schlick, 'The Foundation of Knowledge', *LP* 215.

[4] Carl Hempel, 'On the Logical Positivist's Theory of Truth', 58, 59.

[5] Moritz Schlick, 'The Foundation of Knowledge', *LP* 213.

[6] Carl Hempel, 'The Empiricist Criterion of Meaning', *LP* 108–10.

[7] Carl Hempel, 'On the Logical Positivist's Theory of Truth', 51.

[8] Note 49 to 'Studies in the logic of Confirmation', in *Aspects of Scientific Explanation*.

realize in the light of Tarski's work, is a legitimate semantic notion, and should not be treated as a matter of coherence. Confirmation, on the other hand, was of two sorts, *relative* and *absolute*. The logical study of confirmation was the study of the extent to which an arbitrary set of sentences confirmed a hypothesis. In this context, one could only say that relative to a set of sentences (whatever its provenance), a hypothesis was confirmed or disconfirmed. Absolute confirmation, on the other hand, depended on a 'pragmatic' decision to treat certain sentences as true. Neurath and Carnap, Hempel suggests, were thinking of relative confirmation, which invites a coherence theory. Schlick, and Hempel in 1950, were thinking of absolute confirmation.

This important distinction of Hempel's is revealing, since it does seem at times that early discussions of protocol sentences vacillated between treating such sentences as any sentences with a specified syntax, and treating them as sentences that were accepted, perhaps on the basis of observation or experience. But the distinction cannot reconcile all the differences. The differences that remained were these: Schlick held, while Neurath denied, that protocol sentences may be established as true once and for all; Schlick claimed, while Neurath denied, that a sentence could intelligibly be said to be compared to reality. There were also differences over the question of the proper subject matter of protocols, and the question whether they reported something private or something public. Obviously, these various points are closely related to one another.

One way to approach our central problem is to ask what the nature of *evidence* is: does it consist of objects, events, facts, experiences, sensations, beliefs, propositions, or sentences? Almost every one of these possible answers can be found in the writings of the Vienna Circle.

I observe two pieces of green paper [writes Schlick] and determine that they have the same color. The proposition which asserts the sameness of color is verified, among other ways, by the fact that at the same time I have two experiences of the same color. The proposition: 'there are two spots of the same color before me now' cannot be reduced to others; it is verified by the fact that it describes the given.[9]

What exactly does the verifying? Schlick says it is the fact that he has certain experiences that are veridical. But if the same experiences were not veridical, would they still verify the same proposition? The

---

[9] Moritz Schlick, 'Positivism and Realism', *LP* 92–3.

fact that I see a piece of paper implies that there is a piece of paper, but here we do not move from evidence to hypothesis in an interesting way; we merely deduce an entailed proposition. Elsewhere, Schlick insists that we must start with statements that 'have their origin' in observation sentences; and he elaborates this as: 'they derive, as one may confidently say in the traditional way of speaking, "from experience" '.[10] In the same essay he declares that 'It is clear, and is so far as I know disputed by no one, that knowledge in life and science in *some* sense *begins* with confirmation of facts, and that the "protocol statements" in which this occurs stand in the same sense at the *beginning* of science.'[11] In another passage he says that everything goes back to what is 'immediately observed'.[12] As Ayer put it, some propositions can be 'directly confronted with the facts'.

Let me try to bring out in one further way the apparently puzzling question of the ontological status of evidence. We say that laws are confirmed by their positive instances; so the positive instances are, presumably, evidence for the laws they confirm. Suppose, for the sake of clarity in one direction, that we identify laws with universally quantified conditional sentences—sentences which are, needless to say, interpreted. What is a positive instance? Let the law have the form '$(x)(Fx \rightarrow Gx)$'. Then, Hempel suggests, it is reasonable to suppose that an *object* that is F and G confirms the law.[13] (Goodman often talks this way in *Fact, Fiction, and Forecast*.) Hempel then explains that instead of viewing confirmation as a 'relation between an object or an ordered set of objects, representing the evidence, and a sentence, representing the hypothesis', he will take it to be a relation between a sentence that describes the evidence, and the hypothesis. Thus, 'The evidence adduced in support or criticism of a scientific hypothesis is always expressed in sentences, which frequently have the character of observation reports . . . The evidence . . . consists, in the last analysis, in data accessible to what is loosely called direct observation and such data are expressible in the form of "observation reports" '.[14] What are accessible to observation are objects and events. These are not the same things as facts nor, of course, as sentences. Sentences can, in some loose sense, express facts (i.e. true propositions), and describe objects. None of what I say

[10] Moritz Schlick, 'The Foundation of Knowledge', *LP* 215.   [11] Ibid. 210.
[12] Ibid. 220.
[13] Carl Hempel, 'Studies in the Logic of Confirmation', in *Aspects of Scientific Explanation*, 14.   [14] Ibid. 21–2.

is criticism of Hempel's exemplary work on confirmation as a relation between sentences; I am using the distinction among various ways of describing positive instances of laws (or lawlike sentences) in order to emphasize the very different ways in which it is natural to talk of evidence.

Perhaps it is not strange to call a black raven—some actual bird— an *instance* of a law, but it does seem odd to say the bird is *evidence* for the law. At best this seems to be shorthand for saying it is the *fact* that this bird is a black raven that constitutes the evidence; or we could speak of the truth of the proposition, or of some appropriate sentence. So far, however, we have not touched on the epistemological issue, the question what it means for *someone* to have a reason to accept the law, to *possess* evidence. Neither the existence of the black raven nor the truth of the proposition or sentence that says there is a black raven in itself gives anyone a reason to believe there is a black raven, much less a reason to believe all ravens are black. For someone to have a reason to believe all ravens are black, it is necessary for him to *believe*, for example, that here is a black raven.

We are off on a well-worn track. Surely it is not enough simply to believe that here is a black raven; not enough, either, that the belief should also be true. For both of these conditions together do not add up to evidence unless the person has an adequate reason for holding the belief. If the reason must be another belief, we are faced by an infinite regress or a circle. A regress would make knowledge impossible, while a circle would lead to the difficulties of a pure coherence theory of knowledge. I'll come back to the latter in a moment.

At this point we come to the various attempts to find states of mind that bridge or eliminate the gap between sensation, where no question of truth can arise, and judgement, which is plausibly a source of evidence. Quasi-sentences like 'Black here now' have been proposed as expressing such states of mind. And perhaps we will be persuaded that there are such states of mind if we overlook the fact that the verb has been omitted (since putting it in would push things too far in the direction of judgement) and that words like 'here' and 'now' cannot be understood except as involving a reference to an agent. In any case, the attempt to base science on such states of mind is doomed, since no one has ever succeeded in showing how to base knowledge of an objective, common world on such 'evidence'. Even Schlick, who somehow hoped to back protocol sentences of the form 'A experiences black at time *t*' by whatever it is that is expressed by

'Black here now' as said or thought by A at *t*, did not believe in a construction of science or a public world, with the construction based on 'immediate experiences'.

It should be obvious that no appeal to perception can clear up the question what constitutes a person's ultimate source of evidence. For if we take perception to consist in a sensation caused by an event in the world (or in the body of the perceiver), the fact of causality cannot be given apart from the sensation, and the sensation cannot serve as evidence unless it causes a belief. But how does one know that the belief was caused by a sensation? Only further beliefs can help. If perception is expressed by locutions like 'A perceives that there is a black raven', then this can certainly serve as evidence.This does not solve the problem, it only transfers it to the concept of perception, since to perceive that there is a black raven is to be caused by a raven, and *in the right way*, to believe that there is a black raven.

One is struck, in reading early writings of the members of the Vienna Circle, by the embarrassed way in which they refer to experience, what is immediately given, what is directly observed. Thus Schlick says that all meaning goes back to ostensive situations, 'and this means, in an obvious sense, reference to "experience" or "possibility of verification" '.[15] In 'The Turning Point in Philosophy' he says 'The act of verification in which the path to the solution finally ends is always of the same sort: it is the occurrence of a definite fact that is confirmed by observation, by means of immediate experience';[16] but in 'Positivism and Realism' he expresses grave doubts about terms like 'the given' (*das Gegebene*), and worries that if we use the word 'experience,' we will 'presuppose a distinction between what experiences and what is experienced'.[17]

There is, then, good reason to conclude that there is no clear meaning to the idea of comparing our beliefs with reality or confronting our hypotheses with observations. This is not, of course, to deny that there is an ordinary sense in which we perform experiments and note the results, or discover in our everyday pursuits that some of our beliefs are true and others false. What should be denied is that these mundane events are to be analyzed as involving

[15] Moritz Schlick, 'Meaning and Verification', 148.
[16] Moritz Schlick, 'The Turning Point in Philosophy', *LP* 56.
[17] Moritz Schlick, 'Positivism and Realism', *LP* 84.

evidence that is not propositional in character—evidence that is not some sort of belief. No wonder Neurath and Carnap were attracted to the idea of a coherence theory!

Of course, coherence theories of knowledge are not without difficulties, and these, Schlick was, as we have seen, quick to point out. Let me pause here for a moment to make the obvious distinction between a coherence theory of knowledge and a coherence theory of truth. In his 1935 paper 'On the Logical Positivist's Theory of Truth' Hempel had barely distinguished between the two; understandably, since he was not then aware of Tarski's method for defining truth semantically. He therefore was at the time inclined to think the only sense we can make of the phrase 'Sentence S is true' is 'S is highly confirmed by accepted observation reports'.[18] But the concept of being highly confirmed by accepted observation reports belongs rather in the domain of epistemology; and when coupled with the idea that protocol statements 'may only be characterized by the historical fact' that they are accepted (i.e. believed true), leads directly to a coherence theory of knowledge. This is the theory to which Schlick objected.

Schlick agreed with Neurath that protocols belong, in a general way, to the hypotheses of science. They are objective, and therefore intersubjectively understood and testable. They are *about* observations or experiences, but they don't attempt to *express* them. They take the form, roughly at least, of sentences like 'A saw a black raven at time t'. It is clear that one cannot be certain of the truth of such sentences—not even A at time t can be certain he is seeing a black raven; or, leaving the question of certainty aside, it is clear that anyone who judges such a sentence to be true may be wrong. Further evidence is always relevant, and may come to outweigh the evidence of the moment. Where Schlick disagreed with Neurath is on the question whether there are indisputable grounds on the basis of which we judge protocols to be true.[19]

The objection to Neurath's coherence theory was the standard objection to all such theories: consistency is not enough, since it leaves no basis on which to choose between various and conflicting consistent theories. Perhaps a theory of this kind banishes the last

[18] Carl Hempel, 'Studies in the Logic of Confirmation', in *Aspects of Scientific Explanation*, 42.

[19] Moritz Schlick, 'The Foundation of Knowledge', *LP* 213. The following seven quotations are from *LP* 218–25.

remnant of absolutism from philosophy, as Schlick said of Neurath's claims, but it leaves us with no basis for judging truth. Schlick insisted that we must have, and do have, indubitable grounds for choosing some sentences as the true ones rather than others. There are statements that are *not* protocol statements, which 'express facts of one's own "perception" ('or whatever you like to call it', he adds). Schlick then admits that 'in spite of the fact that statements of this sort seem so simple and clear, philosophers have found themselves in a hopeless labyrinth the moment they actually attempted to use them as the foundation of all knowledge'. But he thinks we can steer clear of the familiar difficulties if we remember that 'one's *own* statements in the end play the only decisive role'.

One must admit that Schlick's attempt to explain his view ends in obscurity. The observation 'sentences' that constitute the 'ultimate criterion' of all knowledge are not really sentences, being always of the form 'Here now so and so'. Such sentences cannot be written down (since they lose their certainty in a moment); they express a 'feeling of *fulfillment*, a quite characteristic satisfaction: we are *satisfied*'. 'One cannot build any logically tenable structure upon such confirmations, for they are gone the moment one begins to construct.' Finally, 'the occasion of understanding [observation statements] is at the same time that of verifying them: I grasp their meaning at the same time as I grasp their truth'. One can sympathize with Neurath for rejecting this last step. But then one is left with a coherence theory.

Hempel calls the Neurath–Carnap position a 'restrained' coherence theory. The reason is that Neurath and Carnap do provide us with a criterion for picking out one scientific theory from among the consistent ones. The criterion is that it is the consistent theory that maximizes agreement with the statements historically held true by 'mankind especially the scientists of our culture circle'.[20] In the end, protocol sentences have no pride of place; like any others they may be abandoned if they conflict with too much else we hold true.

Thus it turns out, rather surprisingly, that both Schlick and Neurath held views that could be called 'restrained' coherence theories. They agreed that everything in the corpus of science, including protocol sentences, must be viewed as only tentatively established at any stage in the progress of science, and all sentences remain open

[20] Carl Hempel, 'On the Logical Positivist's Theory of Truth', 57.

to revision in the light of new evidence. They likewise agreed that when revision was called for, there were no strict rules for deciding where the revision should be made; it was a matter for 'decision'. Their sole important difference concerned the question how the whole pattern of sentences accepted at a given time by science was to be related to experience, observation, or the real world. And on this score their answers were less than clear or satisfactory.

Schlick's answer was unsatisfactory because it ended with something so private that even its meaning could only be given at a moment for an individual. How such a basis could warrant belief in a public objective world was not explained. Neurath rejected the idea of a confrontation between a belief about the world and the world itself as well as the idea of an incorrigible subjective basis for scientific knowledge. But his suggestion as to how to 'restrain' a coherence theory is unappealing. He suggests that we start with protocols of the form 'A sees a black raven at t', and he dismisses the idea that such protocols are any more the basis of A's knowledge than of B's. This guarantees the intersubjective aspect of the language of science right down to the protocols (since, as Neurath said, '*every* language *as such* is inter-subjective'[21]—clearly a crack at Schlick and his observation statements, whose meaning is revealed to only one person, and then only for a moment). Neurath imagines all protocols being thrown into one great machine; a bell rings if a contradiction arises; something must then be thrown out, either one or more protocols, or perhaps a law or other theoretical statement; but '*who* rebuilds the machine, or *whose* protocol sentences are thrown into the machine is of no consequence whatsoever'.[22]

There is an obvious difficulty here. If protocol sentences are known only by their form, throwing them *all* in the machine will mean each sentence *and* its negation will be thrown in, as well as 'A sees a black raven at spot s at t' and 'B sees a non-black raven at spot s at t.' No basis for science can emerge from this, just endless consistent systems. If, on the other hand, the protocols are limited to the sentences that express *beliefs*, it *will* matter who mends the machine and whose protocols are thrown in or out. For each person will weigh the sentences he accepts (whether protocols or not) in accord with the strength of his beliefs—that's what it means to say they are *his*

---

[21] Otto Neurath, 'Protocol Sentences', *LP*. 205.   [22] Ibid. 207.

beliefs. He will give weight to other people's protocols to the extent that he believes they are true, just as Schlick maintained.

I would not dwell at such length on the familiar epistemological problems that beset Schlick and Neurath and their followers if I thought philosophy had now rejected them or solved them. On the contrary, I think the members of the Vienna Circle and their friends emphasized in a particularly useful way, even if partly in spite of themselves, a central unsettled problem in epistemology. And I think we can find a number of ideas and intuitions in the writings I have been discussing that point in the direction of a new view of the old problem.

The central problem may be stated as a dilemma in the theory of knowledge. Each person has a complex network of beliefs. Knowledge requires at least these two things: that some of these beliefs are true of the public world, and that each person has adequate reasons for holding these beliefs. I am willing to assume that the first condition is satisfied; the hard problem concerns the second issue, the way in which the system of beliefs is related to the world not merely semantically, but epistemologically. The dilemma arises because if we take as the connecting link something self-certifying (like Schlick's observation statements or events), it is so private as to lack connection with the sentences of the public language that alone are capable of expressing scientific, or even objective, claims. But if we start with sentences or beliefs already belonging to the public language (or what can be expressed in it), we find no intelligible way to base it on something self-certifying (Neurath's problem). In short, the foundations of knowledge must be subjective and objective at once, certain and yet open to question.

The problems I am rehearsing belong, we all know, to the foundations of epistemology, and in one form or another the problems are ancient. The logical positivists, one senses at once in their writings, were impatient with such problems, which they felt verged on the meaningless, or were to be solved by mere 'conventions' or 'decisions'. This attitude now seems to us, rereading these bold classics, cavalier. But the giddy conviction that a clear and correct line would somehow open up in the face of all that enthusiasm and intellectual power did produce some profoundly novel and valuable hints. What on the surface now may seem naive and failed attempts contained deeply suggestive intuitions of radical new ideas.

Given the positivists' tendency to remain within the vocabulary of intersubjective ideas and hypotheses, the flirtations of Neurath, Schlick, Hempel, and Carnap with some form of epistemological coherence theory is not surprising. But coherence theories have always been bedeviled by failure to distinguish between coherence theories of truth and coherence theories of knowledge. This is natural enough, since if knowledge, which is of the true, demands nothing but coherence of belief, how can truth require anything more than a set of coherent propositions? Thus one is invited to dismiss the difference between coherence of beliefs and coherence of sentences (or statements or propositions) as tests of knowledge and truth. But while we find this confusion in the writings of Schlick and Neurath, we also find moments when the distinction is clearly made. Neurath, we remember, hoped to destroy any aura of subjectivity in protocol statements by insisting that though it may be a 'historical accident' that one person is more inclined to accept his own protocols than those of someone else, in fact both are to be accepted on the same level. This leads him to the picture of the impersonal sorting machine into which protocol sentences are thrown. In proposing this idea, Neurath never hints that it is only sentences held to be true by someone that are to count. It is this fact that occasioned Schlick's outburst: 'The astounding error of the "coherence theory" can be explained only by the fact that its defenders and expositors were thinking only of such statements as actually occur in science.'[23] Here Schlick means, of course, such as occur as *assertions*. Yet in spite of much that we find in Neurath's article on protocol sentences, can he really be accused of having forgotten the difference between the coherence of an arbitrary set of sentences and the coherence of a set of sentences held true? The famous metaphor of the ship which must be rebuilt at sea piece by piece proves he was aware that it is beliefs that are at stake, not mere sentences, for if we were dealing with an arbitrary set of sentences, nothing would stop us from putting them all in dry dock simultaneously. And Hempel, as I mentioned above, makes the distinction clear.

Since standard objections to coherence theories of knowledge parallel standard objections to coherence theories of truth, it is not immediately apparent why it is so important to distinguish between them. But of course beliefs are not historically or causally arbitrary; even if our *reasons* for our beliefs are always other beliefs, the *causes* sometimes lie elsewhere. Some appreciation of the

[23] Moritz Schlick, 'The Foundation of Knowledge', *LP* 215.

importance of this point must, as we will see, be credited to the logical positivists.

The logical positivists preferred to talk of sentences or 'statements' rather than beliefs, and we can easily enough make this switch as long as we remember that the sentences that correspond to beliefs are (1) sentences held true by someone, and (2) sentences that have an interpretation. Someone else can know what I believe if he knows what sentences I hold true, and what those sentences mean. Let me review some of the logical positivists' views in the light of these simple considerations.

There is Schlick's idea that observation sentences are understood in the act of grasping their truth. This may well seem extreme or obscure, but it is related to the correct doctrine that an interpreter is constrained to take first person present tense attributions of attitude as presumptively true. Such sentences (of English) as 'I believe I now see a black raven', if held true by a speaker, require of an interpreter that he assign a high a priori probability to their truth. This means: so interpret such sentences as to make them true when possible.

Hempel comments on the fact that the protocol statements 'produced' by different men might not admit the construction of a unique system of scientific statements. He goes on: 'but fortunately this possibility is not realized: in fact, by far the greater part of scientists will sooner or later come to an agreement, and so, as an empirical fact, a perpetually increasing and expanding system of coherent statements and theories results from their protocol statements'.[24] Again, we must assume that protocol statements are not any sentences written down, or uttered; they must be sentences their speakers believe to be true, or at least that a hearer believes the speaker to have held true. But it is surely odd to consider it merely 'fortunate' that there is a large degree of consensus: and why should we expect agreement to increase over time?

Schlick has an even more surprising discussion of the possibility that someone might discover that all his own observations in no way substantiate the assertions made about the world by other men. He says that under these circumstances one would not, as Neurath's protocol machine would, simply sacrifice one's own protocol statements. Instead, one would cling to a

---

[24] Carl Hempel, 'On the Logical Positivist's Theory of Truth', 57.

system of knowledge into which one's own observations fitted unmutilated. And I can always construct such a system. I need only view the others as dreaming fools, in whose madness lies a remarkable method, or—to express it more objectively—I would say that the others live in a different world from mine . . . In any case no matter what world picture I construct, I would test its truth always in terms of my own experience.[25]

This is a remarkable admission from someone who has objected that a coherence theory leaves us with an unacceptable relativism.

Elsewhere in Schlick, however, we find a rather different way of viewing the possibility of massive disagreement. He notes a basic contrast between a disagreement over whether two pieces of paper are the same color, and a disagreement over what color both pieces are. With respect to the first he says that 'by virtue of linguistic usage the proposition expresses just that experience'—i.e. the experience of sameness. But in the case of color, there is no objective way—that is, no way—to tell if you and I experience the same color. Schlick says that even if all your expressed judgements about color agree entirely with mine, I cannot infer from this that you experience the same quality. As long as the inner order of your experiences agrees with mine, we will understand each other perfectly.[26]

Schlick seems in the end to reject the view that the experiences may be undetectably different. '. . . the statement that different individuals have the same experience has its sole verifiable meaning in the fact that all their assertions . . . exhibit certain agreements . . . the statement *means* nothing but this.'[27] It is not easy to tell from this passage whether Schlick thinks the experiences might be qualitatively different while we could not in principle discern this, or meaningfully claim it; or whether he thinks no such situation could arise. The radical suggestion, which it is not impossible to read into Schlick's attack on the coherence theory, is that interpersonal agreement, and hence objectivity, are built into the way in which we determine the meanings of other people's utterances, and hence the contents of their beliefs.

I mentioned above Hempel's remark that 'fortunately' the protocol statements of different people allow the construction of a unique system of science. He adds that Carnap has 'perhaps provided us a

[25] Moritz Schlick, 'The Foundation of Knowledge', *LP* 219.
[26] Here I paraphrase Schlick, 'Positivism and Realism', *LP* 93.
[27] Ibid. 93.

possibility of explaining this fortunate fact'.[28] The possible explanation lies in the fact that 'young scientists are conditioned' to produce
true protocol statements, and he adds, 'Perhaps the fact of the general
and rather congruous conditioning of scientists may explain to a
certain degree the fact of a unique system of science.'[29]

It would be mysterious if people were first taught what various
sentences mean, and *then* were conditioned to 'produce' the true
ones; this would amount to teaching them, on the one hand, how to
be better observers, and, on the other hand, how to be honest. But the
situation may be seen rather as a matter of conditioning people, as we
surely do, to hold certain sentences true under publicly observable
conditions, and fixing on the interpretation of utterances of the
sentences in accord with the success of the conditioning. This would
explain interpersonal agreement on the main features of the environment in a natural way.

Carnap at one point seems clearly to take this line. In 'Psychology
in Physical Language' (written in 1932) Carnap flatly rejects
Neurath's idea that I must or can treat your protocol sentences on a
par with my own.

Generally speaking [he writes], a psychologist's spoken, written, or printed
protocol sentences, when they are based on so-called introspection, are to be
interpreted by the reader, and so figure in inter- subjective science, *not
chiefly as scientific sentences, but as scientific facts.* The epistemological
confusion of contemporary psychology stems, to a large extent, from this
confusion of facts in the form of sentences with the sentences themselves
considered as parts of science.[30]

The inferences we are permitted to draw from the fact that someone
else utters a sentence are not the deductive consequences that flow
from that sentence as interpreted, but rather the sort of inference we
can draw from observing the movements of a voltmeter, or the movements of a raindrop. The point is not that others do not mean
anything by the sentences they utter, but that we cannot take for
granted that we know in advance *what* they mean; and interpretation
is explicitly called for or implicitly assumed.

I think that by following out this line, along with several other
suggestions drawn from passages I have been quoting, we can

[28] Carl Hempel, 'On the Logical Positivist's Theory of Truth', 57.
[29] Ibid. 58.
[30] Rudolph Carnap, 'Psychology in Physical Language', *LP* 195.

discover the outline of a correct view of the foundations of empirical knowledge, a view that reconciles Neurath's coherentist theory with Schlick's insistence on a basic tie to experience and observation.

From here on, although I shall be borrowing in many and obvious ways on ideas of Schlick, Neurath, Hempel, and Carnap, I am stating my own position. This is a position deeply influenced by Quine, though it is not Quine's position.

Neurath was right in rejecting the intelligibility of comparing sentences or beliefs with reality. We experiment and observe, but this is not 'comparing' in any but a metaphorical sense, for our experimentation bears no epistemological fruit except as it *causes* us to add to, cling to, or abandon our beliefs. This causal relation cannot be a relation of *confirmation* or *disconfirmation*, since the cause is not a proposition or belief, but just an event in the world or in our sensory apparatus. Nor can such events be considered in themselves to be evidence, unless, of course, they cause us to believe something. And then it is the belief that is properly called the evidence, not the event.

Neurath was also right in saying that, given this situation, we may as well admit that protocols, like any other propositions of science or common sense, can be wrong; we stand ready to tinker where tinkering does the most good. As Hempel observed, no epistemological priority is left to protocols— they are like the rest. All this is, of course, the line Quine was later to exploit in arguing against the analytic–synthetic distinction.

We are left, then, as Neurath insisted, in a situation where our only evidence for a belief is other beliefs; this is not merely the *logical* situation, but also the pragmatic situation. And since no belief is self-certifying, no set of beliefs can supply a certain basis for the rest. How then can we escape Schlick's objection that this makes 'arbitrary fairy stories to be as true as a historical report'? He concludes: 'Thus the coherence theory is shown to be logically impossible . . . for by means of it I can arrive at any number of consistent systems of statements which are incompatible with one another.'[31] It's not clear what it means to say I could 'arrive' at various systems, since I do not invent my beliefs; most of them are not voluntary. Still, the point of the criticism would seem to remain in the form of a challenge to say what reason I have to consider the bulk of my beliefs true.

---

[31] Moritz Schlick, 'The Foundation of Knowledge', *LP* 216.

The key to the answer lies, I think, in generalizing Carnap's two suggestions that we are conditioned to produce (hold true) specific sentences under particular conditions, and that we cannot use other people's statements as evidence until we have interpreted them. Carnap said this only about protocol sentences, but the same should be said about all language.

Language is in its nature, as Neurath insisted, intersubjective; what someone else's words mean on a given occasion is always something that we can in principle learn from public clues. Consider how we discover what some simple sentence means, say 'There's a table' or 'Here's a piece of green paper'. Our basic evidence is that the speaker is caused to assent (not just on this occasion, but generally) to these sentences by the presence of tables or pieces of green paper, while the absence of these objects causes him (generally) to dissent from the same sentences. I do not think of assent and dissent as overt speech acts, but as attitudes towards sentences sometimes revealed in speech and sometimes in other ways. My main point is that our basic methodology for interpreting the words of others necessarily makes it the case that most of the time the simplest sentences that speakers hold true *are* true. It is not the *speaker* who must perform the impossible feat of comparing his belief with reality; it is the *interpreter* who must take into account the causal interaction between world and speaker in order to find out what the speaker means, and hence what that speaker believes. Each speaker can do no better than make his system of beliefs coherent, adjusting the system as rationally as he can as new beliefs are thrust on him. But there is no need to fear that these beliefs might be just a fairy tale. For the sentences that express the beliefs, and the beliefs themselves, are correctly understood to be about the public things and events that cause them, and so must be mainly veridical. Each individual knows this, since he knows the nature of speech and belief. This does not, of course, tell him *which* of his beliefs and sentences are true, but it does assure him that his overall picture of the world around him is like the picture other people have, and is in its large features correct.

Neurath, Carnap, and Hempel were right, I believe, in abandoning the search for a basic sort of evidence on which our knowledge of the world could rest. None is available, and none is needed. What they perhaps failed to appreciate is *why* it is not needed. It is not needed because the causal relations between our beliefs and speech, and the world also supply the interpretation of our language and of our beliefs. In this rather special sense, 'experience' is the source of all knowledge. But this is a sense that does not encourage us to find a mental or inferential bridge between external events and ordinary beliefs. The bridge is there all right—a causal bridge that involves the sense organs. The error lies, as Neurath saw, in trying to turn this causal bridge into an epistemological one, with sense data, uninterpreted givens, or unwritable sentences constituting its impossible spans.

There are of course some beliefs that carry a very high degree of certitude, and in some cases their content creates a presumption in favor of their truth. These are beliefs about our own present propositional attitudes. But the relative certitude of these beliefs does not suit them to be the foundation of empirical knowledge. It springs, rather, from the nature of interpretation. As interpreters we have to treat self-ascriptions of belief, doubt, desire, and the like as privileged; this is an essential step in interpreting the rest of what the person says and thinks. The foundations of interpretation are not the foundations of knowledge, though an appreciation of the nature of interpretation can lead to an appreciation of the essentially veridical nature of belief.

12 *Epistemology and Truth*

Everyone agrees that what is known must be true, but beyond this there is little agreement on the epistemic status of truth. Many philosophers in recent decades have held that truth is an epistemic concept; even when they have not explicitly held this thesis, their views have often implied it. Coherence theories of truth are usually driven by an epistemic engine, as are pragmatic characterizations of truth, Dummett and Crispin Wright's antirealism, Peirce's idea that the truth is what science will end up believing, Richard Boyd's claim that truth is what explains the success of science, and Hilary Putnam's internal realism. Quine also, at least at times, has maintained that truth is internal to a theory of the world and so to that extent dependent on our epistemological stance. Relativism about truth is perhaps always a symptom of infection by the epistemological virus; this seems to be true in any case for Quine, Goodman, and Putnam.

Apparently opposed to all these views is the intuitive idea that truth, aside from a few special cases, is entirely independent of our beliefs; as it is sometimes put, our beliefs might be just as they are and yet reality—and so the truth about reality—be very different. According to this intuition, truth is 'radically non-epistemic' (so Hilary Putnam characterizes 'transcendental realism'), or 'evidence-transcendent' (Michael Dummett).

If we were to look for a short description of these two views of truth, we might well hit on the words 'subjective' and 'objective'; the assertion of an essential tie to epistemology introduces a dependence of truth on what can be verified by finite rational creatures, while the denial of such dependence makes truth objective. Perhaps the words 'immanent' and 'transcendent' also suggest the same basic division.

And since the question of truth cannot be separated from questions about the nature of reality, 'antirealism' and 'realism' have often been used to make a closely related distinction. For reasons that will become clear as I go along, my preference is for 'subjective' and 'objective'; but I realize that some parties to the dispute will find this terminology tendentious.

In this talk I outline an approach to the concept of truth which I think undermines the dispute between the two views of truth. I do not aim to reconcile the two views, but to question their clarity, and so leave us free to give up the search for the 'right' theory of truth. That both views, while no doubt answering to powerful intuitions, are fundamentally mistaken is at least suggested by the fact that both invite skepticism. Subjective theories are skeptical in the way idealism or many versions of empiricism are skeptical; they are skeptical not because they make reality unknowable, but because they reduce reality to so much less than we believe there is. Objective theories, on the other hand, seem to throw in doubt not only our knowledge of what is 'evidence-transcendent', but all the rest of what we think we know, for such theories deny that there is any link between belief and truth.

Let us consider first Tarski-style truth definitions, with an eye to deciding whether they are objective or subjective or neither.[1] The first thing to be clear about is that Tarski did not define, nor show how to define, the concept of truth; what he did was define truth for a specific language, and indicate how to define truth for other languages of a specific sort. Tarski's basic insight was to make use of the apparently trivial fact that sentences of the form ' "Snow is white" is true in L if and only if snow is white' must be true if the sentence quoted is a sentence of the language used to state the platitude. Let us call such platitudes T-sentences. Tarski observed that a definition of 'is true in L' which entailed a T-sentence for every sentence of L would pick out just the true sentences of L; and he further observed that the definition would be just as correct if the truth predicate were in a language that did not contain L, and the entailed T-sentences had a translation of the quoted sentence in place of that sentence itself to the right of the biconditional. The hard work came in providing a correct definition, given the constraints Tarski imposed. (None of this survey is quite accurate, but my inaccuracies are irrelevant to the discussion.)

---

[1] Alfred Tarski, 'The Concept of Truth in Formalized Languages'.

It is clear that no definition in Tarski's style is a definition of truth; each such definition is a definition of truth *in a particular language*. If we think that it is the same concept of truth that is involved in each of Tarski's definitions, this can only be because we have a grasp of that concept that is independent of Tarski's work.[2] In fact this is entirely clear; Tarski's condition on satisfactory definitions of truth for particular languages rests on the recognition that T-sentences are obviously true, and this recognition depends on our prior understanding of the concept of truth. The triviality of T-sentences is a guarantee of their truth, and this guarantee is passed on by Tarski's work to the 'partial definitions' of truth he provides. T-sentences are trivially true only if we know that the sentence described is identical with, or a translation of, the sentence that gives its truth conditions; but this is enough to display the sense in which we have a firm grasp of the general concept of truth.

Tarski's definitions are sometimes called 'merely translational' or 'disquotational'. They are indeed disquotational in the special case where truth is being defined for a language in a language that contains it; in such cases, T-sentences show how to remove the quotation marks and get a sentence that provably has the same truth value. But this feature can be known to be present only when the object language is known to be contained in the metalanguage. The idea that such truth definitions are translational rests on a mistake. If one knows how to translate a language L into one's own language, it does not follow that one can automatically produce a truth definition. Translation relates languages to one another; truth, even in Tarski's limited editions, relates a language to the world.

Tarski's definitions are reached through several steps. The notion of a well-formed expression (particularly a closed sentence) is defined; there is a recursive definition of a satisfaction relation (satisfaction is a highly generalized version of reference); truth is defined on the basis of the concepts of sentence and satisfaction; the recursive definitions are turned into explicit definitions. For present purposes it is best to forget the last step. What we are then left with is not a proper definition at all, but a recursive characterization of an undefined concept, that of satisfaction; and since truth is defined in terms of satisfaction, which is a semantic concept, it can no longer

---

[2] As far as I know this point was first made by Max Black, 'The Semantic Definition of Truth'. Also see Michael Dummett, 'Truth', in *Truth and Other Enigmas*.

be said that truth has been defined, even for a particular language, in nonsemantic terms. Let us think of the result, then, as an axiomatized theory with the basic semantic notions undefined.

Which semantic concept we take as basic is open to choice. Truth, as Tarski showed, can be defined on the basis of satisfaction; but equally satisfaction can be taken to be whatever concept yields a correct account of truth. Tarski's work, despite appearances, is ultimately neutral concerning the question what semantic concept is basic. He assumes, as we have seen, a grasp of the concept of truth, and shows how this intuition can be implemented in detail for particular languages. The implementation requires the introduction of the relation of satisfaction, which relates (a bit indirectly) words and things. The story about truth traces the pattern of logical forms in a language, or grammar properly conceived, and hence the pattern of logical dependencies. There is no way to tell this story (for a language of any appreciable richness) without assigning semantical roles to the parts of sentences.

There is a strong tradition which sees things differently. According to this tradition, we could never come to understand sentences in their infinite or indefinitely large array unless we understood the words that make them up. Therefore, the semantic properties of words must be learned before we understand sentences, and the semantic properties of words have conceptual priority because it is they that explain the semantic properties—above all the truth conditions—of sentences. I think this line of argument, which starts with a truism, ends with a false conclusion; so something in the reasoning must be wrong. The mistake is to confuse the order of explanation that is appropriate once the theory is in place with the explanation why the theory is correct. The theory is correct because it yields correct T-sentences; its correctness is tested against our grasp of the concept of truth as applied to sentences. Since T-sentences say nothing about reference, satisfaction, or expressions that are not sentences, the test of the correctness of the theory is independent of our intuitions concerning these concepts. Once we have the theory, though, we can explain the truth of sentences on the basis of their structure and the semantic properties of the parts. The analogy with theories in science is impressive: in order to organize and explain what we directly observe, we posit unobserved or indirectly observed objects and forces; the theory is tested by what is directly observed.

The perspective on language and truth that we have gained is this: what is most open to observation is sentences and their uses, and truth is the semantic concept we understand best. Reference and related semantic notions like satisfaction are by comparison theoretical (as are the notions of word, predicate, sentential connective, and the rest); there is no question about their 'correctness' beyond the question whether they yield a satisfactory account of the truth conditions of sentences and the relations among sentences.

These observations invite us to focus on the centrality of the concept of truth in the understanding of language; it is our grasp of the contents of this concept that permits us to make sense of the question whether a theory of truth for a language is correct. There is no reason to look for a prior, or independent, account of some referential relation. The other main consequence of these reflections is that they provide an opportunity to say fairly sharply what is missing, as an account of truth, in a theory of truth in Tarski's style.

What is missing is the connection with the users of a language. Nothing in the world would count as a sentence, and the concept of truth would therefore have no application, if there were not creatures that used sentences by uttering or inscribing tokens of them. Any complete account of truth must therefore relate it to actual linguistic intercourse. Put more precisely: a Tarski-style theory of truth is true for a given language only if the sentences of that language have a meaning prior to the construction of the theory (otherwise the theory is not a theory in the ordinary sense, but a description of a possible language). Or to return to the definitional form which Tarski favored: if the question can be raised whether the definition is correct for a given language, the language must have a life independent of the definition (otherwise the definition is merely stipulative: it specifies, but is not true of, a language). So if the issue of correctness can be raised, the theory must be viewed as empirically true or false. The one exception is the case we considered before, where it is assumed that the object language is contained in the metalanguage; in this case the only test is formal, and no empirical issue is at stake. There is a question, though, when this assumption is justified. If I have a theory of truth for your language, the assumption would be obviously correct only if it were obvious that you and I mean the same thing by every sentence we do or might speak. I doubt if this is ever obvious, but in any case the assumption is certainly empirical. It is even a question whether the formal test of correctness is guaranteed to be all that is needed to tell if my theory of truth, couched in my own words, is correct for my own language; this is, however, a point I shall not discuss here.

If we knew what makes a theory of truth true for a speaker or group of speakers, we could plausibly be said to understand the concept of truth; and if we could say what makes such a theory true, we could give an explicit account, if not a definition, of truth. The ultimate *evidence*, as opposed to a criterion, for the correctness of a theory of truth we must presume lies in available facts about how speakers use the language. When I say available, I mean publicly available—available not only in principle, but available in fact to anyone who is capable of understanding the speaker or speakers of the language. Since all of us do understand some speakers of some languages, all of us must have adequate evidence for attributing truth conditions to the utterances of some speakers; all of us have, there-fore, a competent grasp of the concept of truth as applied to the speech behavior of others.

Have we now settled the question whether truth is radically nonepistemic, as objectivists claim, or basically epistemic, as subjec-tivists claim? It may seem so, since we have followed a course of argument that leads to the conclusion that it is how language is used that decides whether a theory of truth for that language is correct.

But in fact the matter is not settled, for it may be held by objec-tivists that the question whether the theory is true for a given language or group of speakers is indeed empirical, but only because the question of what the words mean is empirical; the issue of truth, it may be held, remains to be answered, whether by the theory itself or in some other way.

Does the theory itself contain the answer? It does if a Tarski-type theory of truth is a correspondence theory, for then the form of the theory in effect defines truth to be correspondence with reality—the classical form of objectivism with respect to truth. I am sorry to say that I have myself argued in the past that theories of the sort Tarski showed how to produce were correspondence theories of a sort. I said this on the ground that there is no way to give such a theory without introducing a concept like reference or satisfaction which relates expressions to objects in the world.[3]

---

[3] Tarski seems to have viewed his truth definitions as implementing the idea of corre-spondence. I foolishly accepted the term in 'True to the Facts', essay 3 in *Inquiries into Truth and Interpretation*.

It now seems to me to have been a mistake to call such theories correspondence theories. Let me explain why I think it was a mistake. The usual complaint about correspondence theories is that it makes no sense to suggest that it is somehow possible to compare one's words or beliefs with the world, since the attempt must always end up simply with the acquisition of more beliefs. This complaint was voiced, for example, by Otto Neurath, who for this reason adopted a coherence view of truth; Carl Hempel expressed the same objection, speaking of the 'fatal confrontation of statements and facts'.[4] Richard Rorty has repeatedly insisted, with Dewey, that a correspondence view of truth makes the concept of truth useless.[5] I have said much the same myself.[6]

This complaint against correspondence theories I now think is a mistake. One reason it is a mistake is that it depends on taking the side of the subjectivists; it would be a legitimate complaint only if truth were an epistemic concept in the way subjectivists claim it is. If this were the only reason for rejecting correspondence theories, the objectivist can simply reply that his position is untouched; he always maintained that truth was independent of our beliefs or our abilities to learn the truth.

The real objection to correspondence theories is simpler; it is that there is nothing for true sentences to correspond to. The point was made long ago by C. I. Lewis; he challenged the correspondence theorist to *locate* the fact or part of reality, or of the world, to which a true sentence corresponded. One can locate individual objects, if the sentence happens to name or describe them, but even such location makes sense relative only to a frame of reference, and so presumably the frame of reference must be included in whatever it is to which a true sentence corresponds. Following out this line of thought led Lewis to conclude that if true sentences correspond to anything at all, it must be the universe as a whole; thus all true sentences correspond to the same thing. Frege, as we know, independently reached the same conclusion through a very similar course of reasoning. Frege's argument, if Alonzo Church is right, can be formalized: starting from the assumptions that a true sentence can't be made to correspond to something different by the substitution of

---

[4] See Otto Neurath, 'Protocol Sentences'; and Carl Hempel, 'On the Logical Positivist's Theory of Truth', 51.

[5] Richard Rorty, *Consequences of Pragmatism*, introd.; also his 'Pragmatism, Davidson and Truth'.   [6] For example, in Essay 10 in this volume.

coreferring singular terms, or by the substitution of logically equivalent sentences, one can show that if true sentences correspond to anything, they all correspond to the same thing. But this is to trivialize the concept of correspondence completely; there is no interest in the *relation* of correspondence if there is only one thing to correspond to since, as in any such case, the relation may as well be collapsed into a one-place predicate: '*x* corresponds to the universe'. Similarly, '*x* corresponds to (or names) the True' or '*x* corresponds to the facts' can less misleadingly be read '*x* is true'. Peter Strawson made the point in his famous exchange on truth with J. L. Austin. He observed that the parts of a sentence may correspond to parts of the world (that is, refer to them), but adds that there is nothing else in the world to which a sentence may be related. He correctly goes on to claim that 'while we certainly say that a statement corresponds to (fits, is borne out by, agrees with) the facts', this is merely 'a variant on saying it is true'.[7]

The correct objection to correspondence theories is not, then, that they make truth something to which we humans can never legitimately aspire; the real objection is rather that such theories fail to provide entities to which truth vehicles (whether we take these to be statements, sentences, or utterances) can be said to correspond. As I once put it, 'Nothing, no *thing*, makes our statements true.' If this is right, and I am convinced it is, we ought also to question the popular assumption that sentences, or their spoken tokens, or sentence-like entities, or configurations in our brains can properly be called 'representations', since there is nothing for them to represent. If we give up facts as entities that make sentences true, we ought to give up representations at the same time, for the legitimacy of each depends on the legitimacy of the other.

I said I regretted ever having said that a Tarski-style truth theory was a form of correspondence theory, and I do. My reason for saying it was not that I had made the mistake of supposing that sentences or utterances of sentences corresponded to anything. But I was still under the influence of the idea that truth is objective; the idea that truth, and therefore reality, are (except for special cases) independent of what anyone believes or can know. Thus I advertised my view as a brand of realism, realism with respect to the 'external world', with respect to meaning, and with respect to truth.

---

[7] Peter Strawson, 'Truth', 194–5.

If the terms were ill chosen, it is because they suggest a positive endorsement of a position, or an assumption, that there is a clear positive thesis to be adopted. Whereas all I was entitled to maintain, all that my position actually entailed with respect to realism and truth, was the negative claim that subjectivism is false. The objective view of truth, if it has any content, must be based on correspondence, correspondence as applied to sentences or beliefs or utterances, entities that are propositional in character, and such correspondence cannot be made intelligible. To the extent that realism is just the ontological version of a correspondence theory, I must also reject it. All I had in mind in calling my position a form of realism was a rejection of antirealism; I was concerned to reject the doctrine that either reality or truth depends directly on our epistemic powers. Once more, however, I must make clear that I am neither accepting nor rejecting the objectivist-realist slogan that the real and the true are 'independent of our beliefs'. The only evident positive sense we can make of this phrase that consorts with the intentions of those who prize it derives from the idea of correspondence, and this idea must be rejected. But to reject it is not to say there is no connection whatever between belief and truth; there must be some connection, as we have seen, if we are to relate the truth of utterances to their human context. The question is what that connection may be.

Various forms of subjectivism—that is, of views that make truth out to be an epistemic concept—connect human thoughts, desires, and intentions to truth in quite different ways, and I cannot pretend to do justice to all such views. The best I can do is explain why, despite the differences, it makes sense to group many of them together, and to indicate the reasons for being dissatisfied with them.

I have classified coherence theories as subjective, and this needs an explanation. A pure coherence theory of truth would hold, I suppose, that all the sentences in any consistent set of sentences are true. I doubt if anyone ever held such a theory, for it is obviously false. Those who have proposed coherence theories, for example Neurath and Carnap (at one time), have usually made clear that it was sets of *beliefs*, or of sentences held to be true, whose consistency was enough to make them true; this is why I class coherence theories with other subjective views; they tie truth directly to what is believed. But unless something further is added, this view seems as wrong as Schlick held it to be (he called it an 'astounding error'[8]). The obvious objection is that many different consistent sets of beliefs are possible which are not consistent with one another.

There are theories not usually, or perhaps properly, thought of as coherence theories which have much the same drawback. Quine holds that the truth of some sentences, which he calls observation sentences, is tied directly to sensory input; further sentences derive their empirical content from their connections with observation sentences and their logical relations to one another. The truth of these further sentences (call them theoretical sentences) depends on nothing but how well they serve to explain or predict observation sentences on the basis of other observation sentences. Quine holds (plausibly) that there could be two theoretical structures which are equally capable of accounting for all true observation sentences, and yet such that neither can be reduced to the other (each theory contains at least one predicate that cannot be defined using the resources of the other theory). Quine has at different times embraced two different ways of thinking of this situation. According to one thesis, both theories are true. To this I have no objection. According to the other view, a speaker or thinker at a given time operates with one theory, and for him at that time the theory he is using is true and the other theory false. If he shifts to the other theory, then *it* is true and the other theory false. This position seems to be what Quine has meant on occasion when he has said that truth is 'immanent'.[9] This conception of the immanence or relativity of truth should not be confused with the pedestrian sense in which the truth of sentences is relative to the language in which they occur. Quine's two theories can belong to, and be stated in, the same language. It is not easy to see how the same sentence (without indexical elements), with meaning unchanged, can be true for one person and not for another, or for a given person at one time and not at another. The difficulty seems due to the attempt to import epistemological considerations into the concept of truth.

Putnam's 'internal realism' also makes truth immanent, though not, as Quine's view does, to a theory, but to the entire language and

[8] Moritz Schlick, 'The Foundations of Knowledge'.

[9] W. V. Quine, *Ontological Relativity and Other Essays*. For Quine's problem about empirically equivalent, mutually irreducible theories, see his 'On Empirically Equivalent Systems of the World', 313–28, *Theories and Things*, 29–30, and Quine in Hahn and Schilpp (eds.), *The Philosophy of W. V. Quine*, 156–7.

conceptual scheme a person accepts. Of course, once again, if all that this means is that the truth of sentences or utterances is relative to a language, that is familiar and trivially correct. But Putnam seems to have something more in mind, for example that a sentence of yours and a sentence of mine may contradict each other, and yet each be true 'for the speaker'. It is hard to think in what language this point can be persuasively stated. The source of the trouble is once again the felt need to make truth accessible. Putnam is clear about this. He identifies truth explicitly with idealized justified assertability. He calls this a form of realism because there is 'a fact of the matter as to what the verdict would be if the conditions were sufficiently good, a verdict to which opinion would "converge" if we were reasonable'. He adds that his view is 'a *human* kind of realism, a belief that there is a fact of the matter as to what is rightly assertable for us, as opposed to what is rightly assertable from the God's eye view so dear to the classical metaphysical realist'.[10] One suspects that if the conditions under which someone is ideally justified in asserting something were spelled out, it would be apparent either that they allow the possibility of error or that they are so ideal as to make no use of the intended connection with human abilities. It is also striking that Putnam seems to have no argument for his position except that the alternative ('metaphysical realism', i.e. a correspondence theory) is unacceptable. He does not argue that there can be no other position.

Putnam describes his position as close to Michael Dummett's on the main point, the epistemological status of truth. One difference is that Putnam is less certain than Dummett that truth is limited to what is definitely ascertainable, and therefore he is less sure that the principle of bivalence must be abandoned; this perhaps explains why Putnam calls his view a form of realism while Dummett calls his position antirealism. Putnam also thinks he differs from Dummett in tying truth to *idealized* justified assertability instead of justified assertability; but here I think a close reading of Dummett would show that he has much the same idea; certainly Crispin Wright does. If Dummett does not insist on something similar to Putnam's ideal conditions, then I think a criticism of Dummett that Putnam once formulated applies: if truth depends simply on justified assertability, truth can be 'lost', and this must be wrong.[11] Dummett says he agrees

[10] Hilary Putnam, *Realism and Reason*, p. xviii.
[11] Hilary Putnam, 'Reference and Understanding' and 'Reply to Dummett's Comment', in Margarit (ed.), *Meaning and Use*.

that truth can't be lost, but he fails to give a clear idea of how warranted assertability can be both a fixed property *and* one that depends on the actual ability of human speakers to recognize that certain conditions are satisfied. Actual abilities wax and wane, and differ from person to person; truth does not.

Why does Dummett endorse this view of truth? There are a number of reasons, but one seems to be this: We have seen that a theory of truth in Tarski's style neither defines nor fully characterizes truth; there is no way to tell if the theory applies to a speaker or group of speakers unless something is added to relate the theory to the human uses of language. Dummett thinks the way (perhaps the only way) to do this is to make truth something humanly recognizable. The human use of language must be a function of how people understand the language, so if truth is to play a role in explaining what it is to understand a language, there must be something that counts as a person having 'conclusive evidence' that a statement is true. One can appreciate the force of this idea while finding it difficult to accept. I have given my chief reason for rejecting it; that it is empty, or makes truth a property that can be lost. But there are other strong intuitions that would also have to be sacrificed if Dummett were right. One is the connection of truth with meaning: on Dummett's view we can understand a sentence like 'A city will never be built on this spot' without having any idea what it would be for this sentence to be true (since the sentence, or an utterance of it, has no truth value for Dummett). Another is the connection of truth with belief: on Dummett's view I can understand and believe a city will never be built on this spot, but my belief will have no truth value.

I might be tempted to go along with Dummett if I thought we must choose between what Putnam calls transcendental realism, i.e. the view that truth is 'radically non-epistemic', that all our best researched and established beliefs and theories may be false, and Dummett's identification of truth with warranted assertability, since I find the former view, essentially the correspondence view, incomprehensible, while I find Dummett's view merely false.

But I see no reason to suppose that realism and antirealism, explained in terms of the radically nonepistemic or the radically epistemic character of truth, are the only ways to give substance to a theory of truth or meaning. Let me suggest a way that seems to me different from either of the two ways we have been discussing. First, I assume that there are inescapable and obvious ties among the concepts of truth, belief, and meaning. If a sentence *s* of mine means that P, and I believe that P, then I believe that *s* is true. What gives my belief its content, and my sentence its meaning, is my knowledge of what is required for the belief or the sentence to be true. Since belief and truth are related in this way, belief can serve as the human attitude that connects a theory of truth to human concerns.

We observed that the evidence for the correctness of a theory of truth must come at the level of the T-sentences; these also constitute the testable predictions of the theory. The evidence that the utterances of a certain sentence by a speaker are true under the conditions provided by a T-sentence consists in facts about the conditions that cause the speaker to hold the sentence true and to take that sentence to express a belief of his. Of course speakers sometimes hold sentences true when they are not; these sentences express mistaken beliefs. So the relation between belief and truth is not simple. But that it exists, and is central to meaning and truth, can be seen from the simplest cases, and their role in understanding other cases. The simplest cases are those where a sentence such as 'That's a book' or 'This is yellow' is caused to be held true by the conspicuous presence of books or yellow things. This is evidence that these sentences *are* true just when books or yellow things are present; the reason is that what determines the meaning of such sentences is what routinely makes them true. Clearly this account must be elaborated in many ways to account for the possibility of error; much more must be said about sentences more remote from direct observation; provision must be made for the truth conditions of sentences held true no matter what is observed; and so forth. I have explored these matters elsewhere. The important matter in the present context is that it is the role of belief that connects truth and meaning; and if this is so, truth is neither radically nonepistemic, nor radically epistemic.

The approach to truth that I recommend is not epistemic in Putnam's or Dummett's sense, nor in the sense of Peirce, or James, or Dewey, for it makes no attempt to tie truth in general to what can be ascertained by rational creatures. But neither is this approach radically nonepistemic, for it does not follow from my view that all our best-attested and widely held beliefs may be false. By paying close attention to what gives content to our beliefs and meaning to our sentences, we see that it is impossible for most of our perceptual beliefs to be false. What we hold true, what we believe, determines what we mean, and thus, indirectly, when our sentences are true. Believing doesn't make it so, but it creates a presumption that it is so.

I have two further observations, and a conclusion. The first observation is that holding a sentence true, or taking it to express a belief, is not a *use* of language, and so it may seem that it cannot provide evidence for what people mean by what they say. The conclusion does not follow. There are obvious relations between holding a sentence true and linguistic (and other) behavior. If we could not often fathom from his linguistic behavior when a speaker held his sentences true, we could not interpret his speech. I have chosen the attitude of belief rather than acts of assertion as providing the central clue to truth not because I deem the actual use of language unimportant, but because I know of no simple relation between the intentions with which we utter or write sentences, and what our words mean. Our speech acts reveal our underlying attitudes towards our sentences; but often indirectly.

The second observation is that my approach to the concept of truth, like my approach to questions about meaning, assumes that what we want is an account of what it is to understand a language. In this I agree with Putnam, Quine, Dummett, and others. But in one important respect Quine and I differ from Dummett, and perhaps Putnam (though I am less sure about Putnam). Dummett, at any rate, thinks of an account of what it is to understand a language as demanding a description of what it is to grasp the meanings of expressions. I have never been sure I understood this metaphor, and have therefore asked instead what it would suffice someone to know if he were to understand an arbitrary utterance of a speaker (my answer: a theory of truth for that speaker's language), plus an account of how someone could come to know that such a theory was true. Dummett's approach looks at language from the subjective point of view, the perspective of the speaker. My approach looks at language from the start as a social transaction and therefore concentrates on what one person can learn about another in the context of a shared world.

The conclusion I promised is this. All attempts to characterize truth that go beyond giving empirical content to a structure of the sort Tarski taught us how to describe are empty, false, or confused. We should not say that truth is correspondence, coherence, warranted assertability, ideally justified assertability, what is accepted in the conversation of the right people, what science will end up maintaining, what explains the success of science or of our ordinary beliefs.

To the extent that realism and antirealism depend on one or another of these views of truth we should refuse to endorse either. Realism, with its insistence on radically nonepistemic correspondence, asks more of truth than we can understand; antirealism, with its limitation of truth to what can be ascertained, unnecessarily deprives truth of its role as an intersubjective standard. If we want to speak the truth about truth, we should say no more than need be.

13 *Epistemology Externalized*

We know in a way no one else can what we believe, fear, want, value, and intend. We know how things seem to us, how they look to us, feel to us, smell and sound to us to be. We know these things in a way we can never know about the world around us. Whether or not we are sometimes wrong about the contents of our own minds, whether or not we can be in doubt about our own sensations and thoughts, one thing is certainly true of such beliefs: they cannot be generally mistaken. If we think we have a certain thought or sensation, there is a strong presumption that we are right.

The special authority that pertains to first person knowledge has seemed to many philosophers to suit it uniquely to the task of supplying a foundation for the rest of knowledge, particularly, of course, for our knowledge of the 'external world' and of the minds of others. Such knowledge stands in need of a foundation, it is thought, precisely because there is no presumption that our beliefs about the world or the minds of others are true.

I have no intention of rehearsing the difficulties this picture of the mind and its place in nature has gotten us into, nor of reminding you of the ingenious but unpersuasive ways that have been proposed for circumventing its obvious failings. In this essay I describe an alternative, an alternative that I think is correct.

Quine has proposed that epistemology be naturalized.[1] By this he has meant that philosophy should abandon the attempt to provide a foundation for knowledge, or otherwise to justify it, and should instead give an account of how knowledge is acquired. Critics have complained that in abjuring the traditional normative task of episte-

---

[1] W. V. Quine, 'Epistemology Naturalized', in *Ontological Relativity and Other Essays*.

mology Quine has simply changed the subject; I suspect that he agrees, and that this is part of what he intended. Of course, the distinction between describing and justifying, between an empirical account of the genesis of knowledge and a statement of the norms belief must satisfy to count as knowledge, is by no means clear, as is perhaps evident from the fact that Quine's naturalized epistemology, while it makes no serious attempt to answer the skeptic, is recognizably a fairly conventional form of empiricism.[2] And in any case, how can one describe knowledge or its origins without deciding what knowledge is? Quine's answer to this question is that we must accept what science and enlightened common sense dictate without trying to justify it; his account of how we came by this knowledge is, however, just the kind of account that has traditionally been taken to constitute an attempt at justification.

I do not accept Quine's account of the nature of knowledge, which is essentially first person and Cartesian. But I do find congenial Quine's resolutely third person approach to epistemology, and to the extent that the naturalization of epistemology encourages or embraces such an approach, I am happy to count myself a naturalized epistemologist.

There is at least a presumption that we are right about the contents of our own minds; so in the cases where we are right, we have knowledge. But any particular item of such knowledge is logically independent of our beliefs about a world outside, and so cannot supply a foundation for science and commonsense beliefs. This is how skeptics, like Hume, reason, and I think they are right: knowledge of the contents of our own minds cannot be the basis for the rest of our knowledge. If this is correct, then our beliefs about the world must, if they are to count as knowledge, stand alone. Yet it has seemed obvious to many philosophers that if each of our beliefs about the world, taken alone, may be false, there is no reason why all such beliefs might not be false.

This reasoning is fallacious. It does not follow, from the fact that any one of the bills in my pocket may have the highest serial number, that all the bills in my pocket may have the highest serial number, or from the fact that anyone may be elected president, that everyone may be elected president. Nor could it happen that all our beliefs

---

[2] For this characterization of Quine's epistemology, see Essay 10 in this volume, and my 'Meaning, Truth and Evidence'.

about the world might be false. Suppose I think I see a mouse disappear behind a chair. Clearly this belief could be mistaken. But would this belief be wrong if I did not truly believe a mouse was a small, four-footed mammal, or a chair an object made for sitting? Perhaps. There may be no saying exactly what other true beliefs I must have in order to have a particular false belief. But it seems clear that a belief of any kind, true or false, relies for its identification on a background of true beliefs; for a concept, like that of mouse or chair, cannot remain the same concept no matter what beliefs it features in. It is possible to try to avoid this conclusion by arguing that a belief such as that a mouse is a small, four-footed animal is true by virtue of the concepts alone—it is an analytic truth—and so is not really about the world. One could then still say all our beliefs about the world might be false. This line is not available to someone who, like me, does not think a clear line between analytic and synthetic truths is there to be drawn. But even if there are indubitably analytic truths, it is not plausible that these serve to eliminate the host of cases in which concepts are individuated by multiple empirical criteria.

Because of the holistic character of empirical belief, then, it is impossible that all our beliefs about the world are false. Reflection on the reasoning that leads to this thesis suggests, however, that it has disturbing limits. What it shows is that we cannot harbor particular false (or true) beliefs about individual objects unless we have many true beliefs about the nature of such objects. This leaves open the possibility that we may be wrong in all our particular beliefs about what exists in the world, and this would be a pretty extreme skepticism, though not quite total.

But could this happen? Suppose I know what a mouse is and what a chair is. How did I arrive at my false belief that I saw a mouse disappear behind a chair? Presumably I interpreted what I saw, or experienced, as I did because it satisfied my criteria for the presence of a mouse and of a chair (and of disappearing). But we have just decided that I cannot be generally mistaken about the criteria. So my mistake could have come about only in this way: the scene that presented itself to me was one that justified my belief, even though the belief was false. This can certainly happen. It is hard, though, to see how it could happen always, or even often. For how could the scenes that present themselves to me justify beliefs none of which are true?

No skeptic will be persuaded by this argument. I will try to make it more persuasive. Allow me for the moment to make an assumption that begs the question of an external world inhabited by other people; let us suppose we have a speaker and someone else who is trying to understand his words. Each time a mouse appears nearby in good light and with the speaker oriented in the direction of the mouse, etc., the speaker utters what sounds to the interpreter like the same expression: 'Ratón'. When the lighting is poor or the speaker inattentive, the response is less firmly correlated with mouse appearances. I think that unless there is a host of evidence against such an interpretation, the competent interpreter will take the speaker to mean by his words, and to believe, that there is a mouse present. What recommends this interpretation is the fact that the presence of a mouse has apparently in each case caused the speaker intentionally to utter the same expression, 'Ratón', and to utter it in an affirmative spirit. Of course an interpreter may make a mistake: he may be in error about the intention of the speaker, or about the true regular and exclusive cause of the speaker's response. The interpreter would be wrong, for example, if a squirrel would provoke the same response in the speaker, for then mice would not be the regular and exclusive cause of utterances of 'Ratón'. But provided the interpreter makes none of these mistakes (nor certain others to be mentioned), his interpretation is correct.

Suppose the speaker sees a skillfully made mechanical mouse and sounds his 'Ratón'. The interpreter must decide whether the speaker's word and concept include mechanical mice, or whether this is a mistake on the speaker's part. Deciding this is not beyond the interpreter's power. He may expose the mechanism to the speaker, for example, and note the response. The careful interpreter will have to learn how the speaker responds to many other classes of objects before he arrives at his final interpretive scheme.

Obviously the matter is subtle and complicated. But as long as we adhere to the basic intuition that in the simplest cases words and thoughts refer to what causes them, it is clear that it cannot happen that most of our plainest beliefs about what exists in the world are false. The reason is that we do not first form concepts and then discover what they apply to; rather, in the basic cases, the application determines the content of the concept. An interpreter who starts from scratch—who does not already understand the language of a speaker—cannot independently discover what an agent's beliefs are about, and then ask whether they are true. This is because the situations which normally cause a belief determine the conditions in which it is true.

These remarks apply directly to some beliefs only. Someone who has learned from books what a guanaco looks like may never have been caused to accede to 'That's a guanaco' by seeing a guanaco, and yet be prepared (having seen pictures of guanacos perhaps) to accede when he does see one. Or, to take a harder case, someone may know, in some reasonable sense, what a guanaco is, and that it is not a llama, and yet be regularly caused to assent to 'That's a guanaco' in the presence of llamas. In both these cases, the contents of the belief that there is a guanaco present is determined, not by exposure to guanacos, but by having acquired other words and concepts, such as those of llama, animal, camel, domesticated, and so forth. Somewhere along the line, though, we must come to the direct exposures that anchor thought and language to the world.

The general approach to the identification of mental states that I am urging has something in common with what is now sometimes called externalism or (by Tyler Burge) anti-individualism; but it also differs from the best-known versions of externalism in important respects. So at this point I want to distinguish my version of externalism from other forms of externalism, particularly those of Hilary Putnam and Tyler Burge.

I return to first person authority, the fact that each person generally knows what he thinks without appeal or recourse to evidence, and thus knows what is in his own mind in a way that no one can know what is in the mind of another person. It has been widely supposed that externalism, which holds that the contents of a person's propositional attitudes are partly determined by factors of which the person may be ignorant, cannot be reconciled with first person authority. Thus Putnam decided that because (a form of) externalism is true, meanings 'just ain't in the head'—and held that the same applied to thoughts generally.[3] Others have come to the same conclusion.[4] The conclusion does not follow, at least for the kind of externalism I have described. I have argued this at length elsewhere,[5] but the reasoning can be summarized as follows. An interpreter must discover, or correctly assume on the basis of indirect

[3] Hilary Putnam, 'The Meaning of "Meaning" ', 227.
[4] For examples, see John Searle, *Intentionality*; and Andrew Woodfield, 'Introduction', in Woodfield (ed.), in *Thought and Object*, p. viii.
[5] In Essay 2 in this volume.

evidence, what the external factors are that determine the content of another's thought; but since these factors determine both the contents of one's thought and the contents of the thought one believes one has (these being one and the same thought), there is no room for error about the contents of one's own thought of the sort that can arise with respect to the thoughts of others.

While I do not think that the main form of externalism that Putnam endorses[6] threatens first person authority, I am not entirely happy with his thesis for other reasons. Putnam's externalism applies mainly to natural kind words like 'water' and 'leopard'. The idea is that if I learn the word 'water' while experiencing H_2O, the word must henceforth refer only to substances with the same microstructure. While I agree, as I said above, that the usual cause of my use of the word determines what it means, I do not see why sameness of microstructure is necessarily the relevant similarity that determines the reference of my word 'water'. (I will say what I think does control the relevant similarity presently.) I also think there is no reason to limit externalism to one, or a few, categories of words. I believe it is characteristic of language and thought quite generally that their ties to the world accrue from the sort of causal connections I have been discussing.

Tyler Burge has argued for two forms of externalism. In his earlier articles[7] he concentrated on the idea that the meanings of a person's words, and the contents of that person's thoughts, depend in part on the linguistic practices of the person's community, even in cases where the individual is mistaken about the relevant practices. Later articles[8] emphasized the ways in which the contents of utterances and thoughts depend on the causal history of the individual, particularly in connection with perception. Let me call the two brands of externalism social externalism and perceptual externalism. As Burge has argued for them, I think they are largely independent in the sense that neither entails the other.

I am not impressed with the arguments for social externalism, for three reasons.

First, it seems to me false that our intuitions speak strongly in

---

[6] I have in mind the sort of externalism inspired by Twin Earth examples rather than those prompted by the 'linguistic division of labor'.

[7] Tyler Burge, 'Individualism and the Mental', 'Other Bodies', 'Two Thought Experiments Reviewed', and 'Individualism and Psychology'.

[8] e.g.'Cartesian Error and the Objectivity of Perception', 'Intellectual Norms and Foundations of Mind', and 'Individualism and Self-Knowledge'.

favor of understanding and interpreting an agent's speech and thoughts in terms of what others would mean by the same words. For one thing, there is the problem of deciding what group is to determine the norms. But more important, we understand a speaker best when we interpret him as he intended to be interpreted; this will explain his actions far better than if we suppose he means and thinks what someone else might mean and think who used the same words 'correctly'.

Second, I think there is a conflict between Burge's social externalism, which ties a speaker's meaning to an élite usage he may not be aware of, and first person authority.

Third, I have a general distrust of thought experiments that pretend to reveal what we would say under conditions that in fact never arise. My version of externalism depends on what I think to be our actual practice.[9]

I turn now to Burge's perceptual externalism. He makes two important points. The first is that we can have perceptual knowledge, say that we are seeing a cow, without having to ascertain independently that we are not deceived in one way or another (a horse painted to look like a cow, a hologram, etc.). When we have such a case of perceptual knowledge, the content of our thought is partly determined by the cause of the thought. Here is what Burge says:

> to think of something as water . . . one must be in some causal relation to water—or at least in some causal relation to other particular substances that enable one to theorize accurately about water. In the normal cases, one sees and touches water. Such relations illustrate the sort of conditions that make possible thinking of something as water . . . To *think* that water is a liquid, one need not *know* the complex conditions that must obtain if one is to think that thought.[10]

It is hard to decide, from this passage, whether the contents of the thought that this is water are determined, in the case where the thought is true, by the fact that it is water that is causing the thought, or whether in this case, as in the cases where the thought is false, the contents are determined by the normal case, the general run of the thinker's causal contact with his environment. I see no obvious difficulty in accepting and combining both these views, though of course there must be a distinction between the role the actual presence of

---

[9] See Essay 2 in this volume.
[10] Tyler Burge, 'Individualism and Self-Knowledge', 653–4.

water plays when it causes me to think this is water, and the role the history of my relations to water play in making a false thought that I am seeing water nevertheless a thought about water. Clearly it is the latter thesis that is essential to externalism. Burge puts it this way: 'The natures of such states are determined partly by normal relations between the person . . . and the environment. Error is determined against a background of normal interaction.'[11]

I am in sympathy both with the epistemological view that perceptual knowledge does not require that we know independently that the enabling conditions obtain, and of course with the view (more important in the present context) that the contents of our thoughts and sayings are partly determined by the history of causal interactions with the environment.

Agreeing on this point comes naturally to someone like me who has for some thirty years been insisting that the contents of our earliest learned and most basic sentences ('Mama', 'Doggie', 'Red', 'Fire', 'Gavagai') must be determined by what it is in the world that causes us to hold them true. It is here, I have long claimed, that the ties between language and the world are established and that central constraints on meaning are fixed; and given the close connections between thought and language, analogous remarks go for the contents of the attitudes.

Burge and I are essentially in agreement, then, on perceptual externalism, but there is a closely related matter on which we differ, and this concerns the question with which I began this essay, the question whether externalism provides an answer to certain sorts of skepticism. Burge says, 'there is no easy argument against skepticism from anti-individualism and authoritative self-knowledge'.[12] In one sense, I agree, but only because I don't see what first person authority has to do with it. But it does seem to me that *if* you accept perceptual externalism, there *is* an easy argument against global skepticism of the senses of the sort that Descartes, Hume, Russell, and endless others have thought requires an answer. Burge says,

Most perceptual representations are formed and obtain their content through regular interaction with the environment. They represent what, in some complex sense of 'normally', they normally stem from and are applied to. It

[11] 'Cartesian Error and the Objectivity of Perception', 125.
[12] 'Individualism and Self-Knowledge', 655 n.

makes no sense to attribute systematic perceptual error to a being whose perceptual representations can be explained as the results of regular interaction with a physical environment . . .[13]

It may seem that this assumes *more* than mere externalism. But I don't see how. Burge considers a case much like standard brain-in-the-vat cases and shows why such a brain cannot (for long) be radically deceived about its environment. I approve of this argument, having often used it myself. If anything is systematically causing certain experiences (or verbal responses), that is what the thoughts and utterances are about. This rules out systematic error. If nothing is systematically causing the experiences, there is no content to be mistaken about. To quote myself: 'What stands in the way of global skepticism of the senses is, in my view, the fact that we must, in the plainest and methodologically most basic cases, take the objects of a belief to be the causes of that belief.'[14] Anyone who accepts perceptual externalism knows he cannot be systematically deceived about whether there are such things as cows, people, water, stars, and chewing gum. Knowing why this is the case, he must recognize situations in which he is justified in believing he is seeing water or a cow. In those cases where he is right, he knows he is seeing water or a cow.

I have rejected social externalism as championed by Burge. Do I therefore think social factors play no role in the externalism of the mental? Not at all. But I would introduce the social factor in a way that connects it directly with perceptual externalism, thus locating the role of society within the causal nexus that includes the interplay between persons and the rest of nature.

Burge and I agree that the cause of certain mental states is relevant to the content of those states. And we agree that one kind of case is especially important: an example is the way the fact that a certain mental state has been typically caused by seeing cows allows us to think 'There's a cow' even when no cow is present. But here a problem arises. What determines the content of such basic thoughts (and what we mean by the words we use to express them) is what has typically caused similar thoughts. But what *has* typically caused them? There are many choices, for example events that occurred before all cows, or events spatially closer to the thinker than any cow. Burge at

---

[13] 'Cartesian Error and the Objectivity of Perception', 131.
[14] Essay 10 in this volume.

one point says that causes antecedent to the 'natural' cause or intermediate between the natural cause and the mental effect ('such as
arrays of light striking the retina') would make the description of the
content 'complicated in ways that have never been fully articulated'.[15] But complicated for whom? Articulated by whom? Of
course all those arrays of light striking the retina have *something* in
common; and so for other classes of causes. It is we humans for
whom these classifications are complicated and impossible to artic-
ulate (except, of course, by cheating in familiar ways). It is we who
class cow appearances together, more or less naturally, or with mini-
mal learning. And even so, another classification is required to
complete the point, for the class of relevant causes is in turn defined
by similarity of responses: we group together the causes of someone's responses, verbal and otherwise, because we find the responses
similar. What makes these the relevant similarities? The answer
again is obvious; it is we, because of the way we are constructed
(evolution had something to do with this), who find these responses
natural and easy to class together. If we did not, we would have no
reason to claim that others were responding to the same objects and
events (i.e. causes) that we are. It may be that not even plants could
survive in our world if they did not to some extent react in ways we
find similar to events and objects that we find similar. This clearly is
true of animals; and of course it becomes more obvious the more like
us the animal is.

The identification of the objects of thought rests, then, on a
social basis. Without one creature to observe another, the triangulation that locates the relevant objects in a public space could not
take place. I do not mean by this that one creature observing
another provides either creature with the concept of objectivity; the
presence of two or more creatures interacting with each other and
with a common environment is at best a necessary condition for
such a concept. Only communication can provide the concept, for
to have the concept of objectivity, the concepts of objects and
events that occupy a shared world, of objects and events whose
properties and existence is independent of our thought, requires
that we are aware of the fact that we share thoughts and a world
with others.

For this reason we cannot resolve the question of the contents of

[15] 'Cartesian Error and the Objectivity of Perception', 126–7.

mental states from the point of view of a single creature. This is perhaps best seen by thinking about how one person learns from another to speak and think of ordinary things. Put in greatly simplified terms, a basic aspect of such learning can be described in this way: the learner is rewarded, whether deliberately or not, when the learner makes sounds or otherwise responds in ways the teacher finds appropriate in situations the teacher classes together. The learner is subsequently caused to make similar sounds by situations the learner instinctively classes together. Corrections are possible, of course. Success at the first level is achieved to the extent that the learner responds with sounds the teacher finds similar to situations the teacher finds similar. The teacher is responding to two things: the external situation and the responses of the learner. The learner is responding to two things: the external situation and the responses of the teacher. All these relations are causal. Thus the essential triangle is formed which makes communication about shared objects and events possible. But it is also this triangle that determines the content of the learner's words and thoughts when these become complex enough to deserve the term. The role of the teacher in determining the content of the learner's attitude is not just the 'determine' of causality. For in addition to being a cause of those thoughts, what makes the particular aspect of the cause of the learner's responses the aspect that gives them the content they have is the fact that this aspect of the cause is shared by the teacher and the learner. Without such sharing, there would be no grounds for selecting one cause rather than another as the content-fixing cause. A noncommunicating creature may be seen by us as responding to an objective world; but we are not justified in attributing thoughts about our world (or any other) to it.

This brings me back to first person authority. I remarked at the start that first person authority has two closely related features: one is the fact that it yields knowledge that is not based on inference or evidence; the other is the asymmetry between how we know our own minds and how we know the minds of others. It is striking, for example, that Burge's explanation of first person authority fails to account for the fact that the same thing, namely what is in one person's mind, can also be known by someone else, though in a very different way. The missing part of the explanation is filled in, I think, when we recognize the way interaction with other people partly determines the contents of mental states. Knowledge of one's own mind is personal. But what individuates that state at the same time makes it accessible to others, for the state is individuated by causal interplay among three elements: the thinker, others with whom he communicates, and an objective world they know they share.

14 *Three Varieties of Knowledge*

I know, for the most part, what I think, want, and intend, and what my sensations are. In addition, I know a great deal about the world around me, the locations and sizes and causal properties of the objects in it. I also sometimes know what goes on in other people's minds. Each of these three kinds of empirical knowledge has its distinctive characteristics. What I know about the contents of my own mind I generally know without appeal to evidence or investigation. There are exceptions, but the primacy of unmediated self-knowledge is attested by the fact that we distrust the exceptions until they can be reconciled with the unmediated. My knowledge of the world outside of myself, on the other hand, depends on the functioning of my sense organs, and this causal dependence on the senses makes my beliefs about the world of nature open to a sort of uncertainty that arises only rarely in the case of beliefs about our own states of mind. Many of my simple perceptions of what is going on in the world are not based on further evidence; my perceptual beliefs are simply caused directly by the events and objects around me. But my knowledge of the propositional contents of other minds is never immediate in this sense; I would have no access to what others think and value if I could not note their behavior.

Of course all three varieties of knowledge are concerned with aspects of the same reality; where they differ is in the mode of access to reality.

The relations among the three sorts of empirical knowledge, particularly questions of conceptual priority, have long headed the list of philosopher's epistemological concerns, and they are my subject here. Many familiar approaches to the question how the three sorts of knowledge are related take self-knowledge as primary, perhaps because of its directness and relative certainty, and then attempt to derive knowledge of the external world from it; as a final step, they try to base knowledge of other minds on observations of behavior. This is not, needless to say, the only direction the derivation can take: one may instead accept knowledge of the external world, at least in some of its manifestations, as basic, and try to relate or reduce the other forms of knowledge to it. The elaboration of such reductive proposals, and the demonstration of their failure, constitutes much of the history of philosophy from Descartes to the present. If many philosophers have turned away from these problems in recent years, it is not because the problems are thought to have been solved, but because the problems seem intractable. There is also, of course, the wistful hope that the problems themselves are illusory.

This cannot be the case. There are compelling reasons for accepting the view that none of the three forms of knowledge is reducible to one or both of the others. Here I give my own reasons for believing this; but I take the hopelessness of finding effective modes of reduction to be apparent from the almost universal rejection of standard reductionist programs. Skepticism in various of its familiar guises is our grudging tribute to the apparent impossibility of unifying the three varieties of knowledge: one form of skepticism springs from the difficulty of accounting for our knowledge of the external world on the basis of our knowledge of our own minds; another recognizes that our knowledge of other minds cannot consist only in what we can observe from the outside. The intractability of the mind-body problem is another such tribute.

It is striking the extent to which philosophers, even those who have been skeptics about the possibility of justifying beliefs about the external world, have put aside these doubts when they have come to consider the problem of other minds; striking, since the latter problem can arise only if knowledge of behavior, and hence of the external world, is possible. Holding the problems apart has the unfortunate effect of obscuring the fact that the two problems rest on a common assumption. The assumption is that the truth concerning what a person believes about the world is logically independent of the truth of those beliefs. This certainly seems to be the case, for surely the totality of a person's beliefs and subjective experiences is logically consistent with the falsity of any of those beliefs. So no amount of knowledge of the contents of one's own mind insures the truth of a belief about the external world. The logical independence of the mental works equally in the other direction: no amount of knowledge of the external world entails the truth about the workings of a mind. If there is a logical or epistemic barrier between the mind and nature, it not only prevents us from seeing out; it also blocks a view from outside in.

It is sometimes thought that if we separate the problem of knowing what is in a mind from the problem of knowing about anything whatever outside of ourselves, then the problem of knowledge of other minds is solved when we recognize that it is part of the concept of a mental state or event that certain forms of behavior, or other outward signs, count as evidence for the existence of that mental state or event. No doubt it is true that it is part of the concept of a mental state or event that behavior is evidence for it. What is unclear is how this answers the sceptic. For the fact that behavior is evidence for what is in a mind offers no explanation of the asymmetry between the indirect knowledge we have of other minds and the direct knowledge we have of our own mind. The proffered solution insists that behavioral evidence can suffice for the justified attribution of mental states to others, while it recognizes that such evidence is generally irrelevant to self-ascriptions of the same states. But if we are given no explanation of this striking asymmetry, we ought to conclude that there are really two kinds of concepts: mental concepts that apply to others, and mental concepts that apply to ourselves. If the mental states of others are known only through their behavioral and other outward manifestations, while this is not true of our own mental states, why should we think our own mental states are anything like those of others? We might also wonder why, if this answer to the problem of knowledge of other minds is satisfactory, we should not accept an analogous solution to the problem of our knowledge of the external world. Yet it is widely recognized that this answer to general skepticism is unacceptable. Do we distinguish between the problems because we suppose that while we have no access to the outside world except through experience, we nevertheless can intelligibly extrapolate to the experiences of others, since we have access to experience in our own case? But this supposition begs the question, since it assumes without argument that what we call the mental states of others are similar to what we identify as mental states in ourselves.

I have been rehearsing these problems and perplexities because I want, first of all, to stress the apparent oddity of the fact that we have three irreducibly different varieties of empirical knowledge. We need an overall picture which not only accommodates all three modes of knowing, but makes sense of their relations to one another. Without such a general picture we should be deeply puzzled that the same world is known to us in three such different ways. And, second, it is essential to appreciate the extent to which problems that have usually been taken one at a time are interrelated. There are three basic problems: how a mind can know the world of nature, how it is possible for one mind to know another, and how it is possible to know the contents of our own minds without resort to observation or evidence. It is a mistake, I shall urge, to suppose that these questions can be collapsed into two, or taken in isolation.

In trying to form a picture of the relations among the three kinds of knowledge we must do much more than show *that* they are mutually irreducible; we must see *why* they are irreducible. This in turn will involve bringing out the respective conceptual roles played by each of the forms of knowledge, and why each of these three sorts of knowledge is indispensable—why we could not get along without all of them. Of course, if I am right that each of the three varieties of knowledge is indispensable, scepticism of the senses and scepticism about other minds must be dismissed. For the Cartesian or Humean skeptic about the external world holds that it is all too obvious that we can get along without knowledge of the world of nature—what we know of our own mind is self-sufficient, and may be all the knowledge we have. The skeptic about other minds is equally convinced that we can get along without knowledge of other minds—this must be possible if we are forever uncertain whether we have it.

It may seem at first that we could rather easily get along without a form of words to express our beliefs about the mental states of others or of ourselves. I think this is imaginable; but the issue with which I am concerned is primarily epistemic, not linguistic. The epistemic question is whether we could get along without knowledge of minds, both our own and those of others. I shall argue that we could not. What we could not do is get along without a way of expressing, and thus communicating, our thoughts about the natural world. But if we can do this, the transition to also being able verbally to attribute thoughts is relatively simple, and it would be astonishing if this step were not taken. With respect to our own thoughts, it is no more than the difference between saying assertively 'Snow is white'

and saying assertively 'I believe that snow is white'. The truth conditions of these assertions are not the same, but anyone who understands the first assertion knows the truth conditions of the second,
even if he does not command a sentence with those truth conditions.
This is because anyone who understands speech can recognize assertions, and knows that someone who makes an assertion represents
himself as believing what he says. Similarly, someone who says to
Jones that snow is white knows the truth conditions of 'Jones
believes that snow is white' (even if he does not know English nor
has a way of expressing belief).

Belief is a condition of knowledge. But to have a belief it is not
enough to discriminate among aspects of the world, to behave in
different ways in different circumstances; a snail or a periwinkle
does this. Having a belief demands in addition appreciating the
contrast between true belief and false, between appearance and reality, mere seeming and being. We can, of course, say that a sunflower
has made a mistake if it turns towards an artificial light as if it were
the sun, but we do not suppose the sunflower can think it has made
a mistake, and so we do not attribute a belief to the sunflower.
Someone who has a belief about the world—or anything else—must
grasp the concept of objective truth, of what is the case independent
of what he or she thinks. We must ask, therefore, after the source of
the concept of truth.

Wittgenstein put us on the track of the only possible answer to this
question, whether or not his problem was as broad as ours, and
whether or not he believed in answers to philosophical problems.
The source of the concept of objective truth is interpersonal communication. Thought depends on communication. This follows at once
if we suppose that language is essential to thought and we agree with
Wittgenstein that there cannot be a private language.[1] The central
argument against private languages is that, unless a language is
shared, there is no way to distinguish between using the language
correctly and using it incorrectly; only communication with another

---

[1] Of course there can be a private code based on a publicly acquired language. I have
no idea how broadly Wittgenstein intended his thesis about private languages to be interpreted; perhaps he intended his argument to apply only to those concepts which are necessarily private. But I, like Saul Kripke in *Wittgenstein on Rules and Private Language*, think
the argument applies to language quite generally, and so (I would say) to propositional
thought. But while I accept the idea that communication is the source of objectivity, I do
not think communication depends on speakers using the same words to express the same
thoughts.

can supply an objective check. If only communication can provide a check on the correct use of words, only communication can supply a standard of objectivity in other domains, or so I shall argue. We have no grounds for crediting a creature with the distinction between what is thought to be the case and what is the case unless the creature has the standard provided by a shared language; and without this distinction there is nothing that can clearly be called thought.

In communication, what a speaker and the speaker's interpreter must share is an understanding of what the speaker means by what he says. How is this possible? It might help if we knew how language came into existence in the first place, or at least could give an account of how an individual learns his first language, given that others in his environment are already linguistically accomplished. Failing such knowledge or account, what we can do instead is ask how a competent interpreter (one with adequate conceptual resources and a language of his own) might come to understand the speaker of an alien tongue. An answer to this question should reveal some important features of communication, and throw indirect light on what makes possible a first entry into language.

The intrepid interpreter, working without a bilingual trot, seeks to assign a propositional content to the utterances of a speaker. In effect he assigns a sentence of his own to each of the sentences of the speaker. To the extent that he gets things right, the interpreter's sentences provide the truth conditions of the speaker's sentences, and hence supply the basis for the interpretation of the speaker's utterances. The result can be thought of as a recursive characterization of truth, by the interpreter, of the sentences, and hence actual and potential utterances, of the speaker.

An interpreter cannot directly observe another person's propositional attitudes; beliefs, desires, and intentions, including the intentions which partly determine the meanings of utterances, are invisible to the naked eye. The interpreter can, however, attend to the outward manifestations of these attitudes, including utterances. Since we are all able to discover from such manifestations what an agent thinks and means, there must be an intelligible relation between evidence and attitude. How do we bridge this gap? I know of only one way: an interpreter can perceive, often enough, that an agent has a certain sort of attitude towards an object or event the interpreter perceives. If the interpreter could in this way directly *individuate* the attitudes of someone else, the problem would be solved, but only by assuming the interpreter is a mind reader. It would not beg the question, however, to assume the interpreter can detect one or more nonindividuating attitude. Examples of the kind of special attitude I have in mind are: holding a sentence true at a time, wanting a sentence to be true, or preferring that one sentence rather than another be true. The assumption that we can detect such an attitude does not beg the question of how we endow the attitudes with content, since a relation such as holding true between a speaker and an utterance is an extensional relation which can be known to hold without knowing what the sentence means. These attitudes are nonindividuative, for though they are psychological in nature, they do not distinguish the different propositional contents different utterances express.

In *Word and Object* Quine appealed to the nonindividuative attitude of prompted assent. Since someone assents to an utterance, or holds a sentence true, in part because of what he believes and in part because of what the utterance or sentence means in his language, Quine's problem was to separate out these two elements on the basis of evidence that combined their influence. If the separation succeeds, the result is a theory of both belief and meaning for the speaker, for it must yield an interpretation of the speaker's utterances, and if one knows both that the speaker assents to the utterance, and what it means in his mouth, one also knows what he believes.

The process of separating meaning and opinion invokes two key principles which must be applicable if a speaker is interpretable: the Principle of Coherence and the Principle of Correspondence. The Principle of Coherence prompts the interpreter to discover a degree of logical consistency in the thought of the speaker; the Principle of Correspondence prompts the interpreter to take the speaker to be responding to the same features of the world that he (the interpreter) would be responding to under similar circumstances. Both principles can be (and have been) called principles of charity: one principle endows the speaker with a modicum of logic, the other endows him with a degree of what the interpreter takes to be true belief about the world. Successful interpretation necessarily invests the person interpreted with basic rationality. It follows from the nature of correct interpretation that an interpersonal standard of consistency and correspondence to the facts applies to both the speaker and the speaker's interpreter, to their utterances and to their beliefs.

Two questions now obtrude. The first is: why should an interpersonal standard be an objective standard, that is, why should what people agree on be true? The second is: even if it is the case that communication assumes an objective standard of truth, why should this be the only way such a standard can be established?

Here is a way of answering these questions. All creatures classify objects and aspects of the world in the sense that they treat some stimuli as more alike than others. The criterion of such classifying activity is similarity of response. Evolution and subsequent learning no doubt explain these patterns of behavior. But from what point of view can these be called patterns? The criterion on the basis of which a creature can be said to be treating stimuli as similar, as belonging to a class, is the similarity of the creatures's responses to those stimuli; but what is the criterion of similarity of responses? *This* criterion cannot be derived from the creature's responses; it can only come from the responses of an observer to the responses of the creature. And it is only when an observer consciously correlates the responses of another creature with objects and events of the observer's world that there is any basis for saying the creature is responding to those objects or events rather than any other objects or events. As would-be interpreters of the verbal behavior of the speaker of an alien language, we group distinct verbal acts of the speaker together: 'Mother', 'Snow', 'Table', when repeated as one-word sentences, sound similar if we are appropriately attuned. When we discover kinds of objects or events in the world that we can correlate with the utterances of a speaker, we are on the way to interpreting the simplest linguistic behavior.

If we are teaching someone a language, the situation becomes more complex, but more clearly interpersonal. What seems basic is this: an observer (or teacher) finds (or instills) a regularity in the verbal behavior of the informant (or learner) which he can correlate with events and objects in the environment. This much can take place without developed thought on the part of the observed, of course, but it is the necessary basis for attributing thoughts and meanings to the person observed. For until the triangle is completed connecting two creatures, and each creature with common features of the world, there can be no answer to the question whether a creature, in discrim- inating between stimuli, is discriminating between stimuli at the sensory surfaces or somewhere further out, or further in. Without this sharing of reactions to common stimuli, thought and speech would have no particular content—that is, no content at all. It takes two points of view to give a location to the cause of a thought, and thus to define its content. We may think of it as a form of triangulation: each of two people is reacting differentially to sensory stimuli streaming in from a certain direction. Projecting the incoming lines outward, the common cause is at their intersection. If the two people now note each other's reactions (in the case of language, verbal reactions), each can correlate these observed reactions with his or her stimuli from the world. A common cause has been determined. The triangle which gives content to thought and speech is complete. But it takes two to triangulate.

Until a base line has been established by communication with someone else, there is no point in saying one's own thoughts or words have a propositional content. If this is so, then it is clear that knowledge of another mind is essential to all thought and all knowledge. Knowledge of another mind is possible, however, only if one has knowledge of the world, for the triangulation which is essential to thought requires that those in communication recognize that they occupy positions in a shared world. So knowledge of other minds and knowledge of the world are mutually dependent; neither is possible without the other. Ayer was surely right when he said, 'it is only with the use of language that truth and error, certainty and uncertainty, come fully upon the scene'.[2]

Knowledge of the propositional contents of our own minds is not possible without the other forms of knowledge since there is no propositional thought without communication. It is also the case that we are not in a position to attribute thoughts to others unless we know what we think since attributing thoughts to others is a matter of matching the verbal and other behavior of others to our own propositions or meaningful sentences. Knowledge of our own minds and knowledge of the minds of others are thus mutually dependent.

It should now be clear what insures that our view of the world is, in its plainest features, largely correct. The reason is that the stimuli that cause our most basic verbal responses also determine what those verbal responses mean, and the content of the beliefs that accompany them. The nature of interpretation guarantees both that a large number of our simplest perceptual beliefs are true, and that the nature of these beliefs is known to others. Of course many beliefs are given content by their relations to further beliefs, or are caused by misleading sensations; any particular belief or set of beliefs about the world

---

[2] A. J.Ayer, *The Problem of Knowledge*, 54.

around us may be false. What cannot be the case is that our general picture of the world and our place in it is mistaken, for it is this picture which informs the rest of our beliefs and makes them intelligible, whether they be true or false.

The assumption that the truth of what we believe is logically independent of what we believe is revealed as ambiguous. Any particular belief may indeed be false; but enough in the framework and fabric of our beliefs must be true to give content to the rest. The conceptual connections between our knowledge of our own minds and our knowledge of the world of nature are not definitional but holistic. The same is true of the conceptual connections between our knowledge of behavior and our knowledge of other minds.

There are, then, no 'barriers', logical or epistemic, between the three varieties of knowledge. On the other hand, the very way in which each depends on the others shows why none can be eliminated, or reduced to the others.

As noted above, we may think of an interpreter who aims to understand a speaker as matching up sentences of his own with the utterances and states of mind of the speaker. The totality of evidence available to the interpreter determines no unique theory of truth for a given speaker, not just because actually available evidence is finite while the theory has an infinity of testable consequences, but because all possible evidence cannot limit acceptable theories to one. Given the richness of the structure represented by the set of one's own sentences, and the nature of the connections between the members of this set and the world, we should not be surprised if there are many ways of assigning our own sentences to the sentences and thoughts of someone else that capture everything of significance.

The situation is analogous to the measurement of weight or temperature by assigning numbers to objects. Even supposing there are no errors of measurement, and that all possible observations have been made, an assignment of numbers to objects that correctly registers their weights is not unique: given one such assignment, another can be produced by multiplying all the numbers by any positive constant. In the case of ordinary temperature (not absolute temperature), any correct assignment of numbers can be converted to another by a linear transformation. Because there are many different but equally acceptable ways of interpreting an agent we may say, if we please, that interpretation or translation is indeterminate, or that there is no fact of the matter as to what someone means by his or her words. In the same vein, we could speak of the indeterminacy of weight or temperature. But we normally accentuate the positive by being clear about what is invariant from one assignment of numbers to another, for it is what is invariant that is empirically significant. The invariant *is* the fact of the matter. We can afford to look at translation and the content of mental states in the same light.[3]

I once thought that the indeterminacy of translation supplied a reason for supposing there are no strict laws connecting mental and physical concepts, and so supported the claim that mental concepts are not even nomologically reducible to physical concepts. I was wrong: indeterminacy turns up in both domains. But one source of indeterminacy in the case of the mental is that the line between empirical truth and truth due to meaning cannot in general be clearly defined on behavioral grounds; and behavioral grounds are all we have for determining what speakers mean. It is here that the irreducible difference between mental concepts and physical concepts begins to emerge: the former, at least insofar as they are intentional in nature, require the interpreter to consider how best to render the creature being interpreted intelligible, that is, as a creature endowed with reason. As a consequence, an interpreter must separate meaning from opinion partly on normative grounds by deciding what, from his point of view, maximizes intelligibility. In this endeavor the interpreter has, of course, no other standards of rationality to fall back on than his own. When we try to understand the world as physicists, we necessarily employ our own norms, but we do not aim to discover rationality in the phenomena.

How does the normative element in mental concepts prevent their reduction to physical concepts? Perhaps it is obvious that definitional reduction is out of the question; but why can't there be laws—strict laws—that connect each mental event or state with events or states described in the vocabulary of an advanced physics? When writing about this twenty years ago I said, in effect, that one can hope for strict connecting laws only when the concepts connected by the laws are based on criteria of the same sort, and so a strict law could not combine normative with nonnormative concepts.[4] This answer still seems to me right as far as it goes, but

---

[3] Here I accept Quine's thesis of the indeterminacy of translation, and extend it to the interpretation of thought generally. The analogy with measurement is my own.

[4] In 'Mental Events', essay 11 in *Essays on Actions and Events*.

it has understandably been found inconclusive by critics. I now want to add some further considerations.

One further consideration is this: strict laws do not employ causal concepts, while most, if not all, mental concepts are irreducibly causal. An action, for example, must be intentional under some description, but an action is intentional only if it is caused by mental factors such as beliefs and desires. Beliefs and desires are identified in part by the sorts of action they are prone to cause, given the right conditions. Many of the concepts that feature in commonsense explanations are causal in this way. An accident was caused by the fact that the road was slippery; something is slippery if it causes appropriate objects to slip under appropriate circumstances. We explain why the wing of an airplane does not break when it bends by noting that it is made of elastic materials; a material is elastic if there is something about it that causes it, under appropriate conditions, to return to its original shape after deformation. Such explanations do not lend themselves to precision for two reasons: we cannot spell out in detail when the circumstances are appropriate, and the appeal to causality finesses part of what a full-scale explanation would make manifest. Descriptions of objects, states, and events that are needed to instantiate strict, exceptionless laws do not contain causal concepts (which is not to say that laws which contain only noncausal concepts are not causal laws).

In the case of causal properties like elasticity, slipperiness, malleability, or solubility, we tend to think, rightly or wrongly, that what they leave unexplained can be (or already has been) explained by the advance of science. We would not be changing the subject if we were to drop the concept of elasticity in favor of a specification of the microstructure of the materials in the airplane wing that cause it to return to its original shape when exposed to certain forces. Mental concepts and explanations are not like this. They appeal to causality because they are designed, like the concept of causality itself, to single out from the totality of circumstances which conspire to cause a given event just those factors that satisfy some particular explanatory interest. When we want to explain an action, for example, we want to know the agent's reasons, so we can see for ourselves what it was about the action that appealed to the agent. But it would be foolish to suppose that there are strict laws that stipulate that whenever an agent has certain reasons he will perform a given action.

The normative and the causal properties of mental concepts are related. If we were to drop the normative aspect from psychological explanations, they would no longer serve the purposes they do. We have such a keen interest in the subject's reasons for acting and for his or her changes of belief that we are willing to settle for explanations that cannot be made to fit perfectly with the laws of physics. Physics, on the other hand, has as an aim laws that are as complete and ˌprecise as we can make them; a different aim. The causal element in mental concepts helps make up for the precision they lack; it is part of the concept of an intentional action that it is caused and explained by beliefs and desires; it is part of the concept of a belief or a desire that it tends to cause, and so explain, actions of certain sorts.

Much of what I have said about what distinguishes mental concepts from the concepts of a developed physics could also be said to distinguish the concepts of many of the special sciences such as biology, geology, and meteorology. So even if I am right that the normative and causal character of mental concepts divides them definitionally and nomologically from the concepts of a developed physics, it may seem that there must be something more basic or foundational that accounts for this division. I think there is.

Knowledge of the contents of our own minds must, in most cases, be trivial. The reason is that, apart from special cases, the problem of interpretation cannot arise. When I am asked about the propositional contents of my mind, I must use my own sentences. The answer is usually absurdly obvious: my sentence 'Snow is white', like my thought that snow is white, is true if and only if snow is white. My knowledge of the contents of another mind is possible, I have argued, only in the context of a generally correct, and shared, view of the world. But such knowledge differs from the knowledge I have of my own mind since it is necessarily indirect in that it depends, among other things, on observed correlations between the speech and other behavior of the person, and of events in our communal environment.

The fundamental difference between my knowledge of another mind and of the shared physical world has a different source. Communication, and the knowledge of other minds that it presupposes, is the basis of our concept of objectivity, our recognition of a distinction between false and true belief. There is no going outside this standard to check whether we have things right, any more than we can check whether the platinum–iridium standard kept at the

International Bureau of Weights and Standards in Sèvres, France, weighs a kilogram. (This comparison was valid when the standard in Sèvres defined the kilogram.) We can, of course, turn to a third party and a fourth to broaden and secure the interpersonal standard of the real, but this leads not to something intrinsically different, just to more of the same.

I spoke before of an analogy between how we assign numbers to keep track of the relations among objects with respect to temperature or weight and how we use our own sentences to identify the contents of the thoughts and utterances of others. But the analogy is imperfect: the nature of the scaling device differs in the two cases. We depend on our linguistic interactions with others to yield agreement on the properties of numbers and the sort of structures in nature that allow us to represent those structures in the numbers. We cannot in the same way agree on the structure of the sentences or thoughts we use to chart the thoughts and meanings of others, for the attempt to reach such an agreement simply sends us back to the very process of interpretation on which all agreement depends.

It is here, I suggest, that we come to the ultimate springs of the difference between understanding minds and understanding the world as physical. A community of minds is the basis of knowledge; it provides the measure of all things. It makes no sense to question the adequacy of this measure, or to seek a more ultimate standard.

We have dwelt at length on the inescapability of the objective aspect of all thought. What remains of the subjective aspect? Clearly we have not obliterated the difference between self-knowledge and knowledge of other minds: the first remains direct and the second indirect. Objectivity itself we have traced to the intersections of points of view—for each person, the relation between his own reactions to the world and the reactions of others. These differences are real. Our thoughts are 'inner' and 'subjective' in that we know what they are in a way no one else can. But though possession of a thought is necessarily individual, its content is not. The thoughts we form and entertain are located conceptually in the world we inhabit, and know we inhabit, with others. Even our thoughts about our own mental states occupy the same conceptual space and are located on the same public map.

The philosophical conception of subjectivity is burdened with a history and a set of assumptions about the nature of mind and meaning that sever the meaning of an utterance or the content of a thought from questions about external reality, 'my' world from the world as it appears to others. This popular conception holds that the subjective is prior to the objective, that there is a subjective world prior to knowledge of external reality. It is evident that the picture of thought and meaning I have sketched here leaves no room for such priority since it predicates self-knowledge on knowledge of other minds and of the world. The objective and the intersubjective are thus essential to anything we can call subjectivity, and constitute the context in which it takes form. Collingwood put it succinctly:

> The child's discovery of itself as a person is also its discovery of itself as a member of a world of persons . . . The discovery of myself as a person is the discovery that I can speak, and am thus a *persona* or speaker; in speaking I am both speaker and hearer; and since the discovery of myself as a person is also the discovery of other persons around me, it is the discovery of speakers and hearers other than myself.[5]

It may seem that if sharing a general view of the world is a condition of thought, the differences in intellectual and imaginative character among minds and cultures will be lost to sight. If I have given this impression, it is because I have wanted to concentrate on what seems to me primary, and so apt to go unnoticed: the necessary degree of communality essential to understanding another individual, and the extent to which such understanding provides the foundation of the concept of truth and reality upon which all thought depends. But I do not want to suggest that we cannot understand those with whom we differ on vast tracts of physical and moral opinion. It is also the case that understanding is a matter of degree: others may know things we do not, or even perhaps cannot. What is certain is that the clarity and effectiveness of our concepts grows with the growth of our understanding of others. There are no definite limits to how far dialogue can or will take us.

Some philosophers worry that if all our knowledge, at least our propositional knowledge, is objective, we will lose touch with an essential aspect of reality: our personal, private outlook. I think this worry is groundless. If I am right, our propositional knowledge has its basis not in the impersonal but in the interpersonal. Thus, when we look at the natural world we share with others, we do not lose contact with ourselves, but rather acknowledge membership in a society of minds. If I did not know what others think, I would have

---

[5] R. G. Collingwood, *The Principles of Art*, 248.

no thoughts of my own and so would not know what I think. If I did
not know what I think, I would lack the ability to gauge the thoughts
of others. Gauging the thoughts of others requires that I live in the
same world with them, sharing many reactions to its major features,
including its values. So there is no danger that in viewing the world
objectively we will lose touch with ourselves. The three sorts of
knowledge form a tripod: if any leg were lost, no part would stand.

Contents List of Volumes of Essays by Donald Davidson

Volume 2

Inquiries into Truth and Interpretation

Volume 3

Subjective, Intersubjective, Objective

Volume 4

Problems of Rationality

Volume 5

Truth, Language and History

Bibliographical References

AGASSI, JOSEPH, *Science in Flux* (Dordrecht: Reidel, 1975).

ALSTON, WILLIAM, 'Varieties of Privileged Access', *American Philosophical Quarterly*, 9 (1971).

AVRAMIDES, ANITA, 'Davidson and the New Sceptical Problem', in U. Zeglen (ed.), *Donald Davidson: Truth, Meaning and Knowledge* (London: Routledge, 1999).

AYER, A. J., *The Problem of Knowledge* (London: Macmillan, 1956).

AYER, A. J. (ed.), *Logical Positivism* (New York: Free Press, 1959).

AYER, A. J., 'Privacy', in *The Concept of a Person and Other Essays* (New York: Macmillan, 1963).

BENNETT, JONATHAN, *Linguistic Behavior* (Cambridge University Press, 1976).

BLACK, MAX, 'The Semantic Definition of Truth', *Analysis,* 8 (1948).

BRENTANO, FRANZ, *Psychology from an Empirical Standpoint*, ed. O. Kraus, trans. A. Rancurello, D. B. Terrell, and L. L. McAlister (London: Humanities Press, 1973).

BURGE, TYLER, 'Individualism and the Mental', in P. A. French, T. E. Uehling, and H. K. Wettstein (eds.), *Midwest Studies in Philosophy* (Minneapolis: University of Minnesota Press, 1979).

BURGE, TYLER, 'Two Thought Experiments Reviewed', *Notre Dame Journal of Formal Logic*, 23 (1982).

BURGE, TYLER, 'Other Bodies', in A. Woodfield (ed.), *Thought and Object* (Oxford University Press, 1982).

BURGE, TYLER, 'Individualism and Psychology', *Philosophical Review*, 95 (1986).

BURGE, TYLER, 'Cartesian Error and the Objectivity of Perception', in P. Petit and J. McDowell (eds.), *Subject, Thought, and Context* (Oxford University Press, 1986).

BURGE, TYLER, 'Intellectual Norms and Foundations of Mind', *Journal of Philosophy*, 83 (1986).

BURGE, TYLER, 'Perceptual Individualism and Authoritative Self-Knowledge', in R. Grimm and D. Merrill (eds.), *Contents of Thought* (Tucson: University of Arizona Press, 1988).

BURGE, TYLER, 'Individualism and Self-Knowledge', *Journal of Philosophy*, 85 (1988).

CARNAP, RUDOLF, 'Psychology in Physical Language', *Erkenntnis*, 3 (1932–3).

CHAN, WAI PANG, FREDERICK PRETE, and MICHAEL H. DICKINSON, 'Visual Input to the Efferent Control System of a Fly's "Gyroscope" ', *Science*, 280 (10 Apr. 1998).

CHOMSKY, NOAM, *Knowledge of Language: Its Nature, Origin and Use* (New York: Praeger, 1986).

CHOMSKY, NOAM, *Language and Problems of Knowledge* (Cambridge, Mass.: MIT Press, 1988).

CHURCHLAND, PAUL, *Scientific Realism and the Plasticity of Mind* (Cambridge University Press, 1979).

COLLINGWOOD, R. G., *The Principles of Art* (Oxford University Press, 1938).

DAVIDSON, DONALD, *Essays on Actions and Events* (Oxford University Press, 1980).

DAVIDSON, DONALD, *Inquiries into Truth and Interpretation* (Oxford University Press, 1980).

DAVIDSON, DONALD, 'A Nice Derangement of Epitaphs', in R. Grandy and R. Warner, (eds.), (*Philosophical Grounds of Rationality* (Oxford University Press, 1986).

DAVIDSON, DONALD, 'Meaning, Truth and Evidence', in R. Barrett and R. Gibson (eds.), *Perspectives on Quine* (Oxford: Blackwell, 1990).

DAVIDSON, DONALD, 'The Structure and Content of Truth', *Journal of Philosophy*, 87 (1990).

DAVIDSON, DONALD, 'Three Varieties of Knowledge', in A. P. Griffiths (ed.), *A. J. Ayer Memorial Essays* (Cambridge University Press, 1991).

DAVIDSON, DONALD, ' Pursuit of the Concept of Truth', in P. Leonardi and M. Santambrogio (eds.), *On Quine* (Cambridge University Press, 1995).

DAVIDSON, DONALD, 'Replies', *Critica*, 30 (1998).

DENNETT, DANIEL, 'Beyond Belief', in A. Woodfield (ed.), *Thought and Object* (Oxford University Press, 1982).

DENNETT, DANIEL, 'Real Patterns', *Journal of Philosophy*, 88 (1991).

DUMMETT, MICHAEL, *Truth and Other Enigmas* (London: Duckworth, 1978).

DUMMETT, MICHAEL, *The Interpretation of Frege's Philosophy* (London: Duckworth, 1981).

EVANS, GARETH, *The Varieties of Reference* (Oxford University Press, 1982).

FODOR, JERRY, 'Methodological Solipsism Considered as a Research Strategy in Cognitive Psychology', *Behavioral and Brain Sciences,* 3 (1980).

FODOR, JERRY, 'Cognitive Science and the Twin Earth Problem', *Notre Dame Journal of Formal Logic*, 23 (1982).

FODOR, JERRY, *Psychosemantics* (Cambridge, Mass.: MIT Press, 1987).

FODOR, JERRY, *A Theory of Content* (Cambridge, Mass.: MIT Press, 1990).

FØLLESDAL, DAGFINN, 'Knowledge, Identity, and Existence', *Theoria*, 33 (1967).

GOODMAN, NELSON, *Fact, Fiction, and Forecast*, 4th edn. (Cambridge, Mass.: Harvard University Press, 1983).

GUHRAUER, G., *Gottfried Wilhelm Freiherr von Leibniz: Eine Biographie* (Hildesheim: Gb. Olms, 1966).

HAHN, LEWIS E. (ed.), *The Philosophy of Donald Davidson*, Library of Living Philosophers (Chicago: Open Court, 1999).

HAHN, LEWIS E., and P. A. SCHILPP (eds.), *The Philosophy of W. V. Quine*, Library of Living Philosophers (Chicago: Open Court, 1986).

HEMPEL, CARL, 'On the Logical Positivist's Theory of Truth', *Analysis*, 2 (1935).

HEMPEL, CARL, 'The Empiricist Criterion of Meaning', *Revue International de Philosophie*, 4 (1950).

HEMPEL, CARL, *Aspects of Scientific Explanation* (New York: Free Press, 1965).

HENRICH, DIETER (ed.), *Kant oder Hegel?* (Stuttgart: Klett-Kotta, 1983).

JEFFREY, RICHARD, *The Logic of Decision* (University of Chicago Press, 1965).

KAPLAN, DAVID, 'Quantifying In', *Synthese*, 19 (1968).

KRIPKE, SAUL, 'Naming and Necessity', in D. Davidson and G. Harman (eds.), *Semantics of Natural Language* (Dordrecht: Reidel, 1972).

KRIPKE, SAUL, *Wittgenstein on Rules and Private Language* (Cambridge: Blackwell, 1982).

LEPORE, ERNIE (ed), *Truth and Interpretation: Perspectives on the Philosophy of Donald Davidson* (Cambridge: Blackwell, 1986).

LEWIS, C. I., *Mind and the World Order* (New York: Scribner's, 1960).

LEWIS, DAVID, 'Languages and Language', in K. Gunderson (ed.), *Language, Mind and Knowledge* (Minneapolis: University of Minnesota Press, 1975).

MALACHOWSKI, ALAN (ed.), *Reading Rorty* (Oxford: Blackwell, 1990).

MALCOLM, NORMAN, 'Thoughtless Brutes', *Proceedings and Addresses of the American Philosophical Association*, 46 (1972–3).

MARGALIT, AVISHAI (ed.), *Meaning and Use* (Dordrecht: Reidel, 1979).

MATES, BENSON, *The Philosophy of Leibniz: Metaphysics and Language* (Oxford University Press, 1986).

NAGEL, THOMAS, 'The Objective Self', in C. Genet and S. Shoemaker (eds.), *Mind and Knowledge* (Oxford University Press, 1983).

NEURATH, OTTO, 'Protocol Sentences', *Erkenntnis*, 3 (1932–3).

PUTNAM, HILARY, 'The Meaning of "Meaning" ', in *Philosophical Papers*, ii: *Mind, Language, and Reality* (Cambridge University Press, 1975).

PUTNAM, HILARY, *Meaning and the Moral Sciences* (London: Routledge & Kegan Paul, 1978).

PUTNAM, HILARY, *Realism and Reason* (Cambridge University Press, 1983).

QUINE, W. V., 'Quantifiers and Propositional Attitudes', *Journal of Philosophy*, 53 (1956).

QUINE, W. V., *Word and Object* (Cambridge, Mass.: MIT Press, 1960).

QUINE, W. V., *Ontological Relativity and Other Essays* (New York: Columbia University Press, 1969).

QUINE, W. V., *The Roots of Reference* (La Salle, Ill.: Open Court, 1974).

QUINE, W. V., 'The Nature of Natural Knowledge', in S. Guttenplan (ed.), *Mind and Language* (Oxford University Press, 1975).

QUINE, W. V., 'On Empirically Equivalent Systems of the World', *Erkenntnis*, 9 (1975).

QUINE, W. V, 'Intensions Revisited', in *Theories and Things* (Cambridge, Mass.: Harvard University Press, 1981).

QUINE, W. V., *Theories and Things* (Cambridge, Mass.: Harvard University Press, 1981).

QUINE, W. V., 'Reply to Stroud', in P. A. French, T. E. Uehling, and H. K. Wettstein (eds.), *Midwest Studies in Philosophy* (Minneapolis: University of Minnesota Press, 1981).

QUINE, W. V., 'Events and Reification', in E. Lepore and B. McLaughlin (eds.), *Actions and Events: Perspectives on the Philosophy of Donald Davidson* (Cambridge: Blackwell, 1985).

QUINE, W. V., *Pursuit of Truth*, rev. edn. (Cambridge, Mass.: Harvard University Press, 1992).

QUINE, W. V., *From Stimulus to Science* (Cambridge, Mass.: Harvard University Press, 1995).

QUINE, W. V., and NELSON GOODMAN, 'Steps toward a Constructive Nominalism', *Journal of Symbolic Logic*, 12 (1947), 97–122.

RAMSEY, FRANK, 'Truth and Probability', in *Philosophical Papers: F. P. Ramsey*, ed. D. H. Mellor (Cambridge University Press, 1990).

RORTY, RICHARD, 'Incorrigibility as the Mark of the Mental', *Journal of Philosophy*, 67 (1970).

RORTY, RICHARD, *Philosophy and the Mirror of Nature* (Princeton University Press, 1979).

RORTY, RICHARD, *Consequences of Pragmatism* (Minneapolis: University of Minnesota Press, 1982).

RORTY, RICHARD, 'Pragmatism, Davidson and Truth', in E. Lepore (ed.), *Truth and Interpretation: Perspectives on the Philosophy of Donald Davidson* (Oxford: Blackwell, 1986).

RYLE, GILBERT, *The Concept of Mind* (New York: Barnes & Noble, 1949).

SCHIFFER, STEPHEN, *Remnants of Meaning* (Cambridge, Mass.: MIT Press, 1987).

SCHLICK, MORITZ, 'The Turning Point in Philosophy', *Erkenntnis*, 1 (1930–1).

SCHLICK, MORITZ, 'Positivism and Realism', *Erkenntnis*, 3 (1932–3).

SCHLICK, MORITZ, 'The Foundation of Knowledge', *Erkenntnis*, 4 (1934).

SCHLICK, MORITZ, 'Meaning and Verification', *Philosophical Review*, 4 (1936).

SEARLE, JOHN, *Intentionality* (Cambridge University Press, 1983).

SEARLE, JOHN, 'Indeterminacy and the First Person', *Journal of Philosophy*, 84 (1987).

SELLARS, WILFRED, 'Empiricism and the Philosophy of Mind', in H. Feigl and M. Scriven (eds.), *Minnesota Studies in the Philosophy of Science* (Minneapolis: University of Minnesota Press, 1956).

SHOEMAKER, SIDNEY, *Self-Knowledge and Self-Identity* (Ithaca, NY: Cornell University Press, 1963).

STICH, STEPHEN, 'Autonomous Psychology and the Belief–Desire Thesis', *Monist*, 61 (1978).

STICH, STEPHEN, *From Folk Psychology to Cognitive Science* (Cambridge, Mass.: MIT Press, 1983).

STRAWSON, PETER, *Individuals* (London: Methuen, 1959).

STRAWSON, PETER, 'Truth', in *Logico-Linguistic Papers* (London: Methuen, 1971).

TARSKI, ALFRED, 'The Concept of Truth in Formalized Languages', in J. H. Woodger (ed.), *Logic, Semantics, Metamathematics* (Oxford University Press, 1956).

WALLAS, GRAHAM, *The Art of Thought* (New York: Harcourt Brace, 1926).

WEISS, DONALD, 'Professor Malcolm on Animal Intelligence', *Philosophical Review*, 84 (1975).

WITTGENSTEIN, LUDWIG, *Philosophical Investigations* (New York: MacmMillan, 1953).

WOODFIELD, ANDREW (ed.), *Thought and Object* (Oxford University Press, 1982).

WRIGHT, CRISPIN, 'Kripke's Account of the Argument against Private Language', *Journal of Philosophy*, 81 (1984), 759–78.

Index